GREAT HOME COOKING
IN AMERICA

Heirloom Recipes Treasured for Generations

Other cookbooks by FARM JOURNAL

GREAT HOME COOKING
IN AMERICA

Heirloom Recipes Treasured for Generations

Edited by

The Food Editors of *FARM JOURNAL*

Photographic Design by AL J. REAGAN

Doubleday & Company, Inc.

Garden City, New York

1976

Library of Congress Cataloging in Publication Data
Main entry under title:

Great home cooking in America.

Includes index.
1. Cookery, American.   2. Cookery, International.
I. Farm journal.
TX715.G81144   641.5′973
ISBN 0-385-09930-4
Library of Congress Catalog Card Number 75–26701

CONTENTS

COLOR ILLUSTRATIONS

Part I

OUR 200-YEAR HERITAGE OF AMERICAN COOKING

INTRODUCTION

Our native home cooking originated mainly on the farms of the New World, since most of the population lived on the land. Our cuisine is truly a melting pot of flavors, ingredients and customs, a potpourri of native produce and foreign heirlooms. New England's baked beans, boiled dinners . . . sauerkraut, the sweets and sours of the Pennsylvania Dutch . . . grits, biscuits, fried chicken from the South . . . Swedish rye bread . . . German stollens . . . Bohemian kolaches . . . Russian borscht . . . enchiladas and tortillas from the Southwest.

Immigrants brought with them on the long voyage across the Atlantic precious recipes, a few heirloom dishes or utensils, even seasonings—all these to nourish their spirits as well as their bodies. Favorite family dishes were reproduced as well as possible with new ingredients; some, in fact, improved tremendously with new plenty.

For especially as the settlers moved westward, regional recipes sprang up as new produce was discovered and as immigrants from Europe began pouring into the new land to seek a new life, their ethnic dishes took on the influence of their new homeland.

The Indians had a great influence on our cooking, teaching us to use the bounty of our new land. Early pioneer women learned from the Indians and adapted these new foods to interesting combinations of their own. Even before colonists came to the Atlantic coast, however, Spanish conquerors and colonists brought new foods with them from natives in South America and Mexico. Many of the early food patterns that were established have lasted through the generations.

For almost 100 years country women of many ethnic origins have shared their family recipes and food customs with Farm Journal editors for testing and publication. We proudly bring you 200 years of great home cooking in America from the past to the present.

Chapter 1

AMERICAN
FOOD
ORIGINALS

When you eat a piece of spicy pumpkin pie, baked beans or corn bread, you are enjoying foods that originated in early America. The recipes that follow are for traditionals created during colonial years and for new favorites developed during the 200 years of our Republic, adapting to newly available foods, cooking equipment and to changing life-styles.

Since the first settlers were predominantly English, their early cooking reflected to a degree the foods in homes left behind, but necessity forced changes. Many foods previously used were not available in the new country. Their new neighbors, the Indians, were growing and eating several varieties of maize (corn), beans of many sizes and colors and different kinds of squashes, including pumpkins. Indians also were hunters and fishers dependent on the bounty of the forests, streams and ocean for their protein foods. They introduced wild turkeys to the colonists.

The Indians taught colonists how to grind corn into meal and how to make hominy. They demonstrated baking beans in a small hole in the ground on heated stones. They shared their secret of slashing sugar maple trees early in the year when the sap was running to obtain a sweetener, and of gathering cranberries in the marshes. They hung foods in the summer sunshine to dry and eat during winter. Perhaps the most valuable lesson of all was advising colonists which native foods were edible.

Most of the first cookbooks used and compiled on this side of the Atlantic Ocean were more English than American. The first real American cookbook was compiled by Amelia Simmons, who called herself "an American Orphan." Her *American Cookery* was published in Hartford, Connecticut, in 1796. Reprinted and revised many times during the next 35 years, it was designed for fireplace cooking, which was universal.

Miss Simmons presented the first printed recipes listing cornmeal as an ingredient—five of them. She gave a recipe for American-style gingerbread (see our Index for Honeyed Gingerbread) rather than the kind then baked in Europe.

Other firsts in her cookbook were Hartford Election Cake, the first printed recipe for pumpkin pie, cranberry sauce and "purified potash," a leavening that was the forerunner of baking powder.

Several cookbooks of the 1820s reflected the steady and marvelous expansion of American dishes. Among them was the first regional cookbook, *The Virginia Housewife*. The "receipts," as recipes were called, left much to the imagination and judgment of the cook. They must have defied the beginner. For example, a typical recipe from an 1858 cookbook:

CHERRY PUDDING

"Place 3 or 4 layers of cherries in the bottom of a baking dish, sprinkle with 1 cup of sugar and add a few bits of butter. Take 2 cups sour cream, 2 eggs, 1 teaspoon saleratus, a little salt and flour to make a thin batter. Turn over cherries and bake half an hour. Serve with sauce."

Like most recipes of the 19th century, no mention is made of the size of the baking dish, the number of servings are not given, the cherries are not described as sweet or tart, the accompanying sauce is not identified, the measurements are not definite and no oven temperature is given.

That no baking temperature is specified is hardly surprising, for the first wood- and coal-burning cookstoves of the 1840s had no oven heat indicators. After 1850 cookbooks were designed for cookstoves instead of for fireplace cooking.

Women worked out ways to judge oven heat. The feel of the heat on the hand was one test. Another common practice was to place a little flour in a small pan, put it in the oven and count the minutes required to brown it.

Gas ranges followed wood- and coal-burning cookstoves in about 50 years. Their acceptance was rather slow at first. Some people believed they would "blow up" the house. The first so-called electric kitchen drew curious crowds in 1893 at the World's Fair in Chicago. It was one of the wonders on exhibit, but dependable electric ranges did not reach the market until 20 years later. And now microwave cooking is our newest form.

Problems with leavenings other than yeast plagued early American women. Most cookbooks emphasized that the "purified potash" for which *American Cookery* gave a recipe, could be used when saleratus was not available, but warned that if too much was added the food had an unpleasant taste. Saleratus, or baking soda, worked fine with buttermilk or sour milk. When baking powder was invented the middle of the 19th century, sweet milk came into use.

Changes in cooking followed. One of the striking developments was the creation of beautiful American cakes. They differed from those common in Europe in their lightness and delicacy. These cakes often were baked in layers—chocolate, white, spice, banana, burnt sugar, lemon, orange and coconut—frosted and sometimes filled. The angel food cake was invented and was followed in the 1930s by another American original, the chiffon cake. Then excellent packaged cake mixes came to food stores, making it possible for any woman to bake fine cakes quickly and with a minimum of time and effort, thanks also to the electric mixer.

Busy women switched at least partially to making these "mix cakes." The number of pages in cookbooks devoted to cake recipes dwindled. Pie recipes also decreased proportionately from earlier days when other desserts were scarcer. Women now frequently add their own creative touches to "mix cakes" (see Index for Pumpkin Spice Cake).

Equipment changes contributed to the rise of the American cake. Millers stabilized the quality of their flours. And in the early 20th century, under the leadership of Fannie Farmer, cups and spoons to make level measurements of ingredients were popularized. Electric refrigerators, invented in 1916, gradually came down in cost enough to allow installment on a wide scale. Next in demand, especially in country homes, was the electric freezer.

These changes affected the preparation of many foods. Cake baking is just one example. Hostesses delighted in serving the lovely refrigerator desserts (see Index for Lemon Angel Refrigerator Cake) and ice cream cakes and pies, all of which could be made at least a few days ahead.

Americans have come a long way in cooking during these 200 years. Efficient kitchen equipment, new and improved foods, the knowledge of nutrition and the increase in costs of some products all have had an influence.

What does the future hold? Changes will continue to come: adaptions of the old, but also exciting new dishes. Some women rebel at first at surrendering familiar ways—as they always have —but eventually will join the majority who accept the challenges. As they develop better balanced meals and wonderful but different dishes, more American originals will join the earlier favorites to continue to make good eating one of life's greatest pleasures.

AMERICAN SWISS STEAK

Swiss steak is American with no connection to Switzerland. Originally, round steak cut 1½ to 2″ thick, was the beef cut used, but in our recipe for American Swiss Steak, chuck steak is suggested as an alternative. It costs less and the gentle cooking tenderizes the flavorful meat so that you can cut it with a fork.

AMERICAN SWISS STEAK

Expert seasoning and slow cooking create a great steak

¼ c. flour
1 tsp. salt
½ tsp. dry mustard
¼ tsp. pepper
1½ to 2 lbs. round steak or
   bone chuck steak, cut
   1½" thick
2 tblsp. cooking oil
2 onions, sliced

1 (lb.) can tomatoes, cut up
1 clove garlic, minced
1 tsp. Worcestershire sauce
Water
¼ c. flour
½ tsp. salt
⅛ tsp. pepper
½ c. water

Combine ¼ c. flour, 1 tsp. salt, dry mustard and ¼ tsp. pepper. Spread half of mixture over one side of steak. Pound in with side of saucer or meat mallet. Repeat with other side of steak. Brown steak on both sides in hot oil in skillet. Add onions, tomatoes, garlic and Worcestershire sauce. Cover and simmer 1½ to 2 hours or until meat is tender. Place meat on warm platter and top with onions and tomatoes.

Add enough water to pan juices to make 1½ c. Return juices to skillet. Combine ¼ c. flour, ½ tsp. salt, ⅛ tsp. pepper and ½ c. water in jar. Cover and shake until well blended. Add to meat juices. Bring to a boil, stirring constantly, until mixture is thickened. Makes 6 servings.

YANKEE POT ROAST

This classic New England platter dinner has stood the test of time. Our recipe is practically the same as the one women knew by heart two centuries ago and used at least once a week. They browned the floured meat in fat rendered from salt pork or in beef suet. Sometimes a single bay leaf was added to the water in which the meat and vegetables cooked.

In looking through old, handwritten "receipt" books, it

becomes apparent that the gravy was of prime importance. It had to be rich and brown.

For a perfect Yankee Pot Roast follow the basic rules established long ago: Brown the floured meat slowly so it will be deeply browned. Add a small quantity of water, no more than a cupful. Replenish as needed. Let the meat stick to the utensil at least once during the cooking to insure brown gravy. Simmer slowly in a heavy, tightly covered utensil until pot roast is tender.

YANKEE POT ROAST

While the sliced turnip is traditional, it may be omitted

¼ c. flour
2 tsp. salt
¼ tsp. pepper
1 (3 to 4 lb.) chuck pot roast
3 tblsp. cooking oil
½ c. water
6 medium potatoes, pared and halved
6 medium carrots, pared and halved crosswise
6 small whole onions, or 1 large onion, sliced
1 small turnip, pared and sliced
Salt
Pepper
Water
¼ c. flour
½ tsp. salt
⅛ tsp. pepper
½ c. water

Combine ¼ c. flour, 2 tsp. salt and ¼ tsp. pepper. Pat into both sides of pot roast. Brown meat well on both sides in hot oil in heavy Dutch oven or large skillet 15 to 20 minutes. Add ½ c. water; cover tightly and simmer 1 hour 30 minutes. Add potatoes, carrots, onions and turnip; sprinkle vegetables with salt and pepper. Add more water if needed to prevent sticking. Continue cooking 1 hour or until meat and vegetables are tender. Remove meat and vegetables to platter to keep hot.

Skim part of fat from pan juices. Add enough water to pan juices to make 1½ c. Return to Dutch oven. Combine ¼ c. flour, ½ tsp. salt, ⅛ tsp. pepper and ½ c. water in jar. Cover

OVEN-BARBECUED RIBS

Barbecues are a form of American cooking men enjoy. The method is borrowed from Indians who hundreds of years ago cooked game and fish over embers in a pit or a hole in the ground. Fish were split lengthwise in half, fastened to sticks and leaned against stones near the embers. Pit barbecues still are used to some extent in ranch country.

Today's back-yard barbecues are a simplified form of the old-style gatherings. Men often continue as the chefs. They marinate the meat, poultry or fish in highly seasoned sauces and brush the sauce on the food as it grills. The flavor of the smoke is one of the best tastes of barbecued foods.

In many areas where weather prohibits outdoor cook-outs, meat is "barbecued" in ovens. The sauce provides pleasing flavors, even though different from food cooked over live coals.

Our recipe for Oven-barbecued Ribs is lots less work than outdoor barbecuing. It eliminates the tedious brushing of meat with the sauce. Oven heat is easily controlled. Precooking the ribs reduces the amount of fat, a virtue calorie counters appreciate. And they're delicious!

OVEN-BARBECUED RIBS

For a feast, serve these ribs with baked beans and a green salad

4 lbs. pork back ribs	1 tsp. salt
1 c. chopped onion	¼ tsp. pepper
1 clove garlic, minced	2 tblsp. vinegar
1 c. ketchup	1 tblsp. Worcestershire
¼ c. brown sugar, firmly	sauce
packed	1 tblsp. prepared mustard

Cut ribs in serving-size portions. Place in large saucepan with enough salted water to cover ribs. Cover and simmer about 1 hour or until ribs are nearly tender.

Meanwhile, combine onion, garlic, ketchup, brown sugar, salt, and shake until well blended. Add to meat juices. Bring to a boil stirring constantly, until mixture is thickened. Serve pot roast with gravy. Makes 6 servings.

CHICKEN-FRIED STEAK

Some ranchers insist that the West could not have been won without platters of Chicken-fried Steak and the bowls of brown gravy that came to the table with it. This steak was to its era what hamburger patties are to today.

Fried chicken inspired the specialty. Pieces of thin, round steak pounded to one-fourth inch in thickness, were dredged in flour, and cooked brown and tender in a skillet containing a little melted suet. The gravy gave this dish its special appeal.

CHICKEN-FRIED STEAK

Another name for this beef dish is country-fried steak

1¾ lbs. round steak, cut ½" thick	⅓ c. cooking oil
½ c. flour	3 tblsp. flour
1 tsp. salt	½ tsp. salt
¼ tsp. pepper	⅛ tsp. pepper
	1½ c. light cream

Cut meat in 6 serving pieces. Pound each piece ¼" thick. Coat meat with mixture of ½ c. flour, 1 tsp. salt and ¼ tsp. pepper. Brown meat slowly on both sides in hot oil in large skillet. Cover with tight-fitting lid; cook over low heat 45 to 60 minutes or until tender. Remove meat to platter and keep warm. Skim off fat from pan juices.

Add 3 tblsp. flour, ½ tsp. salt and ⅛ tsp. pepper to drippings in skillet, stirring to loosen browned bits on bottom. Add 1½ c. light cream or milk and cook over low heat, stirring constantly, until mixture comes to a boil and is thickened. Serve steak with gravy. Makes 6 servings.

pepper, vinegar, Worcestershire sauce and mustard in small saucepan. Cover and simmer 10 minutes.

Arrange ribs with meaty side up one layer deep in large, shallow roasting pans. Spoon sauce over ribs.

Bake in 350° oven 25 minutes or until meat is tender. Makes 6 to 8 servings.

DRIED-BEEF CASSEROLE

Lack of refrigeration forced early Americans to cure meats and fish for safekeeping. The top round of beef, cured in a brine and air-dried or smoked, was a great favorite. Women usually simmered the beef, sliced thin and torn in pieces, briefly in water to remove the surplus salt. They drained it and then cooked it briefly in butter before stirring in flour and adding milk to make what they called dried-beef gravy. This was spooned over hot biscuits or baked potatoes.

In our recipe for Dried-beef Casserole we add cooked potatoes to the sauce made with milk. Cheese and hard-cooked eggs boost the protein in this main dish. Chopped onion and green pepper step up flavors. The result is a tasty casserole that is quick and that takes care of itself in the oven and will hold if the meal is delayed.

DRIED-BEEF CASSEROLE

If dried beef is not available, substitute smoked, pressed beef

1 (5 oz.) jar dried beef, or 2 (3 oz.) pkgs. smoked, pressed beef, torn	2½ c. milk
	2 c. shredded process, sharp American cheese (8 oz.)
⅓ c. chopped onion	4 c. cubed, cooked potatoes (4 medium)
⅓ c. chopped green pepper	
6 tblsp. butter or regular margarine	4 hard-cooked eggs, sliced
6 tblsp. flour	½ c. dry bread crumbs
⅛ tsp. pepper	2 tblsp. melted butter or regular margarine

Cook dried beef, onion and green pepper in 6 tblsp. butter in 10″ skillet until beef edges are frizzled. Stir in flour and pepper. Add milk and cook, stirring constantly, until mixture thickens and bubbles. Add cheese and stir until melted. Stir in potatoes and eggs. Turn into greased 2-qt. casserole.

Toss bread crumbs with 2 tblsp. melted butter. Sprinkle over top of casserole.

Bake in 350° oven 30 minutes. Makes 6 servings.

NEW ENGLAND BOILED DINNER

Many enthusiastic gardeners are reviving the old-time New England Boiled Dinner to show off their succulent vegetable crops. They especially like to feature this meal-on-a-platter during autumn when vegetables are at their bountiful best. This is another of those one-pot meals developed by colonial women who had to cook over wood fires.

To serve this early American meal buffet style, give the platter the spotlight. Follow the traditional arrangement: Slices of hot, fork-tender meat in the center bordered with vegetables. With a pot of horseradish, hot yellow corn bread and plenty of butter, you have the makings of a good, old-fashioned dinner. Nothing is more appropriate for dessert than apple pie.

NEW ENGLAND BOILED DINNER

You can cook meat one day and refrigerate it—next day reheat, add vegetables and cook until they're tender

1 (5 lb.) corned beef brisket	1 turnip, pared and sliced
Water	1 medium head cabbage, cut in 6 wedges
6 medium potatoes, pared	12 small beets
6 medium carrots, pared	
6 medium onions or 12 small onions	

Place corned beef in large kettle or Dutch oven. Add enough water to cover corned beef by 1"; bring to a boil. Reduce heat; cover and simmer 3 hours 30 minutes or until meat is tender.

Add potatoes, carrots, onions and turnip. Continue simmering 20 minutes. Remove meat and keep warm. Add cabbage; simmer 15 minutes or until all vegetables are tender.

Meanwhile, cook beets separately until tender. Remove skins.

To serve, slice meat, and arrange on large platter with cooked vegetables. Makes 6 servings with extra meat to make Red Flannel Hash (see Index) or use in other ways.

RED FLANNEL HASH

Red Flannel Hash is a classic example of an early American dish made with leftovers that has held its own in country meals through the years. Some people insist that the New England Boiled Dinner endures from one generation to another because it yields dividends the next day—savory hash, tinted pink-red by beets.

The traditional way to cook the hash is to pan-fry it slowly in a heavy skillet. Or as an old Vermont cookbook directs: "When the underside is brown and the hash is heated thoroughly, make a deep crease across the top with a spatula at right angles to the handle. Tip the skillet and fold the top over the bottom like an omelet. Slip onto a warm platter. Or, when the hash is cooked, invert a platter over the skillet and turn out the hash."

These old methods require patience and most women today prefer to bake the hash in a casserole, as in the recipe that follows. Notice that sour cream substitutes for the traditional sweet cream, giving the hash a marvelous flavor. With this old-fashioned New England country dish, serve mustard pickles and your favorite cabbage or apple salad. Keep hot biscuits coming from the oven, butter and honey or strawberry preserves on the table.

RED FLANNEL HASH

"Waste not, want not" was the maxim heeded in colonial homes where leftovers often evolved into noble dishes like this

¾ c. chopped onion
2 tblsp. melted butter or regular margarine
3 c. chopped, cooked potatoes
2 c. finely chopped corned beef

1½ c. chopped, cooked beets or 1 (1 lb.) can chopped beets, drained
½ c. dairy sour cream
1 tsp. salt
¼ tsp. pepper

Sauté onion in melted butter in small skillet until soft. Combine with potatoes, corned beef, beets, sour cream, salt and pepper. Spoon into greased 2-qt. casserole. Smooth out top.

Bake in 350° oven 35 minutes. Or fry mixture slowly in 3 tblsp. butter or bacon drippings in 12″ skillet until bottom is crusty. Invert platter over skillet and turn out, crusty side up. Makes 6 servings.

SCALLOPED POTATOES WITH PORK CHOPS

Few American foods have experienced a history to equal that of potatoes, a native of Peru. The Spanish took them back to Spain in 1520, where they then were grown. They spread to other European countries, but were not accepted because people believed they caused fevers and other ailments. A Frenchman in 1773 published a pamphlet urging his countrymen to plant and eat potatoes, a healthful, nourishing food. Louis XVI wore potato blossoms in his buttonhole to publicize the tuber and ordered that potatoes be served on the royal tables.

Eventually, the prejudices were overcome and potatoes became an important crop in many European countries. The Irish accepted them long before the English who called them Irish potatoes because they were eaten extensively in Ireland. The name stuck.

Scalloped potatoes, plain or baked with pork chops or ham,

have long been farmhouse specials since many American men are meat and potato fans. This hearty dish is also popular for family reunions, church suppers, picnics and all kinds of co-operative suppers. They carry successfully and can be held without deteriorating.

The sauce for our Scalloped Potatoes with Pork Chops is made with chicken broth instead of milk. It gives the dish an interesting flavor and eliminates the concern many women have about the possible curdling as the potatoes bake.

SCALLOPED POTATOES WITH PORK CHOPS

For a hearty, country dinner serve this dish with broccoli, cranberry salad and pumpkin or banana cream pie

6 pork chops, cut ½" thick	1½ tsp. salt
2 tblsp. cooking oil	¼ tsp. pepper
Salt	2 c. chicken broth
Pepper	6 c. sliced pared potatoes
3 tblsp. butter or regular	1 medium onion, sliced and
margarine	separated into rings
3 tblsp. flour	

Brown pork chops on both sides in hot oil in 12" skillet. Sprinkle with salt and pepper to taste.

Meanwhile, melt butter in saucepan. Stir in flour, 1½ tsp. salt and ¼ tsp. pepper. Add chicken broth, and cook, stirring constantly, until mixture comes to a boil.

Place potatoes in bottom of 11×7×1½" baking dish. Top with onion rings. Pour chicken broth mixture evenly over top. Top with pork chops. Cover with foil.

Bake in 350° oven 1 hour. Remove cover and continue baking 30 minutes or until meat is tender. Makes 6 servings.

BAKED HAM SLICE

Pork was the most plentiful meat in early America and baked, home-cured hams were prestigious. Almost every colony boasted about its hams; Virginians and Georgians attributed the superiority of theirs to hogs fattened on peanuts. Families prized their special cures and choices of wood for smoking the meat. Some Pennsylvanians preferred sassafras, but hickory, oak and apple had the most supporters. Sometimes different kinds were mixed to produce fires that gave the desired smoky taste.

These were country hams that required, as they do today, slow precooking in water with seasonings before baking. Sometimes they simmered in cider instead of water.

Most hams in supermarkets today differ from country hams, which no longer are plentiful and are frequently unavailable. These commercial hams are precooked and need not be baked further unless warm meat with special seasoning and glazes is desired. Baked Ham Slice maintains a link to the past. With spices sprinkled on and cider and maple-flavored syrup poured over, Baked Ham Slice is fine for company dinners.

BAKED HAM SLICE

Serve with sweet potatoes, buttered limas and cabbage salad

1 (3 lb.) ham steak, cut 2" thick	Dash of ground cloves
¼ tsp. ground nutmeg	½ c. apple cider or juice
¼ tsp. dry mustard	¼ c. maple-flavored syrup

Place ham in 11×7×1½" baking dish. Sprinkle nutmeg, mustard and cloves over top. Pour cider and syrup over ham.

Bake in 325° oven 1 hour, basting 2 or 3 times. Makes 8 to 10 servings.

HAM HOCKS WITH COLLARD GREENS

Soul food is Afro-American and it is as southern as greens with pork and sweet potato pie, which bear this identity. Creators of this type of home cooking were brought from Africa to a strange land with strange foods. They took what they could find and used it skillfully in their humble kitchens. At first their dishes were food for the poor, but they tasted so good that other Southerners, including the affluent, adopted them.

Greens were an important ingredient in this cookery. They were cooked just right, which means for a comparatively short time. Pork was a favored teammate.

Collards, one of the great southern greens, are available in supermarkets across the country, a testimony to their wide acceptance. Ham Hocks with Collard Greens is one of the most revered of soul foods. Some women add more seasonings to the greens than our recipe lists, especially one or two little pods of dried red pepper and one or two very thin lemon slices. Add them to our recipe if you like. Serve the main dish steaming hot, with corn sticks.

HAM HOCKS WITH COLLARD GREENS

Do save the pot liquor to use in soups, but first ladle some of it over the greens and ham. Much of the credit for the fame of southern home cooking belongs to the early Afro-Americans

1 lb. crosscut smoked ham hocks	1½ lbs. collard greens
6 c. water	⅛ tsp. pepper
1 c. chopped onion	Salt (optional)

Combine ham hocks, water and onion in Dutch oven or large kettle. Cover and simmer about 2 hours or until ham hocks are tender.

Meanwhile, wash greens. Remove hard center vein and chop greens coarsely.

Remove ham hocks from liquid. Chop, discarding skin and bones. Add ham, greens and pepper to liquid. Cover and simmer 30 to 45 minutes or until greens are tender. Season with salt, if necessary. Makes 6 servings.

JAMBALAYA

Jambalaya is a hash often of leftovers with a rice base. Originating in New Orleans late in the 18th century, it is a dish popular in every state south of the Maxon-Dixon line between the Mississippi River and the Atlantic Ocean. In coastal regions shrimp, oysters and/or other fish are combined with the rice while inland, scraps of leftover cooked pork, ham or chicken are the common additions. Seasonings have much to do with the success of the dish.

In our Jambalaya ham and shrimp, as well as bacon and chicken broth, contribute to flavor.

JAMBALAYA

Cook rice tender, fluffy and dry, never moist or gummy. For company dish serve Jambalaya with green salad and lemon sherbet

6 slices bacon, chopped	1 tsp. salt
1 c. chopped onion	½ tsp. dried thyme leaves
2 medium green peppers, cut in strips	¼ tsp. ground red pepper
2 c. uncooked regular rice	1 lb. cooked, smoked ham, cut in strips
2 cloves garlic, minced	½ lb. cleaned, frozen shrimp, thawed
1 (1 lb. 12 oz.) can tomatoes, cut up	2 tblsp. chopped fresh parsley (optional)
2 c. chicken broth	

Cook bacon in Dutch oven until crisp. Drain on paper towels. Add onion to bacon drippings and cook over low heat, stirring occasionally, 5 minutes. Add green pepper; continue cooking 3 minutes. Add rice; cook over moderately hot heat, stirring frequently, until rice becomes somewhat opaque. Add bacon, garlic, tomatoes, chicken broth, salt, thyme, red pepper and ham. Bring to a boil.

Cover and bake in 350° oven 15 minutes. Stir in shrimp; continue baking 20 to 25 minutes or until rice is tender and liquid absorbed. Serve garnished with parsley, if desired. Makes 6 servings.

SAUSAGE/BEAN SUPPER

Indians were cultivating and eating lima beans, the most popular broad beans, when Europeans arrived in the New World. Champlain, the French explorer, reported that he planted Brazil beans, another name for them, in colonial days. Eventually, "Lima" won over "Brazil" in recognition of the capital city of Peru, the country in which the beans originated. But neither of these names is as poetic as the one the Incas used—"little doves" —because the blossoms of the bean vines resemble little birds.

Pork sausage was a staple item many months of the year in early American and later in pioneer homes. Sausage cakes were served for breakfast, but women also included sausage as an ingredient in many dishes. Sausage/Bean Supper is a contemporary casserole in which sausage and dried lima beans pair off in a hearty dish for cold-weather meals, suggestive of those served long ago in country homes.

SAUSAGE/BEAN SUPPER

A big recipe—freeze the surplus. It will come in handy

2 c. large, dry lima beans	**1 tblsp. salt**
1½ qts. water	**½ tsp. pepper**
2 lbs. bulk pork sausage	**1 (1 lb. 12 oz.) can**
1 c. chopped onion	**tomatoes, cut up**
1 c. chopped celery	**1 (8 oz.) can tomato sauce**
½ c. chopped green pepper	

Wash beans. Combine beans and water in Dutch oven. Bring to a boil; boil 2 minutes. Remove from heat, cover and let stand 1 hour. (Or soak beans overnight.) Drain.

Meanwhile, cook sausage, onion, celery and green pepper in large skillet until sausage is browned and vegetables are tender. Drain off fat.

Combine beans, sausage mixture, salt, pepper, tomatoes and tomato sauce. Turn into 3-qt. casserole.

Bake in 350° oven 1 hour or until beans are tender. Makes 12 servings.

BAKED SAUSAGE STUFFING

Roasting the turkey and the stuffing separately is an increasingly popular custom. The big bird cooks in a little less time when not stuffed and it is easier and quicker to get the turkey in the oven because it can be cooking while the stuffing is being made.

Cooked turkey and chicken, covered with broth, will keep up to six months when frozen, one month without the broth. The stuffing is best refrigerated for no longer than a day or two.

Baked Sausage Stuffing, a casserole, is the adaptation of a similar mixture baked in turkey. Serve it as a side accompaniment, or later to extend the leftover meat. It bakes at the same oven temperature as turkey.

BAKED SAUSAGE STUFFING

This stuffing is on the moist side, highly seasoned and tasty

1 lb. bulk pork sausage	1 tsp. rubbed sage
1 c. chopped onion	½ tsp. dried thyme leaves
1 c. chopped celery	¼ tsp. pepper
Butter or regular margarine	2 eggs, beaten
10 c. soft bread cubes	1 (13¾ oz.) can chicken
1 tsp. salt	broth

Cook sausage, onion and celery in skillet until meat is browned and vegetables tender. Pour off drippings, reserving ¼ c. Add melted butter or regular margarine if necessary to make ¼ c.

Combine bread cubes, sausage mixture, reserved drippings, salt, sage, thyme and pepper in large bowl.

Blend together eggs and chicken broth. Stir into bread mixture. Turn into greased 2-qt. casserole. Cover and bake in 325° oven 40 minutes. Uncover and continue baking 15 minutes. Makes 8 servings.

PERFECT ROAST TURKEY

Prepare the Turkey:

Thaw bird if frozen. Let it thaw unwrapped in refrigerator 2 to 4 days, depending on size. Or if package is watertight, place it under running cold water until bird is pliable, 2 to 6 hours. Rinse inside and out with cold water, drain and pat dry with paper towel. Stuff if you wish. Shake bird to settle stuffing, but do not pack it. Truss turkey; brush with fat.

To Roast Turkey:

Place breast side up on rack in shallow pan. Do not cover pan or add water. Cover turkey loosely with foil; then press the foil tightly at ends of drumsticks and neck; do not let foil touch top or sides of bird. Cook in 325° oven; lift foil to baste occasionally with fat (optional). This way of cooking gives the most attractive roast turkey for carving at the table.

When turkey is two-thirds done (see Roasting Guide), cut band of skin or cord that holds drumsticks against turkey. This shortens cooking time by letting heat penetrate to inside of thighs. If you use a meat thermometer, insert it now and continue roasting.

Roasting Guide for Turkey

Ready-to-Cook Weight	Approximate Cooking Time	Internal Temperature
6– 8 lbs.	3–3½	185°
8–12 lbs.	3½–4½	185°
12–16 lbs.	4½–5½	185°
16–20 lbs.	5½–6½	185°
20–24 lbs.	6½–7	185°

If you do not use a thermometer, test for doneness at least 30 minutes before approximate timetable indicates turkey will be done. If you do not stuff turkey, it cooks a little more quickly. Allow cooked turkey to stand at room temperature about 20 minutes. This makes carving easier.

AMERICAN-FRIED CHICKEN

Fried chicken in early days was a seasonal treat, since a new crop of chickens was started in the spring. When the baby chicks grew into birds weighing about two pounds, the big event—the year's first fried chicken dinner—occurred.

The "spring chickens," as they were called, were killed and dressed for each meal since there was no refrigeration. Chicken pieces were rolled in seasoned flour and cooked in a heavy skillet on the kitchen hearth in sizzling lard, or sometimes in a mixture of lard and butter. Bowls of milk gravy, made in the same skillet, accompanied the chicken. In this respect, American chicken differed from that of most nationalities in which the chicken was partially cooked or served in a sauce. In some American colonies, especially in Maryland, the cream gravy sometimes was poured over the fried chicken on the platter.

What the colonists called fried chicken in the winter was actually precooked not fried. The bird was mature and less tender, usually a hen. Here is a recipe from an 1873 handwritten "receipt" book of an up-state New York woman, which shows how incomplete old-time recipes could be:

"Thompkins Country Fryed Chicken: Boil in water until tender. Take and roll in flour and fry in hot butter. Season highly with salt and pepper."

Later with home refrigeration the chicken pieces were chilled in buttermilk or sweet milk to cover, then drained, rolled in flour and fried. The dipping milk was saved for the gravy. Sometimes herbs or a bit of garlic were added.

The menu for the season's first fried chicken varied with the area. In New York State new potatoes and peas were served, with strawberry shortcake for dessert, while the South preferred fluffy rice and corn pudding. On the frontier, there was no substitute for mashed potatoes, except for potato salad for the rare picnic.

AMERICAN-FRIED CHICKEN

Today's tender broiler-fryer makes frying chicken easy work

⅓ c. flour	Cooking oil
1 tsp. salt	3 tblsp. flour
¼ tsp. pepper	¼ tsp. salt
1 (2½ to 3 lb.) broiler-	Dash of pepper
fryer, cut up	1½ c. milk or light cream

Combine ⅓ c. flour, 1 tsp. salt and ¼ tsp. pepper in paper or plastic bag. Shake several pieces of chicken at a time in bag to coat with flour mixture. Heat ¼″ oil in large heavy skillet. Lightly brown chicken on all sides, 15 to 20 minutes. Cover tightly and cook over low heat 20 to 30 minutes or until chicken is tender. Uncover and continue cooking 10 minutes.

Pour off all but 3 tblsp. pan drippings from skillet, keeping crusty bits in the pan. Stir in 3 tblsp. flour, ¼ tsp. salt and dash of pepper. Add 1½ c. milk or light cream, and cook over low heat, stirring constantly or until mixture comes to a boil. Makes 4 servings.

CHICKEN FRICASSEE WITH SAGE DUMPLINGS

Chicken with dumplings suggests big farmhouses in up-state New York and company arriving after church for Sunday dinner. Many people in rural neighborhoods during the 19th century traditionally served a platter of chicken (usually an older hen), bordered by plump, light-as-a-feather dumplings, moist with broth. Traditional accompaniments were fluffy mashed potatoes, gravy made with the chicken broth, peas when available, home-made relishes and cherry pie. Green tomato and cucumber pickles came off the shelves of the fruit closet. Delicate, quivering grape jelly or sparkling crab apple jelly that had been poured hot into glasses containing a sage leaf were the choices to accompany chicken.

Times have changed. The recipe for Chicken Fricassee with

Sage Dumplings calls for a large broiler-fryer, much more available in supermarkets than stewing hens, a better buy and quick-cooking.

CHICKEN FRICASSEE WITH SAGE DUMPLINGS

This old-time chicken treat will provide a hearty and pleasing dinner that will uphold country cooking's fine reputation

1 (3 to 4 lb.) broiler-fryer, cut up
¾ c. flour
2 tsp. salt
¼ tsp. pepper
½ c. cooking oil
1 c. water
¼ c. chopped onion
1 tsp. parsley flakes
3 tblsp. flour

½ tsp. salt
⅛ tsp. pepper
Milk
1½ c. sifted flour
2 tsp. baking powder
¾ tsp. salt
½ tsp. rubbed sage
3 tblsp. shortening
¾ c. milk

Shake chicken pieces in mixture of ¾ c. flour, 2 tsp. salt and ¼ tsp. pepper. Brown on all sides in hot oil in large skillet, removing pieces as they brown. Drain off fat, reserving 3 tblsp.; set aside.

Return chicken to skillet; add water, onion and parsley. Cover and simmer about 45 minutes or until chicken is tender. Remove chicken from skillet. Pour off cooking liquid and reserve.

Add reserved 3 tblsp. fat to skillet. Blend in 3 tblsp. flour, ½ tsp. salt and ⅛ tsp. pepper. Add enough milk to reserved cooking liquid to make 3 c. Add to flour mixture in skillet and cook, stirring constantly, until mixture comes to a boil. Return chicken to skillet. Sift together 1½ c. flour, baking powder, ¾ tsp. salt and rubbed sage. Cut in shortening until mixture resembles meal. Stir in ¾ c. milk.

Drop dumplings by spoonfuls onto hot chicken. Cook uncovered 10 minutes. Cover and continue cooking 20 minutes. Makes 8 to 10 servings.

Note: If you use a stewing hen, simmer it 3 hours or until chicken is tender. Add more water if necessary.

TURKEY STUFFING CASSEROLE

Some people enjoy the stuffing and gravy as much or more than the roast turkey; so often the leftovers are sparse. Our Turkey Stuffing Casserole recipe tells how to make an excellent bread stuffing and a gravy or sauce with chicken broth to combine with cubes of leftover turkey. Aside from being a quick and thrifty dish, it is truly delicious.

TURKEY STUFFING CASSEROLE

Mildly seasoned, but you can add more seasoning if you like

1 c. chopped onion	3 c. cubed, cooked turkey
1 c. chopped celery	3 tblsp. butter or regular
½ c. butter or regular	margarine
margarine	3 tblsp. flour
2 qts. soft bread cubes	½ tsp. salt
(½″)	1 (13¾ oz.) can chicken
1 tsp. salt	broth
½ tsp. rubbed sage	¾ c. water
½ tsp. poultry seasoning	2 eggs, well beaten
¼ tsp. pepper	2 tblsp. chopped parsley

Sauté onion and celery in ½ c. melted butter until soft.

Combine bread cubes, 1 tsp. salt, sage, poultry seasoning and pepper in greased 3-qt. casserole. Add onion mixture and toss gently. Top with turkey.

Melt 3 tblsp. butter in saucepan, blend in flour and ½ tsp. salt. Add chicken broth and water; cook, stirring constantly, until mixture comes to a boil. Stir hot broth slowly into eggs; add parsley. Pour over turkey in casserole.

Cover and bake in 350° oven 30 minutes. Uncover and continue baking 15 minutes. Makes 8 servings.

TENNESSEE TURKEY HASH

For good turkey hash the cooked meat is cut in cubes, not ground. Leftover gravy is added if available, a little sweet or sour cream if it is not. Potatoes are included only when necessary to stretch the meat. The hash is moist, but never runny, and it's crisp-crusted on the outside.

Tennessee Turkey Hash is the modern adaptation of an old-time dish with dry hashed browns added to increase the number of servings. A sauce of canned cream of mushroom soup and sour cream accompanies the hash.

TENNESSEE TURKEY HASH

For company, garnish this dish with pimiento and egg slices

1 (13¾ oz.) can chicken broth
¾ c. water
1 tsp. salt
⅛ tsp. pepper
1 (5½ oz.) pkg. dry hashed brown potatoes
½ c. finely chopped onion
½ c. finely chopped green pepper

½ c. butter or regular margarine
3 c. chopped, cooked turkey
¼ c. dairy sour cream
1 (10¾ oz.) can condensed cream of mushroom soup
¼ c. dairy sour cream

Combine chicken broth, water, salt and pepper in saucepan; bring to a boil. Remove from heat. Add potatoes and let stand 10 minutes.

Meanwhile, sauté onion and green pepper in butter in large, heavy skillet until soft.

Combine potato mixture, turkey and ¼ c. sour cream. Add to onion mixture in skillet. Fry until golden brown and crusty. Turn with wide spatula.

Meanwhile, combine soup and ¼ c. sour cream. Heat thoroughly, but do not boil. Serve with hash. Makes 6 servings.

CREAMED EGGS SUPREME

The egg-bacon team has had the approval of Americans from early days until now. And, when it comes to ways to combine the two foods, country women are clever.

Creamed Eggs Supreme make a superior supper dish, especially if served on toasted English muffins or on hot biscuits.

CREAMED EGGS SUPREME

New bacon and egg dish with cheese—appetite satisfying

3 tblsp. butter or regular margarine
3 tblsp. flour
¾ tsp. salt
⅛ tsp. pepper
1½ c. milk
1½ c. shredded process sharp American cheese (6 oz.)

6 hard-cooked eggs, chopped
4 slices crisp-cooked bacon, crumbled
Toast, toasted English muffins or hot biscuits

Melt butter in saucepan; blend in flour, salt and pepper. Add milk, and cook, stirring constantly, until mixture comes to a boil. Add cheese and stir until melted. Stir in eggs and bacon; heat thoroughly. Serve over toast. Makes 6 servings.

CURRIED SCRAMBLED EGGS WITH CORN

Along the Atlantic watershed from New England through Georgia, nine out of every ten people in the 17th and 18th centuries lived on family farms. Almost every household eventually had poultry flocks that furnished eggs for kitchen use. No wonder early Americans developed many excellent egg dishes.

The skill of Indians in combining corn with different foods was observed by early Americans. Then when trade developed with faraway places, captains of clipper ships returned home with exotic spices, including curry powder. Used sparingly, it enhanced many chicken and egg dishes. Curried Scrambled Eggs with Corn became a summer favorite.

CURRIED SCRAMBLED EGGS WITH CORN

With frozen corn this is an around-the-year special

1 c. frozen corn	⅓ c. milk
2 tblsp. butter or regular margarine	1 tsp. salt
	¼ tsp. curry powder
8 eggs	⅛ tsp. pepper

Cook corn in melted butter in 10″ skillet until hot.

Beat together eggs, milk, salt, curry powder and pepper; pour into skillet. Cook slowly, scraping bottom and sides of skillet with spatula until eggs are set. Makes 6 servings.

CATFISH GUMBO

A muddle in Carolina Low Country is a fish stew, but when it contains okra, it is called gumbo in some parts of the South. Gumbo is the African name for okra, which was imported from Africa. Gumbos are soul food, created by Afro-Americans, but all Southerners like them. The classic fish stew contains, in addition to fish, tomatoes, onions, pork in some form, salt, pepper, thyme and either bottled hot pepper or Worcestershire sauce.

Some of the favorite fish stews are made with catfish, which is popular not only in the South but also in many parts of the Midwest, where pan-frying is the common method of cooking.

Tributaries of the Mississippi River furnished fresh catfish for many years. Catfish "farming" now provides superior catfish for home and restaurant tables. The fingerlings—very small fish—are brought to man-made, fresh-water lakes or ponds and fed a high-protein diet.

CATFISH GUMBO

The classic accompaniment for catfish stew is corn bread; in the South it's usually hush puppies, a corn bread cooked in deep fat

2 beef bouillon cubes
2 c. boiling water
1½ lbs. fresh, skinned
   catfish, or frozen and
   thawed
1 c. chopped onion
½ c. chopped green pepper
½ c. chopped celery
1 clove garlic, minced
3 tblsp. cooking oil or
   bacon drippings

1 (1 lb.) can tomatoes, cut
   up
1 (10 oz.) pkg. frozen okra,
   thawed
2 tsp. salt
¼ tsp. pepper
¼ tsp. dried thyme leaves
¼ tsp. bottled hot pepper
   sauce
1 bay leaf
1 c. uncooked rice

Dissolve bouillon cubes in boiling water in large saucepan. Cut catfish in serving pieces; add to bouillon. Cover and simmer 15 minutes or until fish flakes easily. Remove fish to paper toweling; reserve liquid.

Meanwhile, sauté onion, green pepper, celery and garlic in hot oil in Dutch oven until tender. Add reserved cooking liquid and tomatoes. Cut okra in crosswise slices and add to tomato mixture. Add salt, pepper, thyme, hot pepper sauce and bay leaf. Cover and simmer 30 minutes.

When fish is cool enough to handle, debone and break it in bite-size pieces with your fingers. Add to tomato mixture and simmer 5 minutes. Remove bay leaf.

Cook rice according to package directions. Place ½ c. cooked rice in each of 6 bowls. Fill with gumbo. Makes 6 servings.

OVEN-FRIED FISH

The favorite way to cook fish in midwestern country kitchens is to roll it in cornmeal, biscuit mix or flour and pan-fry it in butter, cooking oil or bacon drippings. Pan-frying takes only about 20 minutes, 10 minutes for each side. Two skillets are required to handle two pounds of fish fillets (enough to make 6 to 8 servings) however, and both need almost constant attention. The fish takes on a crisp, golden crust, but sometimes becomes dry. When close watching is inconvenient, try oven-frying. The fish can be forgotten for 20 to 25 minutes while the rest of the meal is prepared. It is not as crisp as pan-fried but is moist. Cooking fish this way on busy days is a real help.

OVEN-FRIED FISH

Serve with lemon wedges or tartar sauce, and finely shredded coleslaw

½ c. butter or regular
   margarine
2 lbs. fish fillets, fresh or
   frozen and thawed

1 egg, beaten
1 c. cracker crumbs
1 tsp. seasoned salt
¼ tsp. pepper

Melt butter in 15½ ×10½ ×1″ jelly roll pan in 375° oven.

Meanwhile, dip fish fillets in egg, then in mixture of cracker crumbs, seasoned salt and pepper. Place each fillet in pan, turning to coat with butter.

Bake in 375° oven 20 to 25 minutes or until a light golden brown. Makes 6 to 8 servings.

MAINE CORN CHOWDER

"Many people say hamburgers and apple pie are the typical American foods," an Oneida Indian woman recently confided to a Farm Journal food editor. "They are not what we true Americans call native foods," she added. "We think of corn soup, wild rice, milkweed, cowslip, ferns and other greens, and venison."

Corn has the Indians' enduring affection—it is the grain their ancestors believed was the food of gods. They knew from experience how important it was in sustaining life.

A variety of corn soups copied from Indians became standard

fare in colonial homes. When cattle and hog production made headway in the eastern colonies, milk and salt pork joined corn in soup kettles, and chowders were the result. Many women also added potatoes, which thickened the chowders slightly and contributed flavor. Maine Corn Chowder included potatoes, famous product of the region, especially in Aroostook County. Our recipe differs little from those that welcomed families to the supper table long ago, but because bacon and canned corn always are available, we use those ingredients instead of salt pork and fresh or dried corn.

MAINE CORN CHOWDER

Use salt pork instead of bacon, if you have it; fresh or dried corn instead of canned

5 slices bacon, chopped	⅛ tsp. pepper
2 medium onions, sliced	1 (1 lb. 1 oz.) can cream-
3 c. diced pared potatoes	style corn
2 c. water	2 c. milk
1 tsp. salt	

Cook bacon in Dutch oven until crisp. Remove and drain on paper towels. Set aside.

Sauté onion in bacon drippings until soft. Add potatoes, water, salt and pepper. Bring to a boil. Reduce heat; cover and simmer 12 to 15 minutes or until potatoes are tender.

Add corn and milk; heat thoroughly. Garnish with bacon. Makes about 9 cups.

WINTER CORN CHOWDER

Early colonists enjoyed steaming bowls of corn chowder made with dried corn. Many people still believe it tastes best that way (see Index for Oven-dried Corn).

An interesting difference between Winter Corn Chowder and others made with dried corn is that the liquid is chicken broth instead of milk. This produces a chowder in which the flavors of dried corn, bacon, chicken and onion mingle.

WINTER CORN CHOWDER

Serve with pickled beets and eggs, grilled cheese sandwiches and oven-warm gingerbread topped with thick applesauce for dessert

1½ c. Oven-dried Corn (see Index)	2 c. chopped onion
	4 c. milk
2 (13¾ oz.) cans chicken broth	2 tsp. sugar
	½ tsp. salt
6 slices bacon, diced	⅛ tsp. pepper

Rinse dried corn. Combine corn and chicken broth in large saucepan; bring to a boil. Remove from heat and let stand 2 hours. Heat to simmering; cover and cook 45 minutes.

Meanwhile, cook bacon in small skillet until crisp. Drain on paper towels. Sauté onion in bacon drippings until soft. Add to corn mixture and simmer 5 minutes. Add milk, sugar, salt and pepper, and heat thoroughly. Serve garnished with bacon. Makes 2½ quarts.

CHICKEN/CORN SOUP WITH RIVELS

While iron kettles of corn chowder bubbled in New England fireplaces, Pennsylvania Dutch women were dropping rivels into some of their soups. These remarkable cooks rubbed a mixture of flour, salt and egg through their fingers so that it flaked into boiling soup. The rivels held their shape while cooking and had a texture similar to that of boiled rice.

Perhaps the most famous Pennsylvania Dutch soups were those made with chicken and succulent corn cut from the cob. There are many recipes for them but they vary little. Chicken/Corn Soup with Rivels is almost identical to soups made 200 years ago, except that the more available broiler-fryer substitutes for the stewing hen once culled from the farm flock because she was a lazy egg layer. Frozen corn substitutes for the seasonal fresh kernels today.

CHICKEN/CORN SOUP WITH RIVELS

Chopped parsley and hard-cooked egg are traditional garnishes. Add them to soup bowls just before serving

1 (3 to 3½ lb.) broiler-fryer, cut up	1 (10 oz.) pkg. frozen corn, thawed
2 qts. water	¼ c. chopped fresh parsley
1 c. chopped onion	1 c. sifted flour
½ c. chopped celery	¼ tsp. salt
3 tsp. salt	1 egg, beaten
¼ tsp. pepper	

Combine chicken, water, onion, celery, 3 tsp. salt and pepper in Dutch oven. Bring to a boil. Reduce heat; cover and simmer 1 hour. Remove chicken pieces. Cut chicken into bite-size pieces, discarding skin and bones. Return chicken to broth along with corn and parsley.

Combine flour, ¼ tsp. salt and egg to make a crumbly mixture the size of small peas. If necessary, add 1 to 2 tsp. milk. Drop into soup. Cover and simmer 15 minutes. Makes 11 cups.

GREEN BEAN SOUP

This hearty soup, thick with potatoes, chunks of ham and green beans has been a three-generation favorite in a Kansas home. It has been served since the early pioneer days as all the foods were plentiful on Mennonite farms.

GREEN BEAN SOUP

This heirloom recipe has been a favorite for generations

1 meaty ham bone (about 2 lbs.)	¼ c. chopped fresh parsley
2 qts. water	4 sprigs summer savory, chopped, or 1 tsp. dried savory
4 c. cut-up green beans (1″ pieces)	1 tsp. salt
3 c. cubed pared potatoes	¼ tsp. pepper
2 medium onions, sliced	1 c. light cream

Cook ham bone in water in 6-qt. saucepan until tender, for about 1½ hours. Remove meat from bone and cut in chunks. Put back in soup base.

Add green beans, potatoes, onions, parsley, savory, salt and pepper. Bring to a boil; reduce heat and simmer, covered, for 20 minutes or until vegetables are tender. Skim off excess fat.

Just before serving, stir in light cream. Makes about 3½ quarts.

AMERICAN PEA SOUP PLUS

Meals that cooked in one pot were a joy to busy colonial women. It was easier to get a dinner of vegetables and meat in the heavy iron pot, hung over the fire with strong chains or a crane, than to prepare food over hearth coals. One-kettle meals did not disappear with kitchen fireplaces, because they require little watching.

American Pea Soup Plus resembles some old-fashioned dishes that cooked in one pot. The soup and smoked pork simmer together with occasional stirring.

AMERICAN PEA SOUP PLUS

Serve the soup in bowls, the meat on a platter with mustard; add rye bread and apple-cabbage salad to the menu

2 c. dry, split green peas	2 qts. water
3 lbs. smoked pork shoulder roll	½ tsp. whole peppercorns
	¼ tsp. whole allspice
1 c. chopped onion	1 bay leaf
1 c. chopped celery	Salt
1 c. sliced peeled carrots	

Wash peas. Combine peas, pork, onion, celery, carrots and water in Dutch oven. Bring to a boil.

Meanwhile, tie peppercorns, allspice and bay leaf in cloth; add to Dutch oven. Reduce heat; cover and simmer about 1 hour 45 minutes or until meat is tender. Stir occasionally. Remove spice bag and discard. Add salt to taste.

Remove pork from soup; let stand 10 minutes. Slice to serve with soup. Makes about 3 quarts.

DOWN-EAST BEAN SOUP

The Pilgrims made bean porridge, a thick soup, with the red, white, yellow-eyed and speckled beans of all sizes that the Indians grew and cooked. Before the 17th century ended, they were cooking meat with beans in soups as we do in Down-East Bean Soup. Notice that the recipe calls for New England-style beans, the traditional Boston baked beans processed in cans. This saves cooking fuel and speeds up meal preparation. Team with crackers or toast, lettuce salad, mustard pickles, baked apples or other fruit, and cookies and milk to drink for a pleasant meal.

DOWN-EAST BEAN SOUP

You can make this substantial soup in less than 20 minutes

1 c. finely chopped ham	1 tblsp. brown sugar
¼ c. chopped onion	1 tblsp. vinegar
¼ c. chopped green pepper	½ tsp. salt
2 tblsp. bacon drippings	1 (1 lb. 6 oz.) jar New
1 (1 lb.) can tomatoes, cut	England-style baked
up	beans
½ c. water	

Cook ham, onion and green pepper in bacon drippings in large saucepan until meat is browned and vegetables are soft. Add tomatoes, water, brown sugar, vinegar and salt; cover and simmer 10 minutes.

Reserve 1 c. beans from jar. Mash the remainder. Add reserved and mashed beans to soup. Heat thoroughly, stirring occasionally. Makes about 5 cups.

PLANTATION BEAN SOUP

An Englishman visiting Virginia's Roanoke Colony reported on his return that the Indians cooked beans until they fell apart in the broth. This was one of the earliest, if not the first description of American bean soup. It has become an American institution. Every region has favorites. Plantation Bean Soup is an up-to-date southern special.

PLANTATION BEAN SOUP

Turnip greens add subtle flavor, which, when combined with ham, beans and smoked sausage, produces soup that delights everybody

1½ c. dry Great Northern beans	1 tblsp. salt
	¼ tsp. pepper
3½ qts. water	2 c. cubed pared potatoes
1 lb. ham hocks or meaty ham bone	1 (10 oz.) pkg. frozen chopped turnip greens
1 c. chopped onion	¾ lb. smoked garlic sausage
1 c. chopped celery	

Wash beans. Combine beans and water in 8-qt. kettle. Bring to a boil and boil 2 minutes. Remove from heat; cover and let stand 1 hour. (Or soak beans overnight.)

Add ham hocks, onion, celery, salt and pepper to beans. Cover and simmer 1½ hours. Add potatoes, turnip greens and whole sausage; simmer 20 minutes or until vegetables are tender. Remove ham and sausage from soup. Chop ham and cut sausage in ¾″ slices. Return to soup and heat thoroughly. Add more salt if needed. Makes 4½ quarts.

COMPANY BEAN SOUP

Midwesterners like the taste of ham in their bowls of bean soup, and they frequently add tomatoes. Company Bean Soup, as its name suggests, can be the center of interest at a supper party. Serve buffet style: Ladle the soup from a tureen or big bowl into individual bowls and let guests help themselves to relishes and slices of homemade rye and white bread, which can be baked ahead and frozen. For dessert, set a bowl of mixed fruits and a plate of brownies on the buffet and invite guests to "come and get it" while you fill coffee cups.

COMPANY BEAN SOUP

Use condensed chicken broth to add flavor to this soup

2 c. dry navy beans	1 (1 lb.) can tomatoes, cut up
2 qts. water	2 tsp. salt
1½ lbs. ham hocks	¼ tsp. pepper
2 c. chopped onion	1 bay leaf
1 c. chopped celery	2 c. shredded Cheddar cheese (8 oz.)
2 cloves garlic, minced	¼ c. chopped parsley
3 (10¾ oz.) cans condensed chicken broth	
1 qt. water	

Wash beans. Combine beans and 2 qts. water in 8-qt. kettle. Bring to a boil; boil 2 minutes. Remove from heat; cover and let stand 1 hour. (Or soak beans overnight.)

Add ham hocks, onion, celery, garlic, chicken broth, water, tomatoes, salt, pepper and bay leaf. Bring to a boil; reduce heat, cover and simmer 2 hours or until ham and beans are tender.

Remove ham hocks; cut off meat and return it to kettle. Discard bones and bay leaf. Add cheese; cook, stirring, just until cheese is melted. Serve sprinkled with parsley. Makes about 5 quarts.

TUNA CLUB SANDWICHES

Chicken club sandwiches, an American concoction, now are served in many countries. In the beginning they consisted of two slices of bread, toasted and buttered, with a lettuce leaf spread with mayonnaise on the bottom slice of toast. On it were arranged in layers, cooked chicken, tomato and bacon slices. The second piece of toast, buttered side down, made the top. Somewhere and sometime a third slice of toast was inserted in the sandwich, possibly for a heartier version and the idea caught on.

These club sandwiches inspired the development of Tuna Club Sandwiches. Tuna salad assumes the role of chicken, cucumber slices replace the tomatoes and sliced hard-cooked eggs substitute for bacon. You can insert a lettuce leaf on the bottom slice of toast, if you like.

TUNA CLUB SANDWICHES

The availability of canned tuna certainly is a convenience in making this sandwich

2 cucumbers, pared and
    thinly sliced
2 tblsp. salt
2 tblsp. vinegar
2 tblsp. salad oil
⅛ tsp. pepper
⅛ tsp. dried dillweed
2 (7 oz.) cans tuna, drained
    and flaked

1 c. chopped celery
½ c. chopped parsley
½ c. mayonnaise or salad
    dressing
18 slices toast
Butter or regular margarine
6 hard-cooked eggs, sliced

Combine cucumbers and salt. Set aside in strainer to drain 1 hour; rinse with cold water. Place drained cucumbers in bowl. Stir in vinegar, oil, pepper and dillweed. Marinate at least 30 minutes.

Combine tuna, celery, parsley and mayonnaise.

Spread 6 slices toast with butter. Spread each with ½ c. tuna mixture. Top each with a toast slice, then with egg and drained cucumber slices.

Butter remaining 6 toast slices; place over cucumber slices, buttered side down. Cut sandwiches diagonally in halves. Hold layers together with wood pick. Makes 6 servings.

MIDWESTERN TURKEY/CHEESE SANDWICHES

The first Thanksgiving feast gave turkey a place of honor forever after in the American holiday. The birds served on that historic occasion were North American wild turkeys, for the delicate-fleshed bronze or Mexican turkeys domesticated by the Aztecs were unknown to New England Indians. The Pilgrims borrowed the idea of a thanks-giving celebration from their Indian neighbors, who every autumn feasted and gave thanks to their spirits and gods for crops of corn, beans and pumpkins and for an abundance of game.

Roast turkey on American holiday tables guarantees leftovers. Midwestern Turkey/Cheese Sandwiches, a combination main dish and salad, is a favorite in the Midwest. It is an adaptation of a Chicago restaurant's "specialty of the house." First cover rye bread slices with sliced, cooked turkey, then with thin Swiss cheese slices. Arrange mounds of finely shredded lettuce on the cheese and spoon on Easy Thousand Island Dressing. Cross bacon strips over the top. Garnish with tomato quarters.

MIDWESTERN TURKEY/CHEESE SANDWICHES

Build each open-face sandwich on serving plate and take to table

12 slices bacon
12 slices buttered rye bread
Sliced, cooked turkey
Salt
8 oz. Swiss cheese, thinly sliced

6 c. shredded lettuce
3 c. Easy Thousand Island Dressing (recipe follows)
12 tomato wedges (optional)

Cut bacon in half crosswise; pan-fry until crisp. Drain on paper towels; set aside.

On each of 6 plates place 2 slices buttered bread, side by side. Make open-face sandwiches as follows: Cover bread slices with turkey. Sprinkle with salt; cover with cheese slices. Mound 1 c. lettuce over cheese; spoon ½ c. Easy Thousand Island Dressing over. Top each with 4 half slices cooked bacon. Garnish with tomato wedges, if desired. Makes 6 servings.

Easy Thousand Island Dressing: Combine 3 c. mayonnaise or salad dressing, 3 hard-cooked eggs, chopped, ⅓ c. chili sauce, 3 tblsp. chopped dill pickle and 2 tsp. grated onion. Refrigerate several hours to blend flavors. Makes 5 cups.

STUFFED SUGAR PUMPKIN

Herds of deer troubled early colonists and western pioneers. When the pumpkins were ripe, the fleet animals moved in and hollowed them out leaving only the shells. That was a serious loss because pumpkins and winter squash were extremely important in the diet, as expressed by this ditty written in New England in 1638:

> We had pumpkins in the morning
> And pumpkins at noon
> If it were not for pumpkins
> We'd be undone soon.

One of the earliest ways to cook the vegetable was to slice off the top of a small, very ripe pumpkin, scoop out the seeds and stringy substance, fill with milk, put the top on for a lid and bake in the tin or brick fireplace oven 6 to 7 hours. Then milk was added again and the pumpkin was eaten from the shell.

In our recipe for stuffed pumpkin, the natural shell is stuffed with a nourishing meat and rice filling. This makes a spectacular dish to serve to guests.

STUFFED SUGAR PUMPKIN

A moist, flavorful, ground beef filling baked in a pumpkin shell

1 (3 to 4 lb.) sugar pumpkin	1 c. cooked regular rice
1 tsp. salt	¾ tsp. pepper
½ tsp. dry mustard	2 tsp. salt
1 medium onion, chopped	½ tsp. dry mustard
1 lb. ground beef	½ c. water
3 eggs, slightly beaten	

Cut lid out of pumpkin; remove seeds. Prick inside cavity with fork. Rub inside with 1 tsp. salt and ½ tsp. mustard.

Cook onion and ground beef in skillet until lightly browned. Remove from heat. Add eggs, rice, pepper, 2 tsp. salt and ½ tsp. mustard. Stuff pumpkin with mixture (size of cavity will vary with pumpkins—you may need more filling if pumpkin meat is very thick). Replace pumpkin lid.

Place stuffed pumpkin in shallow pan with ½ c. water. Bake in 350° oven 1 hour 30 minutes or until pumpkin is tender. Add more water if necessary. Makes 6 servings.

BOSTON BAKED BEANS

Indians, according to tradition, baked beans in small holes in the ground which they lined with stones. They built fires in the holes and heated the stones. Then they put beans in covered pots in the holes and covered the openings with sod or flat stones to retain the heat. The slow cooking continued for hours.

"Bean-hole Beans," as early colonists explained, tasted different from baked beans containing molasses or brown sugar and salt pork. Ten years after the Pilgrims disembarked from the *Mayflower,* the Puritans from England landed at Boston and Salem less than 50 miles up the coast. They came with more provisions than the Pilgrims—with some utensils, silver, pewter and linens. They installed fireplaces with brick ovens in most houses, which influenced the cooking and originated Boston Baked Beans.

The Puritan Sabbath started at sundown on Saturday and lasted until sundown on Sunday. Their religion forbade cooking but not serving of food during the 24 hours. On Saturday morning they put big pots of beans in their ovens to bake all day. These supplied hot beans for Saturday's evening meal, some still warm for Sunday breakfast, and for another meal, sometimes cold, after church on Sunday.

Although the strict observance of the Sabbath died out in the 19th century, the custom of having Boston Baked Beans for Saturday's evening meal and the leftovers for breakfast on Sunday was so firmly established that it continued and still does in some New England homes.

Recipes for Boston Baked Beans vary from one family to another, but they must contain salt pork and molasses, or a combination of molasses and brown sugar, or maple sugar. And they must cook a long time to develop flavor and a rich brown sauce. There are New Englanders who insist that the supremacy of their baked beans is due to the use of a bean pot—an earthen cooking utensil with a narrow throat and big, bulging sides.

Boston Brown Bread, a steamed bread, was the traditional and still is the favored accompaniment to Saturday night's baked beans. Most families now buy the bread from bakeries.

BOSTON BAKED BEANS

Stick two or three whole cloves in onion for subtle spicy taste, and give beans time to bake gently to perfection

2 c. dry navy beans	**2 tsp. dry mustard**
6 c. cold water	**⅓ c. brown sugar, firmly**
1 tsp. salt	**packed**
¼ lb. salt pork	**¼ c. molasses**
1 medium onion (optional)	

Wash beans. Combine beans and cold water in large kettle. Bring to a boil; boil 2 minutes. Remove from heat and let stand 1 hour. (Or soak beans overnight.)

Add salt; simmer about 1 hour or until beans are tender. Drain, reserving 1¾ c. bean liquid. Add water if necessary; set aside.

Cut a slice from salt pork and put it in bottom of bean pot or Dutch oven. Add beans. Place onion in center of beans.

Mix mustard, sugar and molasses into reserved bean liquid; pour over beans.

Cut 3 gashes in remaining salt pork; place on beans, rind side up.

Cover and bake in 300° oven 5 to 7 hours, adding more

water as needed. Remove cover from bean pot the last 30 minutes of baking so pork rind will brown and become crisp. Makes 6 servings.

NEW YORK BAKED BEANS

Boston Baked Beans are famous, but there are Americans who prefer the dried vegetable cooked in the old-time, up-state New York way. Great Northern beans, which do not hold their shape as well as the pea or navy beans cooked in New England, were used and brown sugar took the place of molasses. And the beans baked in a shallow dish, often a crock, instead of a bean pot with a small opening. Sometimes the beans were served cold, cut in squares.

Here are directions as given in an original up-state recipe: "Soak beans in water overnight. Slowly cook them next morning in the water in which they soaked until partly tender, about 2 hours. Add salt pork and sliced onions; simmer until beans are tender, about 1 hour. Add more hot water as needed. Drain, reserving liquid and place beans in a shallow, greased baking dish, covering the salt pork with them. Sprinkle with brown sugar mixed with a little pepper and add bean liquid almost to cover. Bake uncovered in a low oven until a soft, brown crust forms on top and along the sides, or about 2½ hours. As the beans dry out in baking, add more of the reserved liquid or hot water."

NEW YORK BAKED BEANS

A cruet of cider vinegar traditionally accompanies these beans

2 c. dry Great Northern beans	**¼ c. brown sugar, firmly packed**
6 c. water	**2 tblsp. sugar**
2 medium onions, sliced	**1 tsp. salt**
¼ lb. salt pork	

Wash beans. Combine beans and water in Dutch oven. Bring to a boil; boil 2 minutes. Remove from heat and let stand 1 hour. (Or soak beans overnight.)

Add onions, salt pork, sugars and salt. Cover and simmer 2 to 2 hours 30 minutes. Add more water if necessary. Taste beans and add more salt if needed.

Bake in 350° oven 1 hour; uncover and continue baking 1 to 1 hour 30 minutes or until top edges are browned. Makes 6 to 8 servings.

MIDWESTERN BAKED BEANS

In the Midwest, tomatoes and dried beans were cooked together in pioneer kitchens. And since many desired a more pronounced tomato taste, they often topped their servings with ketchup or chili sauce, homemade or commercial, a definite conversion from Boston and New York baked beans. Baked beans are examples of regional food preferences time has not erased.

MIDWESTERN BAKED BEANS

Hot gingerbread or feathery rolls are good with these beans

2 c. dry navy beans	1 medium onion, sliced and
6 c. water	separated into rings
1 (1 lb. 12 oz.) can	⅓ c. brown sugar, firmly
tomatoes, cut up	packed
1 tsp. salt	¼ c. molasses
¼ lb. salt pork, sliced	1½ tsp. dry mustard

Wash beans. Combine beans and water in Dutch oven. Bring to a boil; boil 2 minutes. Remove from heat and let stand 1 hour. (Or soak beans overnight.)

Add tomatoes and salt; bring to a boil. Reduce heat; cover and simmer 1 to 1 hour 30 minutes or until beans are tender and skins burst.

Stir in salt pork, onion, brown sugar, molasses and mustard. Turn into 3-qt. casserole or bean pot. Cover and bake in 325° oven 3 hours. Remove cover and continue baking 1 hour or until top edges are browned. Makes 8 to 10 servings.

WINTER CORN PUDDING

Visions of the cruel cold and storms of winter kept early colonists busy during summers storing food to use in the months ahead. Drying vegetables and fruits was a chore not to be neglected. Corn was so important in the diet that practically every household tried to lay by a supply, and the Indians set a good example as they dried food in the sunshine. The habit of drying corn was so firmly established by the end of the first hundred years that it continued long after that. To this day even some country families who freeze corn every year try to dry at least a little because they like the taste.

It is a tradition in some rural households to serve dried corn in Thanksgiving holiday meals. As American as cranberries and turkey! Winter Corn Pudding is one of the best-loved dishes made with dried corn.

WINTER CORN PUDDING

The kernels are soaked in dairy half-and-half instead of in water, for a more flavorful dish

¾ c. Oven-dried Corn (recipe follows)

2 c. dairy half-and-half, scalded

2 eggs, slightly beaten

2 tblsp. chopped green onions

2 tblsp. melted butter or regular margarine

1 tblsp. sugar

1 tsp. salt

⅛ tsp. pepper

Rinse dried corn. Add to hot dairy half-and-half and let soak about 4 hours.

Combine corn mixture with eggs, green onions, butter, sugar, salt and pepper. Pour into greased 1-qt. casserole.

Bake in 325° oven 35 to 40 minutes or until knife inserted in center comes out clean. Makes 6 servings.

Oven-dried Corn: Cook large ears corn in large kettle of boiling water 5 minutes, or just until milk in kernels is set when pricked with fork. Cool. Cut kernels from cob (5 large ears yield about 3 c. kernels; 3 to 4 large ears, about 2 c.). Spread kernels in a single layer in large shallow pan (15½ ×10½ ×1" jelly roll pan will hold 5 c. kernels). Place in oven set at lowest temperature, 150 or 175°. Heat 6 to 7 hours, until kernels are thoroughly dry to touch. Stir several times during drying. Store in covered jars at room temperature (3 c. fresh kernels make ¾ c. dried corn; 2 c. fresh kernels make ½ c. dried corn).

CORN CUSTARD PUDDING

People in all the American colonies ate corn pudding. Like all vegetable dishes, it was seasonal. Southerners had a longer growing season for corn and so enjoyed it more days of a year than Northerners. Most of the corn eaten in America until around 1850 was hard and flinty, although a British army officer visiting western New York State in 1779, discovered the Iroquois Indians were growing sweet corn and obtained some seed.

Corn Custard Pudding is a rich, velvety custard flavored with corn. Although delicate, the custard holds its shape when served —especially congenial with fried chicken.

CORN CUSTARD PUDDING

Frozen corn now makes this pudding a year-round favorite

2 c. frozen corn, thawed, or fresh kernels, cut from cob	**¼ c. flour**
	1 tblsp. sugar
	1 tsp. salt
1 egg	**⅛ tsp. pepper**
1½ c. dairy half-and-half	

Combine all ingredients in electric blender container. Blend at high speed 30 seconds. Pour into ungreased 1½-qt. casserole. Place in pan of hot water.

Bake in 350° oven 1 hour 10 minutes or until knife inserted in center comes out clean. Serve at once. Makes 6 servings.

RED BEANS AND RICE

Red beans and rice have been served in New Orleans since its Spanish and French beginnings. They are to the Crescent City and to many homes in the South what baked beans are to Boston.

Cooking red beans with a ham bone or hocks and serving them over boiled rice was first a dish for low-income families. When hard times came to the South during and immediately after the War Between the States, Red Beans and Rice won acceptance in all social circles. And just as Boston Baked Beans were a Saturday-night special in New England, the bean-rice combination was the main dish in the noon meal on Monday in the South.

RED BEANS AND RICE

This is a nutritious, thrifty, hunger-satisfying and tasty dish, expertly seasoned with red pepper, a New Orleans trademark

2 c. dry red kidney beans	¼ tsp. pepper
2 qts. water	2 cloves garlic, minced
2 c. chopped onion	1 bay leaf
1 tsp. salt	2 lbs. smoked ham hocks
½ tsp. crushed, dried red pepper	2 c. uncooked rice

Wash beans. Combine beans and water in Dutch oven. Cover and bring to a boil; boil 2 minutes. Remove from heat and let stand 1 hour. (Or soak beans overnight.)

Add onion, salt, red pepper, pepper, garlic, bay leaf and ham hocks. Bring to a boil. Reduce heat; cover and simmer about 2 hours 30 minutes or until beans are very tender. Remove bay leaf.

Cut ham hocks into small pieces; discard skin and bones. Slightly mash beans. Return meat to beans; heat.

Meanwhile, cook rice according to package directions. Serve beans over rice. Makes 8 servings.

HOPPING JOHN

To start the year right, people in South Carolina and neighboring states say you must eat Hopping John on New Year's Day. According to a belief that has endured for many generations, the simple dish of black-eye peas and long-grain rice, when eaten on January 1, brings good luck in the year ahead.

Hopping John may be made successfully with fresh, frozen or dry beans (peas). South Carolinians like to cook bacon with them; many Texans prefer hog jowls; Virginians like to serve them with tomatoes.

How Hopping John acquired its name no one knows. One theory is that it derived from an old custom that the children hopped once around the table before the dish was served "to give them something to do and help them work off excess steam."

HOPPING JOHN

As traditional in the South as baked beans are in New England; cook the peas and rice with ham hocks for superior flavor

1 c. dry black-eye peas	**Water**
4 c. water	**1 c. uncooked rice**
½ lb. crosscut ham hocks	**Salt**
½ c. chopped onion	**Pepper**
½ tsp. salt	
⅛ tsp. crushed, dried red	
pepper	

Wash peas. Combine with 4 c. water in Dutch oven. Bring to a boil; boil 2 minutes. Remove from heat; cover and let stand 1 hour. (Or soak peas overnight.)

Add ham hocks, onion, ½ tsp. salt and red pepper. Bring to a boil. Reduce heat and simmer about 1½ hours or until ham and peas are tender. Remove ham hocks. Cut meat in small pieces, discarding rind and bone. Drain peas, reserving liquid. Add enough water to reserved liquid to make 2 c.

Return peas, liquid and ham to Dutch oven. Bring to a boil. Stir in rice. Reduce heat; cover and simmer 20 minutes or until rice is tender and liquid is absorbed. Add salt and pepper to taste. Makes 6 servings as a main dish, 10 as a side dish.

COMPANY MASHED POTATOES

Although potatoes were developed by Indians from wild plants that grew in the highlands of Peru, they came to North America by way of Europe. Records reveal that they arrived in New Hampshire in 1719. They were baked on the hearth in ashes or Dutch ovens in early American homes and were one of the vegetables in the New England Boiled Dinner (see Index). Not until the 19th century were they commonly and extensively used. Even then the South did not favor them but clung to sweet potatoes and rice.

Potatoes came into their own on the western frontier. As soon as pioneers arrived at their destination, they cut blocks of sod to build homes and planted corn and potatoes. Hot mashed potatoes heaped in warmed serving dishes became standard dinner fare.

Company Mashed Potatoes require no gravy. You can make them ahead and refrigerate until baking time, or if they are baked and ready a few minutes before serving time, you can hold them in a low oven. Cheese, onion and sour cream season them delightfully.

COMPANY MASHED POTATOES

You can use fresh or instant potatoes with equal success

4 c. hot, seasoned mashed potatoes	4 oz. sharp Cheddar cheese, cut in ¼" cubes
1 c. dairy sour cream	½ tsp. seasoned salt
⅓ c. chopped, green onions and tops	

Combine potatoes, sour cream, green onions and cheese. Turn into greased 1½-qt. casserole. Sprinkle with seasoned salt.

Bake in 350° oven 25 minutes. Makes 6 servings.

ORANGE-CANDIED SWEET POTATOES

Most Southerners prefer sweet to white potatoes. Old southern cookbooks devote many more pages to them than to Irish potatoes. On the other hand, New England cookbooks devote pages to white potato recipes, but little space to sweets. New Englanders usually combine sweet potatoes with apples or maple syrup; Southerners use sweet potatoes in breads, pies and candied dishes.

Early colonists cooked sweet potatoes in their jackets on the hearth, smothered in ashes and hot coals. Candied sweets emerged before the Revolutionary War, enhanced by the flavor of such ingredients as lemon, orange, coconut, pineapple, apple, raisin, different spices, brown sugar, marshmallow, sherry, rum or bourbon.

ORANGE-CANDIED SWEET POTATOES

Juicy slices of orange and grated peel enhance the sweets

6 medium sweet potatoes, cooked and peeled
1 small orange, peeled and cut in thin slices
⅔ c. brown sugar, firmly packed
1 tsp. salt
1 tblsp. grated orange peel
¼ c. butter or regular margarine

Cut sweet potatoes in ½" slices. Place half the slices in greased 2-qt. casserole. Top with orange slices, then half the brown sugar, salt and orange peel. Dot with half the butter. Add remaining sweet potatoes. Top with remaining brown sugar, salt, orange peel and butter.

Bake uncovered in 375° oven 30 minutes or until glazed. Makes 6 servings.

WINTER SQUASH BAKE

Experts know that many more varieties of squash once flourished in Peru and other places in the Americas. Hairy or woolly squash seeds that no longer exist anywhere have been uncovered in ancient Peruvian graves. Since only the most highly prized foods were placed in Indian graves to feed the spirits after life on this planet ended, squash must have been special.

The number of superior varieties growing widely in the Americas when Europeans arrived was, and is still, great. The Indians, of course, were eating the seeds as well as the flesh of the squash. Among the highly valued types today are the long-necked butternuts and the buttercups that have been bred small enough to serve today's smaller families. Hubbard squash is especially favored in New England. Winter Squash Bake is an excellent dish made with any of these.

WINTER SQUASH BAKE

Onion and sour cream convert the squash flavor into something miraculous

3 lbs. butternut, buttercup or Hubbard squash	1 c. dairy sour cream
	1/3 c. finely chopped onion
2 tblsp. butter or regular margarine	1 tsp. salt
	1/4 tsp. pepper

Cut squash in pieces. Pare and remove seeds. Cook in boiling salted water 15 to 20 minutes or until tender. Mash squash. Stir in butter, sour cream, onion, salt and pepper. Turn into greased 1½-qt. casserole.

Bake uncovered in 350° oven 30 minutes. Makes 8 servings.

BAKED SQUASH SUPPER

An acorn squash cut in half serves a family of two without waste, and more can be baked to fit the number of people to be served. Gardeners find them easy to grow and they usually are the first winter squash ready to use in autumn.

Baked Squash Supper pleases menu planners because individual servings come to the table as half a squash, stuffed with seasoned meat combined with a variety of vegetables and topped with cheese.

BAKED SQUASH SUPPER

Meal-in-a-squash-half; just add an apple salad, a beverage and have homemade spicy molasses cookies for dessert

3 large acorn squash	2 tblsp. melted butter or
1 lb. bulk pork sausage	regular margarine
1 (10 oz.) pkg. frozen mixed	1 c. shredded process sharp
vegetables, thawed	American cheese (4 oz.)
½ tsp. salt	

Cut squash in halves; remove seeds. Place cut side down in 15½ ×10½ ×1″ jelly roll pan. Bake in 350° oven 45 minutes.

Meanwhile, brown sausage, breaking it apart with a fork. Drain off excess fat. Stir in vegetables and salt.

Turn squash cut side up. Brush cavities with butter. Fill with sausage mixture. Continue baking 20 minutes. Sprinkle cheese over tops. Return to oven 2 to 3 minutes or just until cheese is melted. Makes 6 servings.

GREEN BEANS COMPANY STYLE

This vegetable casserole rates high for company dinners and buffet suppers. It is a good selection to take to co-operative meals. The canned bean sprouts and water chestnuts reflect Chinese influence, but the casserole topping is an American favorite, French-fried onions from a can. Flavor and texture contrasts are delightful. The ingredients may be combined in the morning and chilled to bake later in the day when getting the meal—a big advantage for the hostess.

GREEN BEANS COMPANY STYLE

Excellent companion for roast pork, chicken or turkey

2 (9 oz.) pkgs. frozen French-style green beans
1 (8 oz.) can water chestnuts, drained and sliced
1 (1 lb.) can bean sprouts, drained
2 (10¾ oz.) cans condensed cream of celery soup

1 (4 oz.) can mushroom stems and pieces
½ c. sliced green onions
1 tsp. salt
1 (3 oz.) can French-fried onions

Cook beans as directed on package; drain. Combine with water chestnuts and bean sprouts.

Stir together soup, undrained mushrooms, green onions and salt. Stir into bean mixture. Turn into greased 2½-qt. casserole.

Bake in 350° oven 40 minutes. Cover with French-fried onions, and continue baking 5 minutes. Makes 8 to 10 servings.

SWEET-SOUR GREEN BEANS

Few vegetable dishes American women have cooked through the years surpass green beans seasoned with bacon. Originating with the Pennsylvania Dutch, they later won great acclaim at the old-time dinners for threshers in the Midwest. Green beans were then called snap or string beans to indicate they were so fresh they snapped when broken into pieces for cooking, or that there were strings to remove from every pod. The stringless beans available today were unknown.

SWEET-SOUR GREEN BEANS

This dish, attributed to the Pennsylvania Dutch, continues as a summer favorite when the bean vines are bearing generously

1 lb. green beans, cut up
3 slices bacon, cut up
1 c. chopped onion
2 tblsp. vinegar

1 tblsp. sugar
½ tsp. salt
⅛ tsp. pepper

Cook green beans in boiling salted water in large saucepan until tender. Drain.

Meanwhile, cook bacon in small skillet until crisp. Drain on paper towels.

Sauté onion in bacon drippings until tender. Add vinegar, sugar, salt and pepper; heat to boiling. Stir into hot green beans. Spoon into serving dish and sprinkle with bacon. Makes 6 servings.

SQUAW CORN

Squaw Corn may have originated in the East, but lumberjacks in Wisconsin and Minnesota claimed it as their own. Made with other ingredients they had in their camp kitchens, it cheered hungry, hard-working men for many years. The dish also became a favorite with campers. Canned corn eventually replaced the dried kernels. Our Squaw Corn recipe calls for one new ingredient.

SQUAW CORN

Sour cream adds a lot of flavor to this traditional dish

4 slices bacon, diced	**1 tsp. sugar**
¼ c. chopped onion	**½ tsp. salt**
2 (12 oz.) cans whole	**⅛ tsp. pepper**
kernel corn, drained	**½ c. dairy sour cream**

Cook bacon in saucepan until crisp. Drain on paper towels.

Sauté onion in bacon drippings until soft; pour off bacon drippings. Add corn, sugar, salt, pepper and sour cream. Heat thoroughly, but do not boil. Stir in reserved bacon. Makes 6 servings.

EASY CORN RELISH

First-time visitors in Iowa are astonished at the ever-present corn relish wherever they dine. Sometimes the relish served in homes is made during the sweet corn season and canned along with pickles, but more frequently these days it starts with a can of corn from the supermarket.

EASY CORN RELISH

This relish is as popular in Iowa as pickled beets were in Pennsylvania Dutch country during early days

1 (1 lb. 1 oz.) can whole kernel corn, drained	2 tblsp. chopped onion
1 c. chopped celery	2 tblsp. chopped pimiento
½ c. sweet pickle relish	½ c. French dressing
¼ c. chopped green pepper	½ tsp. salt
	⅛ tsp. pepper

Combine all ingredients. Chill several hours in refrigerator. Stir occasionally. Makes about 3½ cups.

SCALLOPED TOMATOES

Scalloped tomatoes, country style, originated in friendly kitchens where thrifty women stretched the all-American fruit (called a vegetable) with cubes of dry bread. Not until after 1850 did people in the United States lose their fear that tomatoes were poisonous. This is about the time love apples, as tomatoes were called, started to disappear from among flowers where they grew as ornamental plants. Gardeners began to set out the plants alongside rows of vegetables to produce food for the table.

How did the Indians find out which fruits and plants growing wild were edible and worthy of development and cultivation? Was it by the taste-test method? When they showed new European arrivals on these shores which ones were safe and good to eat, they extended the truly helpful hand of friendship.

SCALLOPED TOMATOES

For the most attractive dish, put scallop under the broiler two or three minutes to brown the top

½ c. chopped onion	1 tblsp. sugar
3 tblsp. melted butter or regular margarine	1 tsp. salt
3 slices bread, cubed	⅛ tsp. pepper
1 (1 lb. 12 oz.) can tomatoes, cut up	

Sauté onion in butter until soft. Add bread cubes, and toss together.

Combine tomatoes, sugar, salt and pepper. Place half the tomato mixture in greased 1½-qt. casserole. Top with half the bread mixture. Repeat layers.

Bake in 350° oven 50 minutes. Makes 6 servings.

HARVARD BEETS

This dish originated in New England, date unknown, but supposedly after the founding of Harvard University in 1636. Does the color of the vegetable stand for "the red of Harvard," as many people believe?

Beets were important in colonial times and later. They grew successfully in home gardens and stored well during winter months. Without them New England Boiled Dinner would have lacked the cheer of red on the platter, no one would have written eulogies to Red Flannel Hash, and hard-cooked eggs would not have turned red as they did in Pennsylvania Dutch Pickled Red Beets and Eggs (see Index for recipes).

NEW ENGLAND BAKED BEANS, COPIED FROM THE INDIANS. We present an authentic recipe for *Boston Baked Beans* (page 41). In pioneer days beans were baked in iron pots buried in hot ashes in a hole in the ground.

EUROPEAN RECIPES ADAPTED TO MIDWESTERN BOUNTY. From good Kansas cooks, *Green Bean Soup* (page 33), *Amish Vanilla Pie* (page 87) and *Cinnamon Swirl Bread* (page 67) . . . **today's** version of old-time recipes.

ENGLISH POUND CAKE BECAME A SOUTHERN SPECIALTY.   This rich, buttery cake was served at Mount Vernon and at Williamsburg. Our recipe for *Deluxe Pound Cake* (page 95) uses fewer eggs, less butter than the original.

AMERICAN INDIANS SHARED PUMPKINS WITH SETTLERS. Pioneer women concocted their own recipes using this bright orange vegetable new to them. *Stuffed Sugar Pumpkin* (page 40) bakes to goodness in its own shell.

HARVARD BEETS

For Yale beets, substitute orange juice for the vinegar!

⅓ c. sugar
1 tblsp. cornstarch
½ tsp. salt
½ c. vinegar
2 tblsp. butter or regular margarine

2 (1 lb.) cans sliced or diced beets, drained, or 3 c. sliced or diced, cooked beets

Combine sugar, cornstarch and salt in saucepan. Stir in vinegar. Cook over medium heat, stirring constantly, until mixture boils and is thickened. Add butter; stir until it melts. Stir in beets.

Cook over low heat until thoroughly hot, stirring occasionally. Makes 6 servings.

PICKLED BEETS AND EGGS

For a summer picnic or a buffet supper during any season, treat your guests with old-fashioned Pickled Beets and Eggs, a creation of Pennsylvania Dutch kitchens. Serve the beautiful, pink eggs, sometimes called red beet eggs, in the center of a pottery, wooden or crystal bowl or on a plate, and surround them with a wreath of pickled beets cut in quarters or slices. Or cut the eggs lengthwise in quarters and nestle them in crisp celery hearts on the relish tray.

The egg slices—red borders around yellow centers—decorate lettuce salads and contribute nutrition as well as charm. And serve the colorful eggs during the Easter season, an appropriate thing to do since the Pennsylvania Dutch introduced Easter eggs and the Easter bunny to the neighboring colonies.

PICKLED BEETS AND EGGS

The longer the eggs marinate the deeper red their color

10 medium beets	2" stick cinnamon
1½ c. vinegar	6 whole cloves
½ c. water	½ c. vinegar
⅓ c. sugar	8 hard-cooked eggs
2 tsp. salt	

Boil unpeeled beets until just tender. Remove skins and place beets in bowl.

Combine 1½ c. vinegar, water, sugar and salt. Tie cinnamon and cloves in cloth. Add to vinegar mixture. Bring to a boil; boil 3 minutes. Remove spice bag. Pour mixture over beets; cover and refrigerate at least overnight.

Add ½ c. vinegar. Add eggs and refrigerate at least 24 hours. Makes 8 servings.

PERFECTION SALAD

Interest in new foods was high at the time of the St. Louis exposition. Iced tea, ice cream cones and meat patties in buns were first introduced there. And Perfection Salad entered the American cuisine at about the same time as powdered gelatin became commercially available. Earlier, extracting gelatin in home kitchens, usually by boiling calves' feet in water, was a tedious process.

A Pennsylvania homemaker submitted the recipe for Perfection Salad in a cookery contest conducted by Knox Gelatine Inc. and it was one of the winners. The original recipe has changed little, but the method has been simplified. Adding ice water hastens the setting. And instead of letting the gelatin soak in cold water until softened, today we heat the gelatin in water to dissolve it quickly. Here is the recipe for Perfection Salad, a favorite in America for 70 years.

PERFECTION SALAD

Too attractive and refreshing to lose its place in food history

2 envelopes unflavored gelatin	**1½ c. finely shredded cabbage**
1 c. cold water	**1½ c. chopped celery**
½ c. sugar	**¼ c. chopped green pepper**
1 tsp. salt	**2 pimientos, cut in small pieces**
1½ c. ice water	**Salad greens**
½ c. vinegar	
2 tblsp. lemon juice	

Sprinkle gelatin over 1 c. cold water in saucepan. Place over low heat; stir constantly until gelatin dissolves, about 3 minutes. Remove from heat. Stir in sugar and salt.

Add 1½ c. ice water, vinegar and lemon juice. Chill until slightly thicker than consistency of unbeaten egg white. Fold in cabbage, celery, green pepper and pimientos; turn into 1-qt. mold or individual molds. Chill until firm. To serve, unmold and garnish with salad greens. Makes 6 servings.

BRIDE'S PERFECTION SALAD

When any food becomes a great favorite, variations evolve in kitchens across the country. Some women like to put their own touch on the dishes they serve, satisfying their creative urge. This is what happened with Perfection Salad.

Bride's Perfection Salad is a third-generation development of the first Perfection Salad (see preceding recipe). The recipe is shared by a home economist who lives in the Midwest.

BRIDE'S PERFECTION SALAD

Great mixed-vegetable salad to serve with chicken and meats

1 c. boiling water	1 c. finely shredded
1 (3 oz.) pkg. lemon-flavor	cabbage
gelatin	1 c. finely chopped celery
1 tsp. salt	⅓ c. finely chopped green
2 tblsp. lemon juice or	pepper
vinegar	2 tblsp. finely chopped
1 c. cold water	pimiento

Stir boiling water into gelatin and salt; stir until gelatin is dissolved. Add lemon juice and cold water. Chill until slightly thickened.

Fold in cabbage, celery, green pepper and pimiento. Pour into 6 individual molds or 8" square pan. Chill until firm. Makes 6 servings.

CRANBERRY RELISH SALAD

Cranberries may have accompanied turkey at the first Thanksgiving feast after the harvest in 1621. At that season cranberry vines that grew along Cape Cod's shores must have been invitingly red with beautiful, bittersweet berries. Undoubtedly, friendly Indians, who ate cranberries both raw and cooked, had demonstrated they were a native fruit worth consideration. Since sugar was either unavailable or in scant supply to the Pilgrims during the first years in their new homes, cranberry sauce, if they made it, was really sour. This may not have mattered much for in that era Americans, due to heavy diets, relished more tart and less sweet foods than they do today.

When trade between New England and the West Indies had prospered enough that salt fish could be exchanged for sugar, cranberries came into their own. They are popular today not only in Massachusetts, New Jersey, Wisconsin, Washington and Oregon, where they are grown commercially, but also in all states and in all forms—fresh, canned sauce, bottled juice and frozen relishes. Most families consider them essential for Thanksgiving Day. And many household freezers hold a supply for us on the Fourth of July and other special occasions.

Cranberry Relish Salad is a good candidate for holiday and other meals where color and flavor mean so much. It is an ideal choice for carrying to co-operative suppers during the cold weather and family reunions.

CRANBERRY RELISH SALAD

Orange, cranberry and pineapple flavors blend temptingly

1 (3 oz.) pkg. lemon-flavor gelatin	1 (8¾ oz.) can crushed pineapple
1 (3 oz.) pkg. raspberry-flavor gelatin	2 c. fresh cranberries
½ c. sugar	1 small unpeeled orange, quartered and seeded
3 c. boiling water	1 c. chopped celery
1 tblsp. lemon juice	½ c. chopped pecans

Dissolve gelatins and sugar in boiling water. Stir in lemon juice and undrained pineapple. Chill until partially set.

Put cranberries and orange quarters through food chopper. Add to gelatin mixture along with celery and pecans. Turn into 2½-qt. mold or 9″ square pan. Chill until set. Makes 9 servings.

TOMATO ASPIC WITH VEGETABLES

Among the favorite make-ahead salads in country homes is tomato aspic. The universal liking for tomatoes and their cheerful color gives it a high rating. Seasonings give our Tomato Aspic with Vegetables a lively taste, including the olives that sharpen flavors. Finely shredded raw cabbage and carrots and chopped celery, green pepper and onion contribute interest and crispness.

TOMATO ASPIC WITH VEGETABLES

This garden-patch salad boosts good nutrition in meals—a great way to get the family to eat vegetables

2 c. tomato juice
½ c. finely chopped onion
¼ c. finely chopped celery
2 tblsp. brown sugar, firmly packed
1 tsp. salt
2 bay leaves
4 whole cloves
2 envelopes unflavored gelatin
1 c. tomato juice

3 tblsp. lemon juice
1 c. tomato juice
1 c. finely shredded cabbage
½ c. finely chopped celery
½ c. finely chopped green pepper
⅓ c. sliced pimiento-stuffed olives
Lettuce
Salad dressing (optional)

Combine 2 c. tomato juice, onion, ¼ c. celery, brown sugar, salt, bay leaves and cloves in saucepan. Simmer uncovered 5 minutes; strain.

Soften gelatin in 1 c. tomato juice; add to hot mixture and stir to dissolve. Add lemon juice and 1 c. tomato juice. Chill until partially thickened.

Fold in cabbage, ½ c. celery, green pepper and olives. Turn into 1½-qt. ring mold or 11×7×1½″ baking dish. Chill until firm. Cut in serving pieces and arrange on lettuce leaves. Serve with salad dressing, if desired. Makes 8 servings.

PARTY WALDORF SALAD

When that famous New York chef, Oscar of the Waldorf, tossed chunks of apples and sliced celery with mayonnaise, he created a salad that spread across the continent. Even in country kitchens where apples are to this day the mainstay of many winter fruit salads, women depend on new ingredients for interest.

In Party Waldorf Salad—a southern special—dates, walnuts

and marshmallows are the extras. Grapes, bananas and pears frequently are included also. A Waldorf Salad that people in the Ozarks especially like has chopped black walnuts scattered over the top, while in New England a spoonful of cranberry sauce often garnishes individual servings.

PARTY WALDORF SALAD

It's at the peak of perfection made with new-crop apples and celery in autumn. Add your own choice of extra ingredients

2 c. diced unpared apples
2 tblsp. lemon juice
1 c. chopped celery
½ c. coarsely chopped
   walnuts
½ c. chopped dates

½ c. miniature
   marshmallows
⅓ c. mayonnaise or salad
   dressing
1 tblsp. light cream or
   milk

Toss apples with lemon juice to keep color bright. Combine with celery, walnuts, dates and marshmallows. (For an everyday salad, omit dates and marshmallows and increase apples and celery.)

Blend together mayonnaise and light cream. Stir into fruit mixture. Makes 6 to 8 servings.

24-HOUR FRUIT SALAD

Overnight fruit salads were a forerunner of frozen fruit salads, served in important meals, most frequently in holiday and family reunion dinners. Made with canned fruits, they were the first make-ahead salads containing no gelatin.

The syrup, drained from the fruits, cooked with egg and seasoned with a little sugar, vinegar and salt, makes a custard dressing. (Commercial salad dressings were not universally available when overnight salads originated.) The fruits and marshmallows are added to the homemade dressing and whipped cream folded in. Chilled overnight, the salad is spooned into crisp lettuce cups just before serving.

24-HOUR FRUIT SALAD

We add fresh grapes and oranges to canned fruits for flavor

1 (1 lb. 4 oz.) can pineapple chunks	2 oranges, peeled and cut up
1 egg	1 c. green seedless grapes or winter grapes, halved and seeded
2 tblsp. sugar	
2 tblsp. vinegar	2 c. miniature marshmallows
Dash of salt	
1 tblsp. butter or regular margarine	1 c. heavy cream, whipped
1 (1 lb.) can pitted light sweet cherries, drained	

Drain pineapple, reserving 2 tblsp. juice. Beat egg slightly in heavy saucepan. Stir in reserved pineapple juice, sugar, vinegar, salt and butter. Cook over low heat, stirring constantly, until mixture thickens slightly and coats spoon. Turn into small bowl and cool to room temperature.

Combine well-drained pineapple, cherries, oranges, grapes and marshmallows. Pour custard dressing over and mix lightly. Fold in whipped cream. Cover and chill 24 hours. Makes 8 to 10 servings.

4-FRUIT FROZEN SALAD

Just as the first iceboxes revolutionized cooking and eating, mechanical refrigerators introduced new dishes. Hostesses of the 1930s frequently featured frozen fruit salads for club and other guest luncheons. Busy women welcomed these make-ahead specials and liked the idea that fruit salads could serve as dessert as well as salad.

This 4-Fruit Frozen Salad is a rich, special-occasion choice. Sour cream substitutes for the whipped cream incorporated in the first frozen salads. Canned dark cherries and golden apricots brighten the salad and blend their flavors with those of bananas and pineapple. When sliced or cut in individual servings and placed on lettuce-lined plates, 4-Fruit Frozen Salad is a thing of beauty.

4-FRUIT FROZEN SALAD

For a luncheon, serve with hot cheese biscuits and tea or coffee

1 (8 oz.) pkg. cream cheese,
    softened
1 c. dairy sour cream
¼ c. sugar
¼ tsp. salt
1 (8¾ oz.) can crushed
    pineapple
1 banana, diced

1 (1 lb. 1 oz.) can apricot
    halves, drained and cut
    in fourths
1 (1 lb.) can pitted dark
    sweet cherries, drained
1 c. miniature
    marshmallows

Beat cheese in large mixer bowl until fluffy. Beat in sour cream, sugar and salt.

Drain pineapple, reserving juice. Place diced banana in pineapple juice; drain.

Add pineapple, banana, apricots, cherries and marshmallows to cream cheese mixture. Turn into 5-c. mold or 8" square pan. Freeze at least 8 hours.

Remove salad from mold and let stand at room temperature 10 minutes before cutting. Makes 8 servings.

SOUR CREAM COLESLAW

No one can leaf through a Pennsylvania Dutch cookbook without being impressed and tempted by the many recipes for cabbage salads. Many of them originated late in the 18th century. The Pennsylvanians borrowed the name, coleslaw, from their Dutch neighbors to the north in New York, but they developed their own salads. These frugal people were of German descent and the "Dutch" was a misnomer for "Deutsch," or German, and had no connection with Holland.

In our recipe for Sour Cream Coleslaw, a simple country dressing converts finely shredded cabbage into a superior salad.

The modern touch is the spoonful of mayonnaise which contributes a pleasing, although subtle, flavor.

SOUR CREAM COLESLAW

Excellent accompaniment for fried fish, meat and chicken

1 c. dairy sour cream
2 tblsp. sugar
½ tsp. salt
¼ tsp. pepper
2 tblsp. vinegar

1 tblsp. mayonnaise or salad
dressing
6 c. finely shredded
cabbage

Blend together sour cream, sugar, salt, pepper, vinegar and mayonnaise. Stir into cabbage. Makes 6 servings.

WILTED SPINACH SALAD

As early as the Revolutionary War, greens tossed with a hot vinegar-bacon dressing were served at Pennsylvania Dutch tables. Salad content followed the seasons. Thrifty hands gathered tender, young dandelion leaves in spring. Garden lettuce, spinach and endive followed, then cabbage. Despite the name of these salads, they wilt little if correctly made. The hot dressing, doused on crackly leaves, takes away only part of the crispness and adds a lot of flavor.

In our recipe for Wilted Spinach Salad, chopped hard-cooked eggs are an important ingredient as they always have been in Pennsylvania Dutch kitchens.

WILTED SPINACH SALAD

For top success, drain the tender, crisp young spinach well and toss with hot dressing just before serving

6 c. spinach, torn in bite-
size pieces
¼ c. sliced green onions
3 hard-cooked eggs,
coarsely chopped
5 slices bacon, chopped

¼ c. vinegar
2 tblsp. water
2 tblsp. sugar
½ tsp. salt
¼ tsp. pepper

Combine spinach, onions and eggs in salad bowl.

Cook bacon in skillet until crisp. Remove bacon and drain on paper towels. Pour off all but 3 tblsp. bacon drippings.

Add vinegar, water, sugar, salt and pepper to bacon drippings. Heat to boiling, stirring to blend. Pour over spinach mixture; toss gently. Sprinkle with bacon. Makes 6 servings.

CINNAMON SWIRL BREAD

A recipe that has been copied and passed on many times throughout a Kansas neighborhood. Everyone who samples it requests the recipe. A favorite at church suppers and fair entries . . . looks handsome too with the sweet glaze dripping over top and sides of the bread.

CINNAMON SWIRL BREAD

A Kansas homemaker makes lots of these to serve the field crew

1 c. milk	**2 eggs**
¼ c. butter or regular margarine	**5 to 5½ c. sifted flour**
¼ c. sugar	**Melted butter or regular margarine**
1 tsp. salt	**⅓ c. sugar**
1 pkg. active dry yeast	**1 tblsp. ground cinnamon**
¼ c. lukewarm water	**Glaze (recipe follows)**

Scald milk. Stir in butter, ¼ c. sugar and salt. Cool to lukewarm.

Sprinkle yeast on lukewarm water; stir to dissolve. Add yeast, eggs and 2 c. flour to milk mixture. Beat with electric mixer at medium speed until smooth, for about 2 minutes, scraping bowl occasionally. Or beat with spoon until batter is smooth.

Gradually add enough remaining flour, a little at a time, to make a soft dough that leaves the sides of the bowl. Turn onto lightly floured surface and knead until smooth and satiny, about 8 to 10 minutes.

Place in lightly greased bowl; turn dough over to grease top.

Cover and let rise in warm place until doubled, about 1 to 1½ hours.

Divide dough in half. Roll each half into a 10×8″ rectangle. Brush lightly with melted butter. Sprinkle with half of combined ⅓ c. sugar and cinnamon. Roll up like jelly roll, starting at narrow end. Seal long edge. Place seam side down in greased 9×5×3″ loaf pan. Repeat with remaining dough. Let rise until doubled.

Bake in 350° oven 30 minutes or until bread tests done. Remove from pans. Cool on racks. Drizzle with Glaze. Makes 2 loaves.

Glaze: Combine 1 c. sifted confectioners sugar, 4 tsp. milk and ½ tsp. vanilla; blend well.

PIPING HOT BISCUITS

First-time European visitors to America in the 19th century were amazed at the way little pieces of hot bread were hurried from oven to table and the number of times the bread basket was replenished during a meal. That was the golden age for biscuits. While they varied little from one region to another or from mansion to cottage, sod house or log cabin, biscuits in the North were larger and thicker than the biscuits of the South, which often were somewhat richer.

Cowboy biscuits of the Old West were the largest and thickest of all and they were somewhat more "bready." Packaged mixes today make excellent biscuits and they are a convenience. Cowboys invented the first mixes. When a lone cowboy was to be gone from ranch headquarters a few days, he mixed flour, salt and baking powder in a muslin sack and tied it along with his skillet, coffee pot, bacon and coffee to his saddle. When time to eat, he built a campfire, cooked bacon and used the drippings to shorten his biscuits, which he usually mixed with water in the flour sack. He shaped the dough in a roll, pinched off bits of it and baked them in the skillet. He called them pinch-offs.

Our Piping Hot Biscuits are a little richer than many of the hot breads, and touches of sugar and cream of tartar do good things to them.

PIPING HOT BISCUITS

Roll dough half as thick as you like your baked biscuits

2 c. sifted flour	½ tsp. cream of tartar
4 tsp. baking powder	½ c. shortening
2 tsp. sugar	⅔ c. milk
½ tsp. salt	

Sift together flour, baking powder, sugar, salt and cream of tartar. Cut in shortening until mixture resembles coarse crumbs. Add milk all at once. Stir with a fork just until moistened. Knead gently 10 times on lightly floured surface. Roll or pat dough ½" thick. Cut with floured biscuit cutter. Place on ungreased baking sheet.

Bake in 450° oven 10 to 12 minutes or until golden brown. Makes 16.

CINNAMON FLOP COFFEE CAKE

Fertile land and farming skill met in Pennsylvania Dutch country in early America. One of the most remarkable cuisines of the thirteen original states developed there in country kitchens. The abundance of wheat flour started Pennsylvania Dutch women on a gigantic baking spree that lasted many years. Some of America's best breads, cakes, cookies and pies came from their ovens, commonly located outdoors near the kitchen door.

Cinnamon Flop Coffee Cake, a quick bread, tastes as good today as it did a hundred years ago. People in Lebanon County, Pennsylvania, sometimes call it Moravian Coffee Cake, a quick version of Moravian Sugar Cake, which is made with a yeast dough containing mashed potatoes.

CINNAMON FLOP COFFEE CAKE

During baking some of the crumb topping "flops" or permeates the coffee cake, giving it a marbleized look and a great flavor

1 c. brown sugar, firmly packed	¼ tsp. salt
½ tsp. ground cinnamon	2 tblsp. shortening
¼ c. butter or regular margarine	1½ c. sugar
2 c. sifted flour	1 egg
2 tsp. baking powder	1 tsp. vanilla
	1 c. milk

Combine brown sugar and cinnamon; cut in butter until crumbly and well mixed. Set aside.

Sift together flour, baking powder and salt.

Cream shortening in mixer bowl. Gradually beat in sugar. Add egg and vanilla; beat well. Stir in flour mixture by hand alternately with milk, starting and ending with flour mixture. Pour into greased 8″ square pan. Sprinkle with brown sugar mixture.

Bake in 425° oven 30 to 35 minutes or until golden brown. Serve warm. Makes 8 servings.

SPIDER CORN BREAD

We can imagine the problems the first colonial women had when they attempted to bake bread with their homemade yeast and cornmeal. Accustomed to using wheat flour, they probably did not know that cornmeal lacks gluten, a wheat protein that enables a loaf of bread to hold its increased height when baked. Had the Indians along the Eastern Seaboard known of tortillas, the paper-thin cornmeal cakes their Mexican and South American counterparts baked, they could have borrowed the techniques. By experimenting, the new Americans developed their own thin pancake, of which Rhode Island johnnycake became the most famous.

The next step was to leaven with eggs and saleratus and bake the corn bread in spiders, or three-legged iron skillets. The black utensil resembled a spider to imaginative women.

Our Spider Corn Bread is a descendant of the old-time favorites. It is moist and super-delicious. You can bake it in a heavy skillet or a 9″ square baking pan. Serve it with a fork.

SPIDER CORN BREAD

Another name for this is custard corn bread . . . really good

2 tblsp. butter or regular margarine	1 tsp. salt
	1 c. milk
1⅓ c. white cornmeal	2 eggs
⅓ c. sifted flour	1 c. buttermilk
2 tblsp. sugar	1 c. milk
1 tsp. baking soda	Butter, jelly or syrup

Place 2 tblsp. butter in a 9″ iron skillet or 9″ square baking pan. Place in oven and start heating oven to 400°.

Meanwhile, sift together cornmeal, flour, sugar, baking soda and salt into bowl. Beat in 1 c. milk and eggs. Stir in buttermilk. Pour over melted butter in skillet. Pour remaining 1 c. milk over top of batter; do not stir.

Bake in 400° oven 35 minutes or until golden brown. Serve hot from skillet with butter and tart jelly or syrup. Eat with a fork. Corn bread will have a layer of custard. Makes 6 to 9 servings.

SOUTHERN SPOON BREAD

The corn porridge friendly Indians showed early colonists how to make was the forerunner of the southern delicacy, spoon bread. Eggs became available and, incorporated in the porridge, they leavened it, resulting in a fluffy, soft and delicious bread. When baking soda became available early in the 19th century it was added to the cornmeal batter made with buttermilk or sour milk. The spoon bread was still fluffy and light but it had greater stability. Baking powder evolved later and it was also used for leavening spoon breads made with sweet milk. So soft they cannot be sliced, spoon breads are served with a spoon from the dish in which they bake. They are the aristocrats of corn breads.

There are two kinds of spoon breads, those made with cornmeal and with hominy grits. This cookbook contains recipes for both of them. Our recipe for Southern Spoon Bread calls for both baking powder and soda.

SOUTHERN SPOON BREAD

Southerners prefer white cornmeal for making corn breads

1½ c. boiling water	1 tsp. salt
1 c. white cornmeal	1 tsp. baking powder
1 tblsp. butter or regular	¼ tsp. baking soda
margarine	3 egg whites
1 c. buttermilk	Butter
3 egg yolks	

Pour boiling water into cornmeal in large bowl, stirring constantly. Add 1 tblsp. butter and continue stirring until mixture is lukewarm. Stir in buttermilk, then beat in egg yolks. Stir in salt, baking powder and soda.

Beat egg whites just until soft peaks form. Fold into batter. Pour into greased 2-qt. casserole.

Bake in 375° oven 45 to 50 minutes or until golden brown. Serve hot with butter. Makes 6 to 8 servings.

HOMINY SPOON BREAD

Southerners divide on preference for spoon bread of cornmeal or of hominy. In Charleston, South Carolina, a great colonial seaport, and in adjacent communities, hominy spoon bread was —and still is—the favorite.

In Virginia and to a lesser extent in other states, spoon breads are called batter breads. This explains the reference sometimes made to the "batter-bread express" that existed in wealthy plantation homes during the late colonial era. It consisted of the cook's helpers, frequently youngsters, who ran from the kitchen house to the dining room in the big house, carrying baking dishes, wrapped with linen napkins and filled with spoon bread just out of the oven.

HOMINY SPOON BREAD

This tastes best when hot enough to melt butter instantly

½ c. hominy grits	3 eggs, separated
2½ c. water	½ c. white cornmeal
½ tsp. salt	2 tsp. baking powder
1 tblsp. butter or regular margarine	½ tsp. salt
	Butter

Cook grits with water and ½ tsp. salt as directed on package. Stir in butter until melted. Cool slightly. Blend in egg yolks.

Sift together cornmeal, baking powder and ½ tsp. salt. Stir into grits mixture.

Beat egg whites until soft peaks form. Fold into grits mixture. Turn into greased 1½-qt. casserole.

Bake in 350° oven 1 hour or until golden brown. Serve immediately with butter. Makes 4 to 6 servings.

SOURDOUGH BREAD

Homemade sourdough bread's last stand is in Alaska where some people in the more remote areas still bake the tangy loaves, biscuits and pancakes. Sourdough was the bread of the 1849 California gold-rush days and 50 years later in the Klondike. Earthen crocks of sourdough starter went West with pioneers in covered wagons; they baked biscuits and pancakes over campfires along the way. Ranchers of the Mountain West also were expert with these breads in their cow and sheep camps.

The arrival of packaged yeast in grocery stores began the decline of sourdough bread. It was so much easier to reach in the cupboard for a dependable leavening than to pamper a temperamental starter. The success of a starter depends primarily on a blend of yeast and bacterial fermentation, which is determined by the flour and the types of bacteria in the air. It cannot be 100 per cent predictable.

Anyone who has tasted good sourdough biscuits or hotcakes laments their disappearance. So many requests for sourdough recipes came to the FARM JOURNAL COUNTRYSIDE TEST KITCH- ENS over the years that the following recipes for Sourdough Starter, Sourdough Biscuits and Silver Dollar Hotcakes were developed.

SOURDOUGH STARTER

Using your starter often is best for success with sourdoughs. Pio- neers and prospectors used theirs every day

½ pkg. active dry yeast	2 tblsp. sugar
(1¼ tsp.)	2½ c. warm water (110 to
2 c. unsifted flour	115°)

Combine all ingredients in a stone crock or glass or pottery bowl. Beat well with whisk or electric mixer until smooth. Cover with cheesecloth and let stand two days in a warm place free from drafts, such as in an unheated oven.

After using starter, add an equal amount of warm water and flour to the portion not used. Pour into a glass jar or crock with a tightly fitting lid. Cover and store in refrigerator.

SOURDOUGH BISCUITS

Serve these light biscuits hot with plenty of butter. Be sure to replenish starter so the next batch of biscuits will be good

1½ c. sifted flour	¼ c. butter or regular
2 tsp. baking powder	margarine
¼ tsp. baking soda (½ tsp.	1 c. Sourdough Starter
if Starter is quite sour)	Melted butter
½ tsp. salt	

Sift together flour, baking powder, soda and salt. Cut in ¼ c. butter with pastry blender until crumbly. Add Sourdough Starter, and mix.

Turn dough out on lightly floured board. Knead lightly until satiny.

Roll dough ½″ thick. Cut with floured 2½″ cutter. Place biscuits in well-greased 9″ square pan. Brush with melted butter. Let rise about 1 hour in a warm place. (Replenish Starter by stirring in 2 c. warm water and 2 c. flour. Cover tightly and store in refrigerator.)

Bake in 425° oven 20 minutes. Makes 12 biscuits.

SILVER DOLLAR HOTCAKES

These tiny pancakes were named when silver dollars were common. The size is traditional, but you can enlarge the "dollars"

1 c. Sourdough Starter	2 tsp. baking soda
2 c. unsifted flour	2 eggs
2 c. milk	3 tblsp. melted shortening
1 tsp. salt	2 tblsp. sugar

About 12 hours before mealtime, mix Sourdough Starter, flour, milk and salt; let stand in a bowl covered with cheesecloth. Set in a warm place.

Just before baking, remove 1 c. batter to replenish Starter in crock. To the remaining batter in bowl, add baking soda, eggs, shortening and sugar. Mix well.

Bake cakes the size of silver dollars on lightly greased, hot griddle. For thinner hotcakes, add more milk to the batter. Makes about 30 cakes.

BASIC PANCAKES

Call them griddlecakes, flapjacks, or flannel cakes—they are all American names for pancakes. The first cookbook published in the colonies that included recipes using native foods referred to them as slapjacks. (This modest 1796 Connecticut book presented the first printed recipe using maize, the Indian name for corn.) Regardless of what you call the cakes browned on a griddle, they are served hot and usually with butter and maple or other table syrup, which the cowboys called lick.

The American way is to serve pancakes in stacks of two or more. Some Vermont people like to butter seven or eight large pancakes, sprinkle them with maple sugar and stack them. These "shortcakes" are cut in wedges for serving.

Europeans brought their pancake recipes to America, many of which have been widely adapted. The thin crêpes of France, large, thin Swedish pancakes, frequently rolled, and German potato pancakes are different from the American type. Most pancakes today are made from packaged mixes, and with good results.

Some households cling to old-time recipes, which they think are unsurpassable. Basic Pancakes with five variations is a family treasure. Take your choice of apple, bacon, blueberry, buttermilk or corn pancakes.

BASIC PANCAKES

Five variations—good recipe for men's service club, money-raising suppers

2 c. sifted flour	1 egg
2½ tsp. baking powder	1½ c. milk
½ tsp. salt	2 tblsp. cooking oil

Sift together flour, baking powder and salt into mixing bowl. Add egg, milk and oil. Beat with rotary beater just until smooth. Pour ¼ c. batter onto hot, lightly greased griddle for each pancake. Bake until bubbles appear; turn over. Makes 1 dozen 5" pancakes.

Variations

Bacon Pancakes: Add 5 slices crisp-cooked bacon, crumbled, to batter. Bake as directed. Makes about 13.

Blueberry Pancakes: Stir 1 c. fresh or frozen (thawed and drained) or drained canned blueberries into batter. Bake as directed. Makes about 16.

Corn Pancakes: Stir 1 c. drained, canned whole-kernel corn, or cooked fresh corn cut from cob into batter. Bake as directed. Makes about 16.

Apple Pancakes: Add 1½ c. finely chopped, pared, apples to batter. Bake as directed. Makes about 18.

Buttermilk Pancakes: Substitute buttermilk for milk in recipe for Basic Pancakes. Reduce amount of baking powder to 1 tsp. and add ½ tsp. baking soda. Mix and bake as directed. Makes 1 dozen.

CORNMEAL PANCAKES

The first griddlecakes the colonists baked were of meal, ground the Indian way between stones, with salt and water added. These hot cakes baked over coals were known in New England as journey cakes—by taking meal and salt, early travelers in the wilderness could heat water from streams over campfires to make the batter.

The water was poured over the meal and the mixture was allowed to stand until it was absorbed. (Traditional Rhode Island johnnycakes, still made today, contain white cornmeal preferably stone-ground.) The pancakes were crisp on the outside, soft within, and when served hot, spread with butter and doused with maple or other table syrup, they were delicious.

Our Cornmeal Pancakes are an adapted version. Buttermilk replaces the water, and baking soda leavens the batter; a mixture of flour and cornmeal, eggs and a dash of salt complete the list of ingredients.

CORNMEAL PANCAKES

Hot off the griddle and served with sizzling pork sausage, these are farmhouse favorites

½ c. sifted flour	2 c. yellow cornmeal
1½ tsp. salt	2 eggs, beaten
1 tsp. baking soda	2½ c. buttermilk

Sift together flour, salt and baking soda. Stir in cornmeal. Add eggs and buttermilk and beat just until smooth.

Pour ¼ c. batter for each cake onto lightly greased, hot griddle. Bake until golden brown on both sides. Serve hot. Makes about 20.

OLD-FASHIONED APPLE CIDER PIE

Cider presses worked overtime in youthful America. People were thrifty and they made every effort to keep apples from going to waste. Besides, they liked cider. It was a daily drink in many homes, much as orange juice is today. Good cooks also used it as an ingredient in pies, cakes and many other dishes. And from cider they made the year's supply of vinegar in wooden molasses barrels. Molasses was sold by the pint or quart from the big barrel.

Teamed with sliced apples, cider gives piquancy to Old-fashioned Apple Cider Pie, a dessert treat. If you do not have cider, you can use apple juice.

OLD-FASHIONED APPLE CIDER PIE

Good recipe to use when apples have lost their best flavor

1 c. apple cider or juice	2 tblsp. water
⅔ c. sugar	½ tsp. ground cinnamon
6 c. sliced pared apples	1 tblsp. butter or regular
(6 to 8)	margarine
2 tblsp. cornstarch	Pastry for 2-crust 9″ pie

Combine cider and sugar in large saucepan; bring to a boil. Add apples; cook uncovered about 8 minutes or until apples are tender. Drain, reserving syrup. Add enough additional cider to syrup to make 1⅓ c. Return syrup to saucepan.

Blend together cornstarch and water. Add to apple mixture along with cinnamon. Cook, stirring constantly, until mixture comes to a boil. Remove from heat and stir in butter.

Spoon into pastry-lined piepan. Cover with top pastry; flute edges and cut vents. Bake in 400° oven 40 to 45 minutes or until apples are tender. Cool. Makes 6 to 8 servings.

UPSIDE-DOWN APPLE PIE

The fragrance of apples cooking with spices frequently permeated colonial kitchens. The fruit, prepared in a variety of ways, appeared almost daily in meals. New settlers to America soon discovered that no fruit crop was so easy to grow and none was so versatile as apples. Stored in bins and barrels or as strings of dried fruit hanging from attic rafters, they provided the winter supply.

Women baked apple pies by the dozen in cold weather and stored them in cold rooms or sheds where they froze. They thawed and warmed them slowly in brick fireplace ovens and frequently served the pies more than once a day—often for breakfast as well as dinner.

Clever colonial pie bakers created many seasoning tricks to make up for the loss of flavor in apples stored a long time. After Christmas women used a heavier hand with spices and sometimes they added another food to the apples in pies, such as bits of salt pork, maple sugar and cider.

Upside-down Apple Pie is new to this generation, simple to make and delicious. It is a good basic apple pie which bakes on a mixture of brown sugar, butter and pecans. This forms a glaze on the pie when it is inverted.

UPSIDE-DOWN APPLE PIE

An out-of-ordinary apple pie, heritage from colonial days

¼ c. butter or regular
  margarine, softened
½ c. pecan halves
½ c. brown sugar, firmly
  packed
Pastry for 2-crust 9″ pie

6 c. sliced pared apples
½ c. sugar
2 tblsp. flour
½ tsp. ground cinnamon
Dash of ground nutmeg

Spread butter over bottom and sides of 9″ pie pan. Press pecan halves, rounded side down, into butter. Sprinkle evenly with brown sugar; pat in gently.

Roll out enough pastry for bottom crust; place over brown sugar.

Combine apples, sugar, flour, cinnamon and nutmeg. Spoon into pie pan.

Roll out remaining pastry; place over apples. Trim to fit. Seal edges. Flute edges, and prick top with fork.

Bake in 400° oven 50 minutes or until apples are tender. Cool on rack 5 minutes. Place serving plate over pie; invert. Carefully remove pie pan. Serve warm or cool. Makes 8 servings.

GLAZED PEACH PIE

Peaches, originally a Chinese fruit, were plentiful in the South, and southern kitchens specialized in peach desserts. Glazed Peach Pie is an adaptation of an old-time Georgia open-face pie.

GLAZED PEACH PIE

Summer has few table treats to equal this—a peach-orange glaze lines the pastry and covers red and yellow peach slices

6 c. sliced pared peaches
  (6 large)
1 c. sugar
3 tblsp. cornstarch
¼ tsp. ground cinnamon

½ c. orange juice
1 baked 9″ pie shell
Whipped cream or whipped
  dessert topping

Mash enough sliced peaches to measure 1 c. Reserve remaining sliced peaches.

Combine sugar, cornstarch and cinnamon in saucepan. Stir in orange juice and mashed peaches. Cook over medium heat, stirring constantly, until mixture comes to a boil. Boil, stirring, 1 minute. Spread half the glaze over bottom and sides of baked pie shell. Fill with reserved sliced peaches. Pour remaining glaze over fruit; spread to completely cover peaches. Chill at least 3 hours. Serve topped with whipped cream. Makes 8 servings.

STREUSEL PEAR PIE

Some of the world's best pear pie recipes originate in Oregon, where excellent pears are grown. Try this one when pears are available. The brown sugar, butter and delicate spicing do something good to the fruit filling.

STREUSEL PEAR PIE

For an elegant dessert, top servings of this pie with ice cream

½ c. sugar	½ c. butter or regular
1½ tblsp. quick-cooking	margarine
tapioca	1 c. sifted flour
½ tsp. ground cinnamon	1 c. brown sugar, firmly
⅛ tsp. ground mace	packed
2 tblsp. lemon juice	1 unbaked 9″ pie shell
6 c. sliced pared pears	

Combine sugar, tapioca, cinnamon and mace. Stir in lemon juice and pears. Let stand 15 minutes.

Meanwhile, cut butter into mixture of flour and brown sugar until crumbly.

Turn pear mixture into pie shell. Sprinkle crumb mixture evenly over top. Bake in 375° oven 45 to 50 minutes or until golden brown. Makes 6 to 8 servings.

DEEP-DISH PLUM PIE

Purple Italian prune plums come in late summer when many fruits have disappeared. Their superb flavor and their rather firm meat enables them to ship well so they are widely available. Due to their firmness, plums bake successfully. They may be slit and pitted, or left whole with skins and sprinkled with brown sugar and cinnamon. Add a little water and bake until tender or about 25 minutes in a 350° oven. A good supper dessert to serve warm or chilled with homemade cookies. Top the baked plums at serving time with sour cream.

The recipe for Deep-dish Plum Pie is shared by an Idaho woman, who calls the dessert September Plum Pie.

DEEP-DISH PLUM PIE

Add scoops of vanilla ice cream for a scrumptious dessert

1 c. sugar	2 tblsp. butter or regular
¼ c. flour	margarine
¼ tsp. ground cinnamon	Pastry for 1-crust 9″ pie
2½ lbs. prune plums, halved	Milk
and pitted	1 tsp. sugar

Combine 1 c. sugar, flour and cinnamon. Stir into plums. Turn into 8″ square pan. Dot with butter.

Roll pastry into a 9″ square. Place over plums. Turn edges under and seal to edge of pan. Cut steam vents. Brush top with milk.

Bake in 425° oven 45 to 50 minutes or until golden brown. Sprinkle top with 1 tsp. sugar. Serve warm or cold. Makes 6 servings.

CONCORD GRAPE PIE

The most important all-American grape is the blue Concord from which we get the flavorful grape juice. Pies made with Concords are a classic country dessert. Concord grapes are descendants of eastern wild grapes, which the colonists called "fox grapes."

In no area are juicy Concord grape pies more ardently praised than in the Finger Lakes region and in northwestern sections of New York, where the grapes have been grown extensively for years. Our Concord Grape Pie has two crusts with a tart-sweet filling in which the true grape flavor dominates.

CONCORD GRAPE PIE

One of the joys of early autumn, this is a dessert to remember. Some work to make but more than worth the effort

5 c. Concord grapes	1 tsp. lemon juice
1⅓ c. sugar	Pastry for 2-crust 9″ pie
¼ c. flour	2 tblsp. butter or regular
Dash of salt	margarine

Wash grapes. Remove skins by pinching grapes at end opposite stem. Save skins.

Heat grape pulp in saucepan without water until grapes come to a full rolling boil. Press through sieve to remove seeds. Combine pulp and skins.

Stir together sugar, flour and salt. Stir into grape mixture along with lemon juice. Pour grape filling into pastry-lined pie pan. Dot with butter. Cover with top pastry; flute edges and cut vents.

Bake in 425° oven 35 to 45 minutes or until crust is browned and juice begins to bubble through slits in top. Cool. Makes 6 to 8 servings.

RHUBARB/RUM PIE

Rhubarb brought the first taste of spring to the favorite dessert, pie—in fact, early Americans called it pie plant. Sloops and schooners sailed from our eastern seaports with salt fish, barrel staves and hoops of wood and other items of trade to the Caribbean Islands. They returned home with comparatively inexpensive molasses and more costly sugar and rum, all sugar cane products. A little rum was used in cooking to flavor otherwise common desserts. Rhubarb/Rum Pie is a good example.

The Connecticut woman who shares an old family recipe for it, says she thinks the dessert was an outgrowth of chess and other custard pies extensively served in the early days. Regardless of where and when the recipe for the pie originated, the dessert tastes wonderful and the bits of pink rhubarb give it appetite and eye appeal.

RHUBARB/RUM PIE

Extra-delicious when topped with whipped cream

1 unbaked 9″ pie shell	1 c. milk
2 tblsp. butter or regular margarine	2 tblsp. dark rum
	¼ tsp. salt
1 c. sugar	¼ tsp. ground nutmeg
¼ c. flour	¼ tsp. ground cinnamon
2 eggs, separated	Whipped cream or whipped
2 c. cut-up rhubarb	dessert topping (optional)

Bake pastry shell in 350° oven 5 minutes. Remove from oven.

Meanwhile, cream together butter and sugar. Beat in flour, then egg yolks. Stir in rhubarb, milk, rum, salt, nutmeg and cinnamon.

Beat egg whites until soft peaks form. Fold into rhubarb mixture. Turn into pie shell.

Bake in 350° oven 45 to 50 minutes or until rhubarb is tender. Serve topped with whipped cream, if desired. Makes 6 to 8 servings.

SOUR CREAM/RAISIN PIE

When this recipe was invented in early America, fresh fruit was available only for a short season but raisins, like other dried fruits, could be kept on hand in the cupboard. And without refrigeration, sour cream frequently accumulated in kitchens. So this dessert became a favorite and is popular for its great taste today.

Supposedly the pie originated in New England, but raisin pies of many descriptions were served in all the colonies. The Funeral Pie of the Pennsylvania Dutch was the most famous. It was a two-crust pie, often with a lattice pastry top. The pie was served in the big meals that followed funerals, when relatives of the bereaved family gathered, bringing most of the food. Two-crust raisin pies carried more successfully than those topped with meringue.

So well established in Pennsylvania Dutch country was the pie that a dismal saying, still heard in reference to a serious illness, developed: "There will be a raisin pie soon." But our Sour Cream/Raisin Pie is special and sure to bring cheer.

SOUR CREAM/RAISIN PIE

There are many recipes for pie—this is one of the best

1 c. sugar	1½ c. raisins
1½ tblsp. cornstarch	1½ tblsp. lemon juice
½ tsp. ground cinnamon	1 baked 9″ pie shell
¼ tsp. ground nutmeg	¼ tsp. cream of tartar
¼ tsp. salt	6 tblsp. sugar
1½ c. dairy sour cream	½ tsp. vanilla
3 eggs, separated	

Stir together 1 c. sugar, cornstarch, cinnamon, nutmeg and salt in saucepan. Blend in sour cream.

Beat egg yolks slightly. Stir into mixture in saucepan along with raisins and lemon juice. Cook over medium heat, stirring constantly, until mixture thickens and boils. Boil 1 minute. Pour into baked pie shell.

Beat egg whites with cream of tartar until frothy. Beat in the 6 tblsp. sugar, 1 tblsp. at a time, until mixture is glossy and stiff peaks form. Beat in vanilla. Spread meringue over hot filling, sealing well to edge of crust to prevent shrinking.

Bake in 400° oven about 10 minutes or until lightly browned. Cool away from drafts. Makes 6 to 8 servings.

ORANGE/LEMON CHIFFON PIE

Gelatinized refrigerator pies, called chiffon pies because of their tall, light fillings, first came to tables around 40 years ago in an Iowa family restaurant located in the shadow of a railroad trestle. They won nationwide recognition quickly and menu planners still include them in many meals.

Orange/Lemon Chiffon Pie wins first for its beauty.

ORANGE/LEMON CHIFFON PIE

This dessert deserves its reputation. Perfect light finale for an otherwise substantial meal

1 envelope unflavored gelatin	¼ c. water
½ c. sugar	½ tsp. grated orange peel
Dash of salt	½ tsp. grated lemon peel
4 eggs, separated	⅓ c. sugar
½ c. orange juice	1 baked 9" pie shell
⅓ c. lemon juice	Whipped cream or whipped dessert topping

Stir together gelatin, ½ c. sugar and salt in saucepan.

Beat together egg yolks, orange juice, lemon juice and water. Blend into gelatin mixture. Cook over medium heat, stirring constantly, until mixture comes to a boil and gelatin is dissolved. Remove from heat; stir in orange and lemon peels. Chill, stirring occasionally, until mixture is partially set.

Beat egg whites until soft peaks form. Gradually add ⅓ c. sugar, beating until stiff peaks form. Fold into gelatin mixture. Spoon lightly into pie shell; chill until set. Serve garnished with whipped cream. Makes 6 to 8 servings.

AMISH VANILLA PIE

This is a rich dark pie with brown sugar topping that melts on your tongue. A farm woman in Kansas makes this dessert often for her family. The recipe was handed down through several generations of great Amish cooks.

AMISH VANILLA PIE

A real old-fashioned pie that is certain to be a hit with coffee

½ c. brown sugar, firmly packed	½ c. brown sugar, firmly packed
1 tblsp. flour	½ tsp. cream of tartar
¼ c. dark corn syrup	½ tsp. baking soda
1½ tsp. vanilla	⅛ tsp. salt
1 egg, beaten	¼ c. butter or regular
1 c. water	margarine
1 c. unsifted flour	1 unbaked 9″ pie shell

Combine ½ c. brown sugar, 1 tblsp. flour, corn syrup, vanilla and egg in 2-qt. saucepan. Slowly stir in water. Cook over medium heat, stirring constantly, until mixture comes to a boil. Let cool.

Combine 1 c. flour, ½ c. brown sugar, cream of tartar, baking soda, salt and butter; mix until crumbly. Pour cooled mixture into pie shell; top with crumbs.

Bake in 350° oven 40 minutes or until golden brown. Makes 6 to 8 servings.

BLACK BOTTOM PIE

At the start of the 20th century Black Bottom Pie, with creamy chocolate- and rum-flavored fillings layered in a pie shell, was the pride of Gulf Coast hostesses. The chocolate filling, spread on the bottom of the pastry shell, gave its name. Hollywood, during the fabulous movie days, adopted Black Bottom

Pie as the dessert of desserts and it reached "big-time." Our recipe produces a pie that wins praises equal to those it received when it was a new dessert star.

BLACK BOTTOM PIE

Enchanting in flavor and intriguing in looks, this pie is a champion among refrigerator pies featuring a vanilla wafer crust

½ c. sugar
2 tblsp. cornstarch
¼ tsp. salt
2 eggs, separated
2 c. milk
1 envelope unflavored
 gelatin
3 tblsp. cold water
3 tblsp. rum or 2 tsp. rum
 flavoring

1 square unsweetened
 chocolate, melted
¼ tsp. vanilla
Vanilla Wafer Crumb
 Crust (recipe follows)
¼ tsp. cream of tartar
⅓ c. sugar
1 c. heavy cream, whipped
Grated chocolate

Prepare Vanilla Wafer Crumb Crust.

Stir together ½ c. sugar, cornstarch and salt in saucepan.

Beat egg yolks slightly; blend in milk. Add to sugar mixture and cook over medium heat, stirring constantly, until mixture comes to a boil. Remove 1 c. custard mixture and set aside.

Soften gelatin in cold water; add to hot mixture in saucepan. Stir to dissolve. Stir in rum. Chill until mixture mounds slightly when dropped from a spoon.

Combine melted chocolate, vanilla and reserved custard mixture. Spread over bottom of Vanilla Wafer Crumb Crust.

Beat egg whites with cream of tartar until foamy. Add ⅓ c. sugar, 1 tblsp. at a time, beating until very stiff peaks form. Fold chilled custard mixture into meringue. Spread over chocolate mixture in pie shell. Chill at least 3 hours or until set.

Within 30 minutes of serving time spread whipped cream evenly over pie. Garnish with grated chocolate. Makes 6 to 8 servings.

SAVANNAH PECAN PIE

Early colonists in the South found the tall pecan trees, related to the hickory, growing wild. Indians were pounding the nuts into meal for little cakes and other dishes. They called the nuts pegans, which means bone (hard) shells. They bore little resemblance to today's big, thin-shelled pecans (most of the bitter tannin has been eliminated by breeding) now cultivated in Georgia and Florida west through Texas.

Who baked the first pecan pie no one knows, but the English chess pies apparently were adapted to accommodate the new nuts. Cane syrup and light molasses were sweeteners for the filling. Today corn syrup is generally used. Women throughout American history have substituted ingredients at hand in familiar dishes and thus often create new taste delights.

Our Savannah Pecan Pie is so rich and satisfying that one pie serves eight adequately.

SAVANNAH PECAN PIE

Crisp pastry holds jelly-like filling topped with crisp nuts

3 eggs	6 tblsp. melted butter or
⅔ c. sugar	regular margarine
⅛ tsp. salt	1 c. pecan halves or pieces
1 c. dark corn syrup	1 unbaked 9″ pie shell

Beat eggs. Beat in sugar, salt, corn syrup and butter. Add pecans. Pour into unbaked pie shell.

Bake in 350° oven 50 minutes or until knife inserted halfway between center and edge comes out clean. Cool. Makes 8 servings.

FESTIVE PUMPKIN PIE

Even though American Indians never tasted pumpkin pie or saw a jack-o'-lantern before European colonists arrived, practically every tribe grew and ate large quantities of pumpkins and

Vanilla Wafer Crumb Crust: Combine 1½ c. fine vanilla wafer crumbs and 6 tblsp. melted butter or regular margarine. Press into 9″ pie pan. Chill about 45 minutes or until set. Or bake in 350° oven 10 minutes; cool and chill.

CHOCOLATE/PEANUT PIE

Peanuts are believed to have originated in Brazil, but the pre-Inca Peruvians called them, "ground seeds," as appear on the most ancient Peruvian pottery. And almost every Inca mummy has an accompanying supply of peanuts to help the spirit on its way.

Chocolate/Peanut Pie is rich and delicious. The dessert is at its best when served in small portions, eight to a 9-inch pie, and at the end of a light meal.

CHOCOLATE/PEANUT PIE

Filling bakes into layers with crunchy peanuts forming the top. Peanut and chocolate flavors are unusually harmonious

2 squares unsweetened chocolate	½ c. milk
¼ c. butter or regular margarine	¼ c. light corn syrup
¾ c. sugar	1½ tsp. vanilla
½ c. brown sugar, firmly packed	3 eggs
	1 c. coarsely chopped salted peanuts
	1 unbaked 9″ pie shell

Heat together chocolate and butter in heavy saucepan over low heat just until melted, stirring occasionally. Remove from heat and cool slightly.

Combine sugars, milk, corn syrup, vanilla and eggs in medium bowl. Beat with rotary beater until blended. Beat in chocolate mixture. Stir in peanuts. Pour into pie shell.

Bake in 350° oven 45 to 50 minutes or until knife inserted in center comes out clean. Cool thoroughly. Makes 8 servings.

squash. New England Indians considered them almost as important for food as corn and beans. They grew the vegetables around hills of corn.

Different varieties of pumpkins had been enjoyed throughout the Americas for many centuries. On the ceramic ware in graves of Peru's pre-Inca people, much of which is thousands of years old, just about every known variety of squash, including pumpkins, is depicted.

Pumpkin pies were baked in reflector ovens on the kitchen hearth and in fireplace ovens in colonial days. New England women often substituted winter squash for the pumpkin, while in the South sweet potatoes sometimes took the pumpkin role.

Most pumpkin pies today are made with convenient canned pumpkin, although some enthusiastic gardeners grow, cook, and purée the vegetable for their pies. Our Festive Pumpkin Pie is a version of the old-fashioned pie. It is topped with sour cream, sweetened slightly and briefly baked on the pie.

FESTIVE PUMPKIN PIE

Cream cheese is the new note in this all-American treat

1 (8 oz.) pkg. cream cheese, softened	3 eggs
¾ c. brown sugar, firmly packed	1 c. canned pumpkin
1 tsp. ground cinnamon	1 c. milk
½ tsp. ground ginger	1 tsp. vanilla
½ tsp. salt	1 unbaked 9″ pie shell, edges crimped high
¼ tsp. ground cloves	1 c. dairy sour cream
	2 tblsp. sugar

Cream together cream cheese, brown sugar, cinnamon, ginger, salt and cloves. Add eggs, one at a time, beating thoroughly after each addition. Blend in pumpkin, milk and vanilla. Pour into pie shell.

Bake in 375° oven 45 to 50 minutes or until knife inserted halfway between center and edge comes out clean.

Blend together sour cream and sugar. Spread over top of pie.

Return pie to oven 3 to 5 minutes or just until topping is set. Chill before serving. Makes 6 to 8 servings.

HARTFORD ELECTION CAKE

Election cakes were sold by New England stores on town meeting days and women vied with one another to bake the best yeast-leavened and fruited cake. The first printed recipe for an election cake appeared in the 1800 second edition of Amelia Simmons' *American Cookery*. Practically all cakes baked in colonial homes and for another half century were yeast-leavened. The bread doughs baked successfully in brick fireplace ovens; besides other leavenings had not been developed.

About 1830, people started to refer to the Hartford Election Cake because politicians there served it to men who voted a straight party ticket. About the only connection it has with politics now is that it and coffee are traditional American refreshments for informal parties on election days.

HARTFORD ELECTION CAKE

This cake is rich, spicy, full of raisins and nuts, and frosted—a big recipe that makes as many as 16 servings

2 pkgs. active dry yeast	1½ tsp. ground cinnamon
1½ c. warm water (110 to 115°)	¼ tsp. ground cloves
	¼ tsp. ground mace
2 tsp. sugar	½ tsp. ground nutmeg
1½ c. sifted flour	2 eggs
¾ c. butter or regular margarine	1½ c. raisins
	½ c. chopped citron
1 c. sugar	¾ c. chopped nuts
3 c. sifted flour	Confectioners Sugar
1 tsp. salt	Frosting (recipe follows)

Sprinkle yeast on warm water; stir to dissolve. Add 2 tsp. sugar and 1½ c. flour; beat well by hand or 2 minutes with electric mixer at medium speed. Cover and let rise in warm place until bubbly, about 30 minutes.

Meanwhile, cream butter and 1 c. sugar until light and fluffy.

Sift 3 c. flour with salt, cinnamon, cloves, mace and nutmeg.

When yeast mixture is bubbly, add eggs to creamed mixture and beat well. Combine with yeast mixture. Add sifted dry ingredients, a little at a time, beating with spoon after each addition. Beat until smooth.

Stir in raisins, citron and nuts. Pour into well-greased and floured 10″ tube pan. Cover and let rise in warm place until doubled, about 1½ hours.

Bake in 375° oven 1 hour or until done. Cool in pan 5 minutes; turn out on rack to complete cooling. While faintly warm, spread with Confectioners Sugar Frosting. Makes 12 to 16 servings.

Confectioners Sugar Frosting: To 1 c. sifted confectioners sugar add enough milk or light cream to make mixture of spreading consistency. Add ½ tsp. vanilla and dash of salt (or flavor with ½ tsp. lemon juice and ¼ tsp. grated lemon peel). Stir until smooth.

LADY BALTIMORE CAKE

With the arrival of baking powder in 1856, American women had a new incentive for cake baking. That they reached such delicious heights with their productions was an achievement, for their ovens were without reliable heat controls.

The last part of the Victorian era and the first half of the 20th century was the golden age for homemade butter cakes, now known as "from-scratch" cakes to distinguish them from packaged mix cakes. During this period, the oven control regulator was perfected.

Lady Baltimore Cake had its greatest fame during the early 1900s. It had been enjoyed earlier in homes on Maryland's Eastern Shore and Tidewater Virginia but it was in Charleston, South Carolina, that it won wide recognition. At Christmastime hundreds of white boxes carrying tall, round, fragile gift cakes were sent from there to all parts of the country. It was a business in many home kitchens as well as of the Women's Exchange.

Thousands of homes across country prized their own recipes for this special-occasion cake. In some respects the cakes were alike. They were delicate white layer cakes with sides and tops covered with a cooked white frosting. Fillings varied, but most mixed some of the white frosting with such goodies as nuts, chopped raisins and soft dried figs. Sometimes there were two layers, often three. Our Lady Baltimore Cake meets all the criteria of this immortal cake.

LADY BALTIMORE CAKE

Delicate cake layers with fluffy, fruited frosting

2¼ c. sifted cake flour	1½ c. sugar
3½ tsp. baking powder	2 tsp. light corn syrup
1 tsp. salt	⅓ c. cold water
1½ c. sugar	Dash of salt
½ c. shortening	1 tsp. vanilla
1 c. milk	½ c. finely chopped nuts
1½ tsp. vanilla	½ c. raisins, cut up
4 egg whites	½ c. dried figs, cut in strips
2 egg whites	1 c. frosting

Sift together cake flour, baking powder and salt into large mixer bowl. Add 1½ c. sugar, shortening, ⅔ c. milk and 1½ tsp. vanilla. Blend 30 seconds at low speed, scraping bowl constantly. Beat at high speed 2 minutes, scraping bowl occasionally. Add remaining milk and 4 egg whites. Continue beating at high speed 2 minutes. Spread into 2 greased and floured 8 or 9″ round layer cake pans.

Bake in 350° oven 30 to 35 minutes or until done. Cool in pans on racks 5 minutes. Cover another rack with a towel; place towel side down over one cake pan; invert and remove pan. Place original rack on bottom of layer and turn again. Repeat with other cake layer. Cool completely with top side of cake up.

To make frosting combine 2 egg whites, 1½ c. sugar, corn syrup, water and dash of salt in top of double boiler. Blend 30 seconds at low speed with electric mixer. Place over boiling water, making sure bottom of pan does not touch water. Cook, beating constantly at high speed, about 7 minutes or until stiff peaks form. Remove from heat and add 1 tsp. vanilla. If desired, for easier beating, turn into mixing bowl. Continue beating until of spreading consistency. Set aside 1 c. frosting for filling.

To make filling, combine nuts, raisins and figs. Stir in 1 c. frosting.

Spread filling between cooled cake layers. Cover sides and top of cake with frosting. Makes 12 servings.

DELUXE POUND CAKE

This rich, buttery cake was originally English but it is now truly a traditional southern specialty. At Christmastime, there is always a sugar-dusted pound cake on the buffet table along with a bowl of thick, creamy eggnog.

DELUXE POUND CAKE

Excellent, fine-textured pound cake with a buttery flavor

2 c. butter (1 lb.)	**4 c. sifted cake flour**
3 c. sugar	**⅔ c. milk**
6 eggs	**Confectioners sugar**
1½ tsp. vanilla	

Cream together butter and sugar until light and fluffy. Add eggs, one at a time, beating well after each addition. Add vanilla. (Total beating time: 10 minutes.)

Add cake flour alternately with milk, beating well after each addition. Pour batter into well-greased 10″ fluted tube pan.

Bake in 350° oven 1 hour 30 minutes or until cake tests done. (If you use a dark-colored fluted tube pan, reduce temperature to 325°.)

Cool in pan on rack 15 minutes. Remove from pan; cool on rack. Dust with confectioners sugar. Makes 12 servings.

Note: Cake is best if covered and allowed to stand for 24 hours before serving.

LEMON ANGEL REFRIGERATOR CAKE

Original American cakes appeared for the most part after the middle of the 19th century. During the late 17th and 18th centuries large fruitcakes were mixed in the kitchens of the more affluent families and taken to the bake shop for baking. Later settlers from Europe brought their cake recipes, usually for sponge and pound cakes. Then the first angel food cakes were made—this American, soufflé-like cake has had great popularity ever since.

Today this favorite cake usually is made with a packaged mix. Not only does the mix reduce the work and time required to bake a tall and handsome angel food cake, but it does away with the problem of all those leftover egg yolks.

When baking angel food cakes became easier, women began to make other desserts with the cake as a base. Lemon Angel Refrigerator Cake is an example. Lemon Angel consists of angel food cake with lemon custard, combined, molded and chilled in a tube pan. Before serving, you frost it with whipped cream.

LEMON ANGEL REFRIGERATOR CAKE

Hostesses like this yellow and white cake dessert because they can prepare it a day ahead, except for frosting

1 envelope unflavored gelatin	¾ c. lemon juice
¼ c. water	1 (10″) angel food cake
6 eggs, separated	¾ c. sugar
¾ c. sugar	1 c. heavy cream
2 tsp. grated lemon peel	1 tblsp. confectioners sugar

Soften gelatin in cold water.

Beat 6 egg yolks slightly in heavy saucepan. Add ¾ c. sugar, lemon peel and juice. Cook over low heat, stirring constantly, until mixture coats spoon and is slightly thickened. Remove from heat. Add gelatin; stir until dissolved. Cool to room temperature.

Meanwhile, rub surface of cake with hands to remove brown crumbs. Tear cake into bite-size pieces.

Beat egg whites until soft peaks form. Gradually add ¾ c. sugar, beating until stiff peaks form. Fold cooled custard into egg whites. Pour ½″ layer of custard into buttered 10″ tube pan. Add a layer of angel food pieces, then custard. Continue alternating layers, ending with custard. Chill at least 6 hours, or overnight, until firm. Unmold on round platter.

Whip cream with confectioners sugar. Spread over sides and top of cake. Makes 12 to 16 servings.

BOSTON CHOCOLATE CREAM PIE

When is a pie a cake? When it is Boston cream pie. It consists of two layers of a two-egg cake put together with a delicate custard filling and topped with chocolate frosting. Omit the frosting and sprinkle the top layer with confectioners sugar and you have another version. Some women gave the top a fancy design by sprinkling the confectioners sugar through a paper lace doily placed on top.

Keep Boston Chocolate Cream Pie with its custard filling in the refrigerator until serving time. Or make the cake part ahead (freezes too) and add the custard shortly before serving.

BOSTON CHOCOLATE CREAM PIE

This dessert is old enough to be new to many young families

1¼ c. sifted flour	Dash of salt
2 tsp. baking powder	1 egg, slightly beaten
¼ tsp. salt	½ tsp. vanilla
⅓ c. butter or regular margarine	2 tblsp. butter or regular margarine
¾ c. sugar	1 square unsweetened chocolate
2 eggs	2 tblsp. light cream or milk
1 tsp. vanilla	1¼ c. sifted confectioners sugar
½ c. milk	½ tsp. vanilla
1 c. light cream	
¼ c. sugar	
3 tblsp. flour	

Sift together 1¼ c. flour, baking powder and ¼ tsp. salt.

Cream ⅓ c. butter in small mixer bowl; gradually beat in ¾ c. sugar. Beat in 2 eggs, one at a time, beating well after each addition. Beat until mixture is light and fluffy. Beat in 1 tsp. vanilla. Stir in dry ingredients by hand alternately with milk. Spread in 2 greased and paper-lined 8″ layer cake pans.

Bake in 375° oven 20 to 25 minutes. Cool on racks 5 minutes; remove from pans. Cool thoroughly.

Meanwhile, scald 1 c. light cream. Combine ¼ c. sugar, 3 tblsp. flour and dash of salt in double boiler top. Gradually stir in scalded cream. Slowly stir hot mixture into 1 beaten egg. Cook over boiling water, stirring constantly, until mixture thickens. Remove from heat and stir in ½ tsp. vanilla. Cool custard thoroughly.

To make frosting, combine 2 tblsp. butter, chocolate and 2 tblsp. cream in small saucepan. Cook over medium heat until butter and chocolate are melted. Remove from heat. Add sugar and vanilla; beat until smooth and of spreading consistency.

To assemble Boston Chocolate Cream Pie, spread cooled filling between cooled cake layers. Spread chocolate frosting over top of pie. Refrigerate until serving time. Makes 12 servings.

PUMPKIN SPICE CAKE

American Indians made many dishes with pumpkins which they grew on tribal lands. While pumpkin pies took first place with early European settlers, pumpkin cakes also became popular a century and a half ago. The best compliment a woman received for her cake was: "It tastes like pumpkin pie."

Our Pumpkin Spice Cake is a recent recipe made with a packaged spice cake mix and canned pumpkin. The ease and speed with which you can bake this excellent cake would make a colonial woman marvel. She not only grew, cooked and strained the pumpkin, but she added it to a spice cake she made from scratch. No pumpkin cake ever tasted better than our short-cut version.

PUMPKIN SPICE CAKE

A rich, cheese frosting enhances the good pumpkin-pie taste

1 (18½ oz.) pkg. spice cake
   mix
1 (1 lb.) can pumpkin
2 tsp. baking soda

2 eggs
⅓ c. water
Cream Cheese Frosting
   (recipe follows)

Combine cake mix, pumpkin, baking soda, eggs and water in large mixer bowl. Beat as directed on cake-mix package. Spread in 2 greased and floured 9″ round layer cake pans.

Bake in 350° oven 25 to 30 minutes. Let cool 10 minutes, then turn out of pans. Cool.

Spread Cream Cheese Frosting between layers, then frost sides and top of cake. Makes 12 servings.

Cream Cheese Frosting: Cream together ½ c. butter or regular margarine, 1 (8 oz.) pkg. cream cheese and 1 tsp. vanilla until light and fluffy. Gradually add 1 lb. box sifted confectioners sugar, beating well after each addition. If mixture is too thick to spread, add a small amount of milk.

HONEYED GINGERBREAD

Honey, molasses and maple syrup were the most used sweetenings in colonial days. Early Americans watched the flights of wild bees and tried to chart them hoping they would lead to hollow "bee trees," where bees stored honey. Soon they began to domesticate bees into hives.

Plantations in the West Indies used manufacturing methods that could not extract all the sucrose from sugar cane juices. What was left they sold as molasses. It was inexpensive in comparison to costly white and brown sugars. American traders brought home barrels of molasses and the taste lingers especially in New England.

Molasses and honey are both ingredients in Honeyed Gingerbread. Lighter in color than many gingerbreads and mildly spiced, it is a soft gingerbread created in early America. European gingerbreads then were hard. For more than a century people considered gingerbread a hot bread to serve with butter, but today it often is a dessert with a variety of toppings, such as frosting, sweet sauce, whipped cream, ice cream and whipped dessert topping.

HONEYED GINGERBREAD

Easy-to-make, one-bowl gingerbread—heavenly taste

2¼ c. sifted flour	½ c. light molasses
⅓ c. sugar	½ c. honey
1 tsp. baking soda	¾ c. hot water
1 tsp. ground ginger	½ c. shortening
1 tsp. ground cinnamon	1 egg
¼ tsp. salt	

Sift together flour, sugar, baking soda, ginger, cinnamon and salt into large mixer bowl. Add molasses, honey, hot water, shortening and egg. Beat at low speed 30 seconds, scraping bowl constantly. Beat at medium speed 3 minutes, scraping bowl occasionally. Turn into greased 9″ square pan.

Bake in 325° oven 50 to 55 minutes or until cake tests done. Serve warm. Makes 9 servings.

BLACK WALNUT BARS

Native black walnuts, once plentiful in the woods, contribute unique flavor to many foods. Since there are not enough black walnut trees now to meet the demands of the increased population, they are high-priced. Cracking and picking out the meat is a time-consuming job, but well worth it as evidenced by the many recipes from different parts of the country.

Some of the black walnut favorites are: On the Missouri-Kansas line, luscious black walnut pie, in the Ozarks, black walnut muffins; in Tennessee, sweet potato balls with black walnuts, rolled in crushed cornflakes and baked; Hoosier sweet sauces (butterscotch, caramel and chocolate) on ice cream and sprinkled with chopped black walnuts; in Pennsylvania Dutch country, loaf cakes, cookies, gingerbread and baked meringues all containing black walnuts; and in Iowa, fudge and brownies with black walnuts.

This recipe for Black Walnut Bars is from Iowa.

BLACK WALNUT BARS

The crisp bottom of the cookies is buttery and caramel flavored

2 c. sifted flour

1 c. brown sugar, firmly
   packed

1 c. butter or regular
   margarine

4 eggs

2 c. brown sugar, firmly
   packed

2 tsp. vanilla

2 tblsp. flour

½ tsp. baking powder

½ tsp. salt

2 c. chopped black walnuts

Mix together 2 c. flour and 1 c. brown sugar in large bowl. Cut in butter until crumbs form. Press into well-greased 15½×10½×1″ jelly roll pan. Bake in 350° oven 10 minutes. Remove from oven and cool slightly, about 10 minutes. Turn oven temperature to 375°.

Beat eggs until light. Gradually beat in 2 c. brown sugar, then vanilla.

Stir together 2 tblsp. flour, baking powder and salt. Add to egg mixture along with nuts. Spread over baked crust in pan.

Bake in 375° oven about 20 minutes or until light brown. Cool in pan on rack. Cut in 2×1″ bars. Makes 5 dozen.

SNICKERDOODLES

Inventors of old-time recipes used imagination in naming them that present-day food writers and editors sometimes envy. Who could think up a more unforgettable name for cookies than Snickerdoodles? Our recipe is similar to one used in New

England and Pennsylvania Dutch kitchens before baking powder was discovered—baking soda and cream of tartar are the leavening. Originally, hickory nuts frequently were added to the dough.

Balls of the cookie dough, rolled in cinnamon mixed with sugar, puff up in the oven, but settle down to crisp cookies with crinkly tops. When made into small balls these are light and dainty enough to serve at tea parties, or with ice cream.

SNICKERDOODLES

A splendid example of economical cookies that taste wonderful

½ c. butter or regular margarine, softened	2¾ c. sifted flour
½ c. shortening	2 tsp. cream of tartar
1½ c. sugar	1 tsp. baking soda
2 eggs	¼ tsp. salt
1 tsp. vanilla	3 tblsp. sugar
	3 tblsp. ground cinnamon

Mix together butter and shortening. Beat in 1½ c. sugar, eggs and vanilla.

Sift together flour, cream of tartar, baking soda and salt. Blend into creamed mixture. Shape rounded teaspoons of dough into balls.

Combine 3 tblsp. sugar and cinnamon; roll balls in mixture. Place 2″ apart on ungreased baking sheets.

Bake in 400° oven 8 to 10 minutes or until golden brown. Remove from baking sheets; cool on racks. Makes about 6 dozen.

CHOCOLATE CHIP/PEANUT COOKIES

Drop cookies dotted with chocolate were the talk of women's groups in the 1930s. The goodies were called Toll House Chocolate Chip Cookies, which indicates where they first were baked. When the Massachusetts home economist who operated the Toll House Restaurant found she was out of raisins to add to her cookie dough, she reached in desperation for a bar of chocolate, cut bits from it, stirred them into the dough and baked the cookies. When guests exclaimed over their tastiness and asked for more, she knew her improvisation was a winner. Enterprising food processors soon introduced packages of chocolate pieces to grocery stores.

Peanuts, grown extensively in the southeastern states for years, assume the role of nuts in our recipe. These beans (peanuts are not nuts, but legumes) are less expensive than nuts. They add the crunchiness that nuts, such as pecans and walnuts, provided in the first chocolate chip cookies.

CHOCOLATE CHIP/PEANUT COOKIES

The Americas gave the world chocolate and peanuts. Their flavors blend beautifully in these favorite cookies

½ c. butter or regular
   margarine
½ c. sugar
¼ c. brown sugar, firmly
   packed
1 egg
1 tsp. vanilla

1 c. sifted flour
½ tsp. salt
½ tsp. baking soda
1 (6 oz.) pkg. semisweet
   chocolate pieces
½ c. coarsely chopped,
   toasted, salted peanuts

Cream together butter, sugars, egg and vanilla until light and fluffy.

Sift together flour, salt and soda. Add to creamed mixture, blending well. Stir in chocolate and peanuts. Drop by teaspoonfuls about 2" apart on greased baking sheets.

Bake in 375° oven 10 to 12 minutes or until golden brown. Remove from baking sheets; cool on racks. Makes about 3 dozen.

FROSTED DIAMONDS

Although cookie baking flourishes throughout the year in the Bethlehem, Pennsylvania region, the campaign swings into full tilt as Christmas approaches. To ancestors of the Moravians, who founded the city on Christmas Eve 1741, the holiday always has had special importance. And Christmas cookie baking became a custom that thrives today.

Many Bethlehem households have a collection of cookie cutters, some of them antiques, that produce cookies of different sizes and shapes. They represent dolls, houses, eagles, sitting cats, dogs, fish, horses, men on horseback, birds, chickens, bells, stars, angels, camels, sheep, shepherds, Santa Claus and Christmas trees.

Frosted Diamonds sometimes are called Moravian Scotch cookies. The dough traditionally is cut in diamond shapes either with a cutter or knife. If you like the taste of caraway seeds, these cookies are for you.

FROSTED DIAMONDS

Pink sugar decorates tops of these thin cookies frosted white

¼ c. butter or regular margarine	⅛ tsp. salt
	1 tsp. caraway seeds
¼ c. shortening	White Mountain Frosting
½ c. sugar	(recipe follows)
2 eggs	¼ c. coarse pink decorating
1 tsp. vanilla	sugar
3 c. sifted flour	

Beat butter and shortening until light; gradually add sugar, and beat until mixture is fluffy. Beat in eggs and vanilla, blending thoroughly.

Sift together flour and salt; add to creamed mixture. Stir in caraway seeds.

Roll dough thin, not more than ⅛", and cut in 2" diamonds with sharp knife or cookie cutter. Place ½" apart on lightly greased baking sheet.

Bake in 325° oven 10 to 12 minutes. Remove from baking sheets and cool on racks. Spread cookies with White Mountain Frosting; sprinkle with pink sugar. Makes about 6½ dozen.

White Mountain Frosting: Combine 1 c. sugar, ⅛ tsp. cream of tartar and ¼ c. water in small saucepan. Place over heat and stir until sugar dissolves. Continue cooking to soft ball stage (236°) on candy thermometer.

Meanwhile, add ⅛ tsp. salt to 1 egg white; beat until stiff. Pour hot syrup in a fine stream into egg white, beating constantly until frosting is of spreading consistency.

SPICED CHRISTMAS COOKIES

In Bethlehem, Pennsylvania, families on Christmas Eve visit from one home to another to exchange greetings and see the "putz" or Nativity scene. People there call the custom "putzing." Hostesses on these occasions pass a variety of homemade cookies to their callers. Two kinds of cookies usually are a tempting tradition—brown cookies and white cookies. Spiced Christmas Cookies are the brown special.

SPICED CHRISTMAS COOKIES

Big recipe—you can cut it in half and still have a lot of cookies to share with family and friends

½ c. butter or regular margarine	2 tblsp. light cream or dairy half-and-half
½ c. shortening	5 c. sifted flour
1½ c. brown sugar, firmly packed	1 tblsp. ground cinnamon
2 c. molasses	1½ tsp. ground ginger
	½ tsp. ground cloves

Cream together butter and shortening; gradually add sugar, beating until light and fluffy. Beat in molasses; blend in cream.

Sift together flour, cinnamon, ginger and cloves; stir into creamed mixture. Store in covered bowl in refrigerator overnight.

Roll dough thin, using floured pastry cloth on board and rolling pin. Cut in animal shapes. Place 1 to 1½" apart on greased baking sheets.

Bake in 350° oven 10 to 12 minutes. Remove from baking sheets and cool on racks. Makes 19 dozen.

WHITE CHRISTMAS COOKIES

Tradition in Bethlehem, Pennsylvania, decrees that White Christmas Cookies be thin and cut in fancy shapes, with the star most frequently used. Instead of rolling the soft dough, some women today find it easier to shape the dough in rolls, chill it overnight, slice and bake. Sliced or rolled, the cookies are best paper-thin.

WHITE CHRISTMAS COOKIES

These crisp, spicy cookies are straw-colored despite their name; cut the recipe in half for a smaller batch

½ c. butter or regular margarine	4 eggs, beaten 4 c. sifted flour
½ c. shortening	⅛ tsp. ground nutmeg
2 c. sugar	⅛ tsp. ground cinnamon

Cream together butter and shortening; gradually add sugar, beating until light and fluffy. Beat in eggs.

Sift together flour, nutmeg and cinnamon; stir into creamed mixture (dough should be stiff). Store in covered bowl in refrigerator overnight.

Roll dough very thin, using floured pastry cloth on board and rolling pin. Cut in star shapes. Place 1 to 1½" apart on greased baking sheets.

Bake in 350° oven 10 to 12 minutes or until crisp and straw-colored. Remove from baking sheets and cool on racks. Makes 16 dozen.

OZARK APPLE PUDDING

Apples are important in Ozark country. Many of the recipes featuring them came from people of Anglo-Saxon stock who settled in the region before the War Between the States. Ozark Apple Pudding attracted much attention when the recipe for it was circulating across country during the 1940s. Our recipe is a big one—it makes 8 servings.

OZARK APPLE PUDDING

A distinctive feature of this pudding is that it contains no shortening. At its best served warm, topped with vanilla ice cream

1 c. sugar	3 c. chopped pared apples
2 eggs	½ c. chopped pecans
1½ tsp. vanilla	Whipped cream, whipped
⅓ c. flour	dessert topping or ice
1 tblsp. baking powder	cream
⅛ tsp. salt	

Combine sugar, eggs and vanilla; beat until thick. Stir in flour, baking powder, salt, apples and pecans. Spread in greased and floured 9″ square pan.

Bake in 325° oven 30 to 35 minutes. Serve warm with whipped cream. Makes 8 servings.

RHUBARB BREAD PUDDING

Scraps of leftover homemade bread, honestly called stale, were a treasured ingredient in many early American dishes. Exquisite bread puddings of many flavors and descriptions were among them.

Rhubarb Bread Pudding is a classic example of a favorite country meal ending. The recipe went West in covered wagons for pioneer women to use with the first pink rhubarb stalks in their new gardens. It was the kind of food mothers made for their children to signal the long winter had ended.

RHUBARB BREAD PUDDING

Make this with firm bread more nearly like the old-time home-made. Some of today's breads in supermarkets contain chemicals that make the loaves softer, with less body

4 c. diced rhubarb	¼ c. chopped nuts (optional)
3½ c. bread cubes	¼ c. melted butter or
1⅓ c. sugar	regular margarine
½ tsp. ground nutmeg	Cream, whipped cream or
½ tsp. ground cinnamon	vanilla ice cream

Toss together rhubarb, bread cubes, sugar, nutmeg, cinnamon, nuts and melted butter in mixing bowl. Turn into greased 2-qt. casserole.

Cover and bake in 375° oven 45 minutes. Remove cover; continue baking 10 minutes. Serve warm or cold with cream. Makes 6 servings.

SNOW CUSTARDS

While snow custards had their beginning in colonial years, they are new to many people today. Many distinguished guests feasted on this simple, luscious dessert at candlelighted tables in Mount Vernon and Monticello, the elegant plantation homes of George Washington and Thomas Jefferson.

Victorian hostesses called the custards Floating Islands. Almost every farm produced ample milk and eggs for such desserts.

Old, handwritten recipes call for the meringues to be cooked in scalding milk, which then was used to make the custard. A better and easier way, now that ovens are heat-controlled, is to spoon the fluffy egg whites into custard cups and bake them.

SNOW CUSTARDS

Baked meringues are inverted on custards; float like fairy islands

4 eggs, separated	**3 c. milk**
¼ tsp. cream of tartar	**2 eggs**
Dash of salt	**½ c. sugar**
½ c. sugar	**Dash of salt**
½ tsp. vanilla	**1½ tsp. vanilla**

Combine egg whites, cream of tartar and dash of salt in large mixer bowl. Beat at high speed until soft peaks form. Gradually add ½ c. sugar, beating until stiff peaks form. Add ½ tsp. vanilla. Spoon meringue into six 5-oz. custard cups which have been buttered and coated with sugar. With a knife, press mixture gently into cups to remove air pockets. Place in shallow pan containing 1″ hot water.

Bake in 350° oven about 15 minutes or until lightly browned. Place on wire rack. Unmold meringues at once, browned side down, into individual serving dishes or 13×9×2″ pan sprinkled with sugar. Cool and chill.

Place milk in top of double boiler; heat over direct heat until bubbles form around edge.

Meanwhile, beat together egg yolks, eggs, ½ c. sugar and dash of salt. Gradually pour hot milk into egg mixture, beating constantly (a wire whisk is useful). Return mixture to top of double boiler. Cook over hot, not boiling, water. Stir constantly until custard coats a metal spoon. Place top of double boiler in cold water at once and stir to cool custard. Stir in 1½ tsp. vanilla. Chill.

To serve, spoon ½ c. custard around meringue "islands" in individual dishes. Or chill custard in large serving bowl, and just before serving top with meringues that were chilled in pan. Makes 6 servings.

CHERRY CRISP

Oh to be in Michigan when May is here! The concentration of cherry trees around Traverse City is a sight to behold. Pie made with tart cherries probably has been a great American dessert since the days of the Virginia boy's "truth" legend. There are other cherry specials, such as puddings, fritters, cakes, muffins, preserves, salads, sauces, cider, tarts, upside-down cakes, cobblers and the easiest of all, cherry crisps. Cherry Crisp takes about 10 minutes to get ready for the oven, 30 minutes for baking. It is equally good served warm or cold.

CHERRY CRISP

Keep a can of cherry pie filling for this short-notice dessert

1 (1 lb. 5 oz.) can cherry
   pie filling
¾ c. quick-cooking rolled
   oats
⅔ c. brown sugar, firmly
   packed
½ c. flour

¾ tsp. ground cinnamon
½ c. butter or regular
   margarine
Whipped cream, whipped
   dessert topping or vanilla
   ice cream

Place cherry pie filling in greased 8″ square pan.

Combine oats, brown sugar, flour and cinnamon. Cut in butter. Sprinkle mixture evenly over cherries.

Bake in 375° oven about 30 minutes or until topping is golden. Serve warm with whipped cream. Makes 6 servings.

BLUEBERRY CRISP

These little, native, dark berries dusted with soft blue color were—and are—great favorites. The long season encourages their wide use. They grow from the Virginia mountains, where they ripen first, through Pennsylvania and New England in summer and then to northern Maine and Canada. Blueberry country also includes northern Michigan, Wisconsin and Minnesota, as families who combine fishing trips with blueberry picking know so well. They also know how good blueberry pancakes cooked on a camp stove taste in the cool, early morning.

Blueberry Crisp is a simple, easy dessert. Most people today make it with cultivated berries available across country in supermarkets. The berries are juicy, and in this dessert a small amount of tapioca thickens the juice.

BLUEBERRY CRISP

Use fresh or frozen blueberries, wild or cultivated, and serve the dessert hot or cold with vanilla ice cream

4 c. fresh or frozen
    unsweetened blueberries
2 tblsp. tapioca
⅓ c. sugar
1 tblsp. lemon juice
½ tsp. grated lemon peel
⅔ c. brown sugar, firmly
    packed
¾ c. quick-cooking rolled
    oats

½ c. flour
½ tsp. ground cinnamon
⅛ tsp. salt
6 tblsp. butter or regular
    margarine
Cream, whipped cream or
    vanilla ice cream
    (optional)

Stir together blueberries, tapioca, sugar, lemon juice and peel. Place in greased 8″ square pan.

Combine brown sugar, rolled oats, flour, cinnamon and salt. Cut in butter. Sprinkle over blueberries.

Bake in 375° oven 40 minutes. Serve with cream, if desired. Makes 6 servings.

CHRISTMAS AMBROSIA

Among the Christmas delights in the Old South was a simple dessert of peeled and sectioned or sliced oranges, layered in a bowl with freshly grated coconut. It was properly named ambrosia.

Trading ships more than 200 years ago delivered coconuts from the Caribbean Islands to such cities as Savannah and Charleston. Combined with oranges introduced from Spain, the dessert's fame spread to all parts of the South. It became popular in other areas after packaged, shredded coconut became available.

Every old cookbook of the South contains at least one recipe for ambrosia. Here is a typical one from a Savannah cookbook: "Bowls of ambrosia are a sign of the holidays and company. A layer of sliced oranges, a light sprinkling of sugar and a layer of grated coconut and so on, ad infinitum, depending on the size of the bowl and the company. If a little wine is poured over all, it is even better."

Traditional ambrosia is a holiday special today outside the South as well. Through the years other fruits such as fresh or canned pineapple, sliced bananas, dates, grapefruit sections and frozen strawberries have been added. Most Southerners consider such additions rank intruders.

CHRISTMAS AMBROSIA

This recipe for Christmas Ambrosia calls for bananas and convenient canned, flaked coconut, garnished with maraschino cherries

6 oranges
3 bananas, sliced
1 (3½ oz.) can flaked
   coconut

Maraschino cherries
   (optional)

Peel oranges; cut crosswise in thin slices. Place half of orange slices in serving bowl. Top with banana slices and half of coconut. Top with remaining orange slices, then remaining coconut. Garnish with maraschino cherries, if desired. Refrigerate several hours. Makes 8 servings.

VIRGINIA PEANUT BRITTLE

In Virginia, the Carolinas, Georgia, northern Florida and other places where peanuts grow, little boys in summertime once hawked boiled peanuts along the streets. "Dee-licious boiled peanuts," they cried. These regional treats were green peanuts, shells and all, cooked in salted water.

The peanut snack that people across country can enjoy today is peanut brittle. Virginia Peanut Brittle is the choice of many wives of peanut growers in the Old Dominion. They claim raw peanuts make the best candy, but you can use roasted ones.

VIRGINIA PEANUT BRITTLE

Crushed and sprinkled over vanilla ice cream, this brittle adds a crisp, sweet, nutty taste

2 c. sugar	¼ tsp. salt
1 c. light corn syrup	1 tsp. butter or regular
1 c. water	margarine
2 c. unroasted peanuts, cut in pieces	¼ tsp. baking soda

Combine sugar, corn syrup and water in 12″ heavy skillet. Cook slowly over medium heat, stirring constantly, until sugar is dissolved. Continue cooking until mixture reaches soft ball stage (236°) on candy thermometer.

Add peanuts and salt; cook to just beyond the soft crack stage (290 to 300°). Add butter and baking soda, stirring to blend (mixture will foam).

Pour onto 2 large, buttered baking sheets or 2 large, inverted, buttered pans. Lift candy around edges with spatula and run spatula under candy to cool it partially and keep it from sticking. While candy is still warm, but firm, turn it over and pull edges to make the brittle thinner in the center. When cold, break into pieces with knife handle. Makes about 2¼ pounds.

CARAMEL CORN WITH NUTS

Watching Indians pop corn for the first time must have filled the colonists with wonder. Practically all Indian tribes grew several varieties of corn, including one or two that popped over embers. The Cherokees and Senecas, who were good farmers, cultivated as many as a dozen kinds. Early Americans first ate popped corn plain, but soon they served it as a cereal with milk. The Pennsylvania Dutch created a popcorn soup. And popped corn and cranberries were strung to decorate Christmas trees.

Later a hot syrup made with molasses and sugar was poured over popped corn, which was shaped into balls—a holiday treat children adored. As sugar became more plentiful and less expensive, other ingredients were added to the fluffy kernels. Caramel Corn with Nuts is an outgrowth of the early popcorn balls—a company-best version.

CARAMEL CORN WITH NUTS

Substitute toasted pecans for almonds in this American snack

1 c. blanched, whole almonds	½ c. water
	½ tsp. salt
2½ qts. popped corn	¼ c. butter or regular
2½ c. brown sugar, firmly packed	margarine
	2 tsp. vanilla
½ c. dark corn syrup	

Lightly toast almonds in shallow pan in 325° oven 12 to 15 minutes, stirring occasionally. Combine with popcorn in large ovenproof bowl and keep warm in 200° oven.

Combine brown sugar, corn syrup, water and salt in heavy 3-qt. saucepan. Bring to a full, rolling boil. Add butter; cook over medium heat to very hard ball stage (266°). Remove from heat; stir in vanilla. Immediately pour in steady stream over popcorn and nuts, stirring to coat evenly. Turn out on large piece of oiled aluminum foil. Pull apart with two forks to make 3" clusters. Makes about 3½ dozen.

CRANBERRY/GINGER SHERBET

Although the Indians prepared cranberries in many ways, women in colonial days were so pleased with the ruby sauce made from the ripe fruit that they did not branch out much farther. About 50 years ago exploration of uses for cranberries in home kitchens became popular. Among the new dishes was cranberry sherbet.

Hostesses sometimes garnished fruit salads and fruit plates with it for party luncheons. The color and refreshing flavor of the sherbet earned it a place in the main course of many special-occasion meals, especially turkey and chicken dinners.

Cranberry/Ginger Sherbet pampers the flavors of meats and poultry so successfully that the custom of serving such sherbets with them deserves revival, especially since electric beaters and freezers make easy work of preparing them at home.

CRANBERRY/GINGER SHERBET

Makes a colorful dessert especially good with coconut cake

4 c. cranberries	**1 tsp. unflavored gelatin**
2 c. water	**2 c. ginger ale**
2 c. sugar	

Combine cranberries and water; cook uncovered until skins burst. Press mixture through a sieve or food mill.

Meanwhile, combine sugar and gelatin; add to hot cranberry mixture. Stir until sugar and gelatin are dissolved. Cool to room temperature. Add ginger ale. Pour into 9″ square pan. Place in freezer until almost frozen.

Break mixture into chunks and place in chilled mixer bowl. Beat smooth. Return to pan or paper cups. Freeze firm. Serve as dessert or with main dish. Makes 5 cups.

HOT FUDGE SUNDAE SAUCE

Boston is the undisputed home of the bean and the cod, but ice cream devotees there are exceptionally proud also that the first hot fudge sundae originated in Boston—about 1900. The dessert quickly won favor in many states and countries. The woman who created the sundae, a proper Bostonian, insisted that the hot, thick chocolate sauce should cover the top of the vanilla ice cream and spill a little bit over the silver-footed dessert dish in which she served it.

Hot Fudge Sundae Sauce is easy to make. In our recipe evaporated milk helps insure a glossy, satiny smooth sauce. Ladled over scoops of vanilla ice cream, the thick sauce tastes so good that people forget calorie counting.

HOT FUDGE SUNDAE SAUCE

Keep a jar of the sauce in the refrigerator ready to reheat over hot water or very low heat

1 (14½ oz.) can evaporated milk	¼ c. butter or regular margarine
2 c. sugar	1½ tsp. vanilla
4 squares unsweetened chocolate	¼ tsp. salt

Combine milk and sugar in saucepan. Bring to a full, rolling boil, stirring constantly. Boil, stirring, 1 minute. Add chocolate; stir until melted. Beat over heat until smooth. Remove from heat and stir in butter, vanilla and salt. Serve hot or cold over ice cream or other desserts. Store in refrigerator. Makes about 3 cups.

Chapter 2

SOUTHWESTERN SPECIALTIES

Tomato salad, chocolate cake, avocado or chili-bean dip with corn chips—these are all treats that depend on foods grown and enjoyed in Mexico for centuries.

People in the Southwest eat the same foods as do Americans living in other parts of the country, but they particularly like many dishes inspired by south-of-the-border neighbors, and Indians who still live in the area. The recipes in this section of our cookbook are for these specialties, which are gaining acceptance in all parts of our country.

New Mexico and Arizona are the heart of the Southwest, flanked on one side by Texas, on the other by California with the southern third of Colorado also included. Once this area of lofty mountains, fertile green valleys, big ranches and deserts bathed in sunshine was all a part of Mexico. Europeans—Spaniards—explored the region years before the *Mayflower* reached our shores.

Some of the Indians in the Southwest are descendants of the tribes who lived in pueblos and farmed surrounding acres. They have modernized their dishes to fit life today. Recipes for some of their favorites appear on the following pages. Other people in this region, some of whom are ranchers, proudly trace their ancestry to early Spanish settlers, while other Southwesterners crossed over the border to become citizens of the United States. All have helped popularize dishes from Spanish and Mexican kitchens. Many of these have become popular in the West and Middle West. And there are those who predict that Mexican influence will increase in American cooking in the future.

Mexico has one of the most distinguished cuisines in the world and one of the oldest and largest—an estimated 2000 dishes. The rich variety of native foods, many of which now are grown and enjoyed around the world, has contributed to its continuing success.

Indians in Mexico, Central America and northern South America built remarkable civilizations before the Spanish conquistadors arrived early in the 16th century. Many foods, such as corn, beans and squash, were developed from wild plants by the Incas, Mayans, Aztecs and other Indian tribes before Columbus was born.

Other native foods from this early period include tomatoes, potatoes, sweet potatoes, chilies, peanuts, chocolate, avocados and vanilla. Turkeys also were domesticated in Mexico and our Thanksgiving birds are descendants of them. The American wild turkey has never been domesticated successfully. Americans have added their own touches to these foods of Mexican origin.

During the Spanish colonial era in Mexico, which started in the first half of the 16th century, cattle, hogs, sheep and wheat were introduced. The Spaniards also brought cuttings of olives, oranges, peaches, apricots, figs and almonds and planted them. They took back with them what they considered strange foods and introduced them to the Old World.

Southwesterners like the taste of chilies, which they call chili peppers. The sharpness of their flavor reminded the Spaniards of pepper, then obtained in Europe from the Orient. It was one of the spices that lured Columbus and other explorers to attempt to find a short route to the Indies. This explains why they called the vegetable chili peppers. Use of chilies for seasoning is one reason southwestern cooking is different.

Americans commonly use chili powder, made from the dried

pods, for seasoning. And perhaps the most famous dish that it seasons is chili con carne (see Index for American Chili). The hotness of the recipe varies to some extent with the place where it is served, and also from family to family. Practically everyone agrees that chili powder is used more generously in Texas than elsewhere in the Southwest and that the farther from its area of origin the recipe is prepared, the less highly seasoned it becomes.

Canned green chilies are being introduced into more supermarkets every year. As a result, recipes so seasoned are more widely used. One splendid example of the green chili recipes is Alamosa Corn Muffins (see Index).

Among other highly prized imports from Mexico are corn tortillas, those thin, pancake-like breads made with cornmeal. The meal is made by grinding hominy. Tortillas have been eaten for many centuries. In Mexican homes they are served like a hot bread. Americans prefer using them as an ingredient or base.

Tacos, or "Mexican sandwiches," are a favorite for instance (see Index for Easy Tacos). The tortilla, cooked briefly in hot oil until speckled with brown, is folded in half while hot, to make a pocket open at the top. The open top permits filling with shredded lettuce, chopped tomato, green onions, avocado, seasoned with a taco (chili) sauce. This sauce, used also for seasoning other foods in Mexico, usually is made in home kitchens. Our recipe gives an American version of a homemade sauce, but bottled taco sauce may be used as well. The recipe deserves to be called Easy Tacos because packaged taco shells ready for filling can be purchased—today an increasing number of supermarkets are stocking this convenience food. Markets carrying frozen tortillas also are increasing. Tortillas used for making tacos and other dishes in which they are rolled or folded, should be fresh or they will crack.

Wheat tortillas also have a following in Mexico and the Southwest; they are easily made at home. They are especially popular in northern Mexico. Burritos (see Index) are made with wheat tortillas folded around a beef and bean (or only bean) filling. Most burritos in Mexico are fried or baked before serving. Burritos always are served warm.

Beans of many kinds were a staple food in Mexico before anyone dreamed there ever would be a Boston famous for the contents of its bean pots. To this day they are eaten daily south of the border, often in every meal. The bean dish most popular in Mexico and the Southwest is Refried Beans (see Index). It usually is made with pinto or pink beans. Refried Beans improve in flavor when reheated.

Main dishes featuring beans with Mexican seasonings are an old-time favorite in western ranch homes. Excellent examples are Ranch-hand Beans, Ranchero Chili Corn and Chili Chip Bake, a perfect choice for a meal on the lighter side (see Index).

Mexican avocados grow in a variety of sizes. The Indians used them in many ways in pre-Columbian days, as they still do. Avocados now are grown commercially in the United States and are a favorite ingredient for dips and salads (see Index for Mexican Salad Bowl with Avocado Salad Dressing and Guacamole Burgers).

A festive Mexican fruit-vegetable salad served on Christmas Eve south of the border (see Index for Christmas Eve Salad) appears on southwestern tables and buffets during the holidays. Crisp, roasted peanuts are a traditional garnish.

Desserts of Mexico have entered American meals only to an extent. Some of them are tedious and time-consuming to make—sometimes ingredients are not available. The Mexican custom of ending a substantial meal with a bite or two of a sweet, such as a piece of candy, has American followers, however (see Index for Mexican Prune Candy and Buttermilk Pralines).

Caramel-flavored custards are a Mexican favorite and variations are made for special occasions in the Southwest. One example is Caramel Pumpkin Ring (see Index). Notice the lovely custard sauce served over Mexican Flag Dessert (see Index), a make-ahead, gala gelatin dessert that displays the colors of the Mexican flag.

Southwesterners like the Mexican cinnamon-chocolate desserts and hot chocolate (see Index for Mexican Chocolate Cake and Mexican Chocolate). An accompaniment to hot chocolate are the dainty, fiesta-gay Mexican Cookie Rings (see Index).

MEXICAN CHILI CON CARNE ADOPTED IN THE SOUTHWEST.   Each state features its special recipe for this dish. Our *Chili can Carne Pie* (page 126) wreathed with a cornmeal topping provides a nourishing one-dish dinner.

PENNSYLVANIA DUTCH SAUERKRAUT FROM THE OLD COUNTRY. Our thrifty ancestors made *Homemade Sauerkraut* (page 201) to use surplus cabbage. The recipe and method have changed little since homesteading days.

HOT, SPICY ENCHILADAS, AN ANCIENT MEXICAN DISH. *American-style En-chiladas* (page 129) were sampled by a North Dakota farm woman while visiting in the West. Now they're top favorites in her home on the Plains.

EASY TACOS

Tacos, as made north of the border, are a variation of those commonly served in Mexico. This is especially true now that packaged taco shells are an American convenience food. The shells are tortillas folded in half, making pockets ready to be filled. Mexican tacos generally consist of a strip of meat, chicken, beans or other filling, placed in the center of a warm tortilla, which is rolled around the filling and eaten as is or baked or fried until crisp. Accompaniments, some of which may be part of the filling, are shredded lettuce, cheese, taco sauce, radishes and chopped tomato and onion.

For a teen-age gathering, set out platters of tacos with only the meat filling added. Put bowls of chopped tomatoes and onions, shredded cheese and lettuce and guacamole on the table and let the youngsters add the fillings they prefer.

EASY TACOS

Great served with refried beans, either homemade or canned.

1 (15 oz.) can tomato sauce
½ c. chopped onion
1 clove garlic, minced
4 tsp. chili powder
½ tsp. ground cumin
½ tsp. salt
¼ tsp. dried oregano leaves
1 lb. ground beef
1 c. chopped onion

½ tsp. salt
18 taco shells
2 c. shredded lettuce
1½ c. shredded sharp
   Cheddar cheese (6 oz.)
Chopped tomato, cubed
   avocado, chopped onion,
   refried beans

Combine tomato sauce, ½ c. onion, garlic, chili powder, cumin, ½ tsp. salt and oregano in saucepan. Cover and simmer 20 minutes. Remove ¾ c. cooked sauce; set aside.

Cook ground beef with 1 c. onion in skillet until meat is brown. Add reserved sauce and ½ tsp. salt. Cover and simmer 10 minutes. Stir occasionally.

Fill taco shells with meat filling, lettuce and cheese. Pass bowls of tomato, avocado, onion, refried beans and remaining cooked sauce to spoon into tacos. Makes 18 tacos or 6 servings.

CHILI CHIP BAKE

Not all Mexican-type dishes are hot with chilies or chili powder. An excellent example of a superior main dish on the mild side is Chili Chip Bake. The recipe is shared by a Colorado mountain woman who serves the casserole to her family, and to guests at informal company suppers. She also takes it to church suppers and other potluck meals.

The dish reflects three Mexican influences. There is a gentle taste of chilies provided by the sauce, the corn chips provide the crispness and cornmeal flavor of tortillas and the casserole is topped with sour cream.

CHILI CHIP BAKE

Quick main dish bakes in about 35 minutes . . . so easy to fix

1 lb. ground beef
1 (15 oz.) can pinto beans, drained and rinsed
1 (10 oz.) can hot enchilada sauce
1 (8 oz.) can tomato sauce
1 c. shredded process sharp American cheese (4 oz.)
1 tblsp. instant minced onion
1 (6 oz.) pkg. corn chips
1 c. dairy sour cream

Brown ground beef in skillet; drain off excess fat. Remove from heat. Add beans, enchilada sauce, tomato sauce, ½ c. cheese and onion.

Set aside 1 c. corn chips. Crush remaining corn chips and stir into meat mixture. Turn into greased 2-qt. casserole.

Cover and bake in 375° oven 30 minutes. Top with sour cream and sprinkle with remaining cheese. Arrange reserved corn chips around edge. Continue baking 3 to 4 minutes or until cheese melts. Makes 6 servings.

TAMALE SUPPER

The Aztecs called bundles of seasoned food, wrapped and cooked in cornhusks lined with cornmeal mush, *tamalli*. Early families north of the Rio Grande adapted the Mexican special to their taste. They eliminated the raisins, almonds and sweetenings that sometimes are included in Mexican tamales. Wrappers for tamales today usually are of cooking paper instead of cornhusks, although some people lament the loss of flavor they believe corn leaves imparted. The American fillings usually contain beef or chicken. Southwesterners also buy tamales from frozen food cases or in cans.

Our Tamale Supper is a good example of the kind of main dish Americans make with this old-time Indian creation. It is easy to combine the ingredients and they cook quickly—a good dish for busy days.

TAMALE SUPPER

California's contribution to tamales is ripe olives

1 c. chopped onion
2 tblsp. butter or regular margarine
1 (1 lb. 1 oz.) can whole kernel corn, drained
1 (15 oz.) can tomato sauce
1 (15 oz.) can kidney beans, drained

½ c. sliced, pitted ripe olives (optional)
2 tsp. chili powder
2 (15 oz.) cans of beef tamales, drained
1½ c. shredded Cheddar cheese (6 oz.)

Sauté onion in butter in 10″ skillet until soft. Add corn, tomato sauce, kidney beans, olives and chili powder. Bring to a boil; simmer uncovered 5 minutes. Turn into 11×7×1½″ baking pan. Top with tamales.

Bake in 350° oven 15 minutes. Sprinkle with cheese. Continue baking 2 minutes or until cheese is melted. Makes 6 servings.

BEEF TAMALE PIE ARIZONA

Americans took the appetizing tamale ingredients Mexicans wrapped in cornhusks and baked the mixture in casseroles instead. They called it tamale pie.

Chili con carne frequently is the filling for the casseroles, lined and topped with cornmeal mush. Beef Tamale Pie Arizona has a filling of corn and cheese blended with ground beef.

BEEF TAMALE PIE ARIZONA

Make lattice design or drop dabs of mush on pie for fancy top

1 lb. ground beef
1 c. chopped onion
1 c. chopped green pepper
1 (15 oz.) can tomato sauce
1 (12 oz.) can whole kernel corn, drained
1 c. sliced, pitted ripe olives
1 clove garlic, minced
2 tsp. chili powder

1 tsp. ground cumin
1 tsp. salt
1½ c. grated process sharp American cheese (6 oz.)
¾ c. yellow cornmeal
½ tsp. salt
2 c. cold water
1 tblsp. butter or regular margarine

Cook ground beef, onion and green pepper in skillet until beef is browned. Pour off excess fat. Add tomato sauce, corn, olives, garlic, chili powder, cumin and 1 tsp. salt. Cover and simmer 20 minutes. Add cheese; stir until it melts.

Meanwhile, stir cornmeal and ½ tsp. salt into cold water in saucepan. Cook, stirring constantly, until mixture thickens and bubbles. Remove from heat and stir in butter.

Turn meat mixture into greased 2-qt. casserole. Top with cornmeal mush. Bake in 375° oven 40 minutes or until hot and bubbly. Makes 6 servings.

AMERICAN CHILI

Who originated chili no one knows. Some people along the Rio Grande River Valley say it is a "Tex-Mex" creation; others insist it was invented in the Lone-Star State. It is a popular topic of debate along the border.

Chili peppers—the *aji* of the Incas and *chili* of the Aztecs—are the important seasonings in chili con carne. Usually chili powder, made by drying and pulverizing the hot peppers, is used. Sometimes it is supported by cumin and dried oregano. Recipes for this hot beef dish vary from state to state and from home to home in the Southwest. Texas chili, for instance, is more fiery than New Mexican.

Beans are added to chili in many places, while in others, mainly in the Southwest, they are served as Refried Beans in a side dish (see Index). Another point of difference in chili concerns tomatoes—Southwesterners generally do not add them to chili, while elsewhere they are included.

Our recipe for American Chili is the kind most people across the country prefer. Both tomatoes and pinto beans are listed as ingredients, with kidney beans suggested as an alternate if the speckled pinto beans are unavailable. And while ground beef frequently is the meat chosen to make chili, our selection is stew meat cut in small cubes, a gesture to the good judgment of southwestern chili experts who prefer it. Absence of grease is the hallmark of all good chili.

AMERICAN CHILI

Team bowls of hot chili with crackers and a tray of crisp relishes

2 lbs. stewing beef, cut in ½″ cubes	1 beef bouillon cube
2 tblsp. cooking oil	2 tblsp. chili powder
2 c. chopped onion	1½ tsp. salt
2 cloves garlic, minced	1 tsp. dried oregano leaves
1 (1 lb.) can tomatoes, cut up	1 tsp. ground cumin
	2 (15 oz.) cans pinto or kidney beans

Brown meat in hot oil in Dutch oven. Add onion, garlic, tomatoes, bouillon cube, chili powder, salt, oregano and cumin. Cover and simmer 1¾ hours.

Add undrained beans; simmer 15 minutes. Makes 8 servings.

CHILI CON CARNE PIE

Southwestern cooks have a great wealth of recipes using chili con carne as a base ingredient. This recipe is a perfect example of how imagination and creativity can produce a hearty and handsome main dish.

CHILI CON CARNE PIE

Chili con carne casserole topped with corn bread dumplings

½ c. chopped onion	¾ c. cornmeal
1 clove garlic, minced	¼ c. sifted flour
1½ lbs. ground beef	½ tsp. salt
1 (8 oz.) can tomato sauce	1½ tsp. baking powder
1 (1 lb.) can tomatoes, cut up	1 egg
	½ c. milk
1 (20 oz.) can kidney beans, drained	¼ c. soft shortening
	1 tblsp. chopped fresh parsley
1 tblsp. chili powder	
1 tsp. salt	¼ c. Parmesan cheese

Cook onion, garlic and beef until beef is well browned. Stir in tomato sauce, tomatoes, kidney beans, chili powder and 1 tsp. salt. Simmer 10 minutes, stirring occasionally.

Meanwhile, sift together cornmeal, flour, ½ tsp. salt and baking powder. Add egg, milk and shortening. Beat with rotary beater until smooth, about 1 minute. Do not overbeat. Stir in parsley.

Place hot filling in shallow 2-qt. baking dish; sprinkle with Parmesan cheese. Spoon corn bread topping around edge of dish.

Bake in 425° oven 15 to 18 minutes or until golden. Makes 6 servings.

BURRITOS

Burritos (pronounced boo-ree-tos) translated into English means "little burros." They are a form of tacos made with wheat tortillas. Wheat tortillas can easily and successfully be made in your own kitchen.

For a lunch or supper serve Burritos with a tomato or green salad, with baked custard or pineapple rings for dessert. Or omit dessert and have a cabbage-pineapple salad.

BURRITOS

Our filling is on the mild side; for a more aggressive taste add a few drops of hot pepper sauce

1½ lbs. stewing beef, cut in
   ½" cubes
2 tblsp. cooking oil
1 c. chopped onion
1 clove garlic, minced
1½ tsp. salt
1½ c. water
1 (4 oz.) can green chilies,
   drained and chopped

4 c. flour
2 tsp. salt
½ c. shortening or lard
1 c. warm water
1 (15½ oz.) can refried
   beans
1 tblsp. cooking oil
¼ c. shredded Cheddar
   cheese (1 oz.)

Brown meat in 2 tblsp. hot oil in 10" skillet. Add onion, garlic, 1½ tsp. salt and 1½ c. water. Cover and simmer 2 hours until meat is fork tender and begins to fall apart. Gently flake meat with spoon. Add chilies; simmer uncovered until liquid evaporates.

Combine flour and 2 tsp. salt in mixing bowl. Cut in shortening until crumbly. Add 1 c. warm water, mixing until dough holds together. Turn out on lightly floured surface. Knead until smooth and elastic, about 3 minutes. Add more flour if necessary to keep dough from sticking to surface. Divide dough in 12 equal parts and form each into a ball. Cover with plastic wrap.

Roll each ball of dough into an 8" circle on lightly floured surface. Cook each circle of dough in ungreased heavy skillet over moderately high heat 1 minute or until golden brown spots cover it. Turn and cook 30 seconds. Stack in 9" round layer cake pan. Cover with foil. Keep hot in 300° oven.

Meanwhile, add beans to 1 tblsp. hot oil in saucepan. Sprinkle

ese. Cook over medium heat, stirring occasionally, until
melted and mixture hot.

ve, place a heaping tblsp. of meat mixture and of bean
mixture in center of each tortilla. Fold opposite sides of tortilla
over filling. Roll up, starting at unfolded side, to make a
package. Makes 12 burritos, or 6 servings.

SOUTHWESTERN BEEF ENCHILADAS

Cattle and hogs brought by Spanish colonizers revolutionized
Mexican cooking. Combined techniques of Europeans and native Indians resulted in delicious dishes featuring tortillas or Indian corn bread.

Beef enchiladas are a classic example. To make them, tortillas
are dipped in hot oil just until limp and then are filled with a
ground beef mixture. They are rolled up and covered with
tomato sauce and baked long enough to heat thoroughly.

Small tortilla factories dot the landscape in the Southwest.
People buy tortillas uncooked or cooked, the choice depending
on how they plan to use them. Freezer cases in supermarkets in
many parts of the country now supply this corn bread.

Tortillas made from hominy meal and mixed with water to a
dough, called masa, have delighted Americans for thousands of
years. This is still the bread of Mexico; southwestern Americans
eat it frequently. Indians divided the masa into pieces about the
size of an egg and patted them with their hands into cakes about
8″ in diameter and ⅛″ thick. That took patience, practice and
skill.

The first stoves on which they baked the corn bread consisted
of three stones in the center of which burned a hearth fire. They
placed a large clay griddle over the fire, resting it on the stones.
They baked the tortillas on it without fat, until speckled brown
on both sides.

SOUTHWESTERN BEEF ENCHILADAS

Seasonings are less "fiery" than in many southwestern dishes

1 c. chopped onion	1 c. chopped onion
2 tblsp. cooking oil	1 tsp. salt
3 (8 oz.) cans tomato sauce	Cooking oil
2 cloves garlic, minced	18 corn tortillas, canned or
1 tblsp. chili powder	frozen and thawed
½ tsp. ground cumin	Chopped onion
½ tsp. salt	1½ c. shredded sharp
¼ tsp. dried oregano leaves	Cheddar cheese (6 oz.)
1 lb. ground beef	

Sauté 1 c. onion in 2 tblsp. oil in saucepan until soft. Add tomato sauce, garlic, chili powder, cumin, ½ tsp. salt and oregano. Bring to a boil. Reduce heat; cover and simmer 30 minutes. Reserve ½ c. cooked sauce; set aside.

Cook ground beef and 1 c. onion in 10″ skillet until beef is browned. Add reserved sauce and 1 tsp. salt. Cover and simmer 10 minutes.

Pour about ½″ oil into small skillet; heat. Dip each tortilla in hot oil a few seconds until it becomes limp. Remove with tongs. Drain on paper towels.

Place 2 tblsp. meat filling in center of each tortilla; sprinkle with about 2 tsp. chopped onion. Top with heaping teaspoon of sauce. Fold sides over filling and place seam side down in 13×9×2″ pan. Repeat with remaining tortillas. Pour remaining sauce over enchiladas. Sprinkle with cheese.

Bake in 350° oven 15 to 20 minutes or until thoroughly hot. Makes 6 servings.

AMERICAN-STYLE ENCHILADAS

This is truly an American adaptation of a Mexican-based dish. Paper-thin pancakes replace the tortillas and the generous amounts of fiery chili powder used in the Mexican version have been reduced considerably. This is a wonderful do-ahead main dish for company.

AMERICAN-STYLE ENCHILADAS

A great make-ahead company main dish with Mexican influence

6 eggs, well beaten	1 (10 oz.) pkg. frozen
3 c. milk	spinach, cooked, drained
2 c. sifted flour	and chopped
¾ tsp. salt	1 (29 oz.) jar or 2 (15 oz.)
1 lb. ground beef	cans meatless spaghetti
1 lb. bulk pork sausage	sauce
1 c. chopped onion	1 (8 oz.) can tomato sauce
½ c. chopped green pepper	1 c. water
2 cloves garlic, minced	1 tblsp. chili powder
1⅔ tblsp. chili powder	2 c. shredded Cheddar
1 tsp. salt	cheese

Combine eggs and milk. Add flour and ¾ tsp. salt; beat until smooth. Pour about ¼ c. batter into hot greased 6 to 7″ skillet, tilting skillet so batter covers surface. Batter can also be spread into 6″ rounds on greased griddle. Turn pancakes when the surface looks dry. Pancakes can be stacked while remaining pancakes are baked. Makes 30.

Brown ground beef and pork sausage in large skillet. Pour off all but 1 tblsp. fat. Add onion, green pepper, garlic, 1⅔ tblsp. chili powder and 1 tsp. salt. Simmer for 10 minutes. Add spinach; mix well. Let cool.

Combine spaghetti sauce, tomato sauce, water and 1 tblsp. chili powder; set aside.

Spoon scant ¼ c. meat mixture across center of each pancake. Fold sides over about ½″. Starting at end closest to you, roll up each pancake. Place in two 13×9×2″ baking dishes. Pour half of the sauce over the rolled pancakes in each baking dish. Top each with half of shredded cheese.

Bake in 325° oven 30 minutes or until hot and bubbly. Makes 15 servings.

Note: Prepared enchiladas can be frozen. To reheat: Bake in 375° oven 45 minutes or until hot and bubbly.

GUACAMOLE BURGERS

Mexico and California favorites combine in Guacamole Burgers. The yellow-green mashed avocado with a touch of peppery "fire" originated from Mexico, the beef patties in buns north of the border. Serving cooked beef patties in buns supposedly was introduced at the World's Fair in St. Louis in 1904, but it was in the 1920s that "hamburgers" skyrocketed to popularity, especially in California where hamburger stands mushroomed.

GUACAMOLE BURGERS

Beef patties topped with tomato slices, avocado and lettuce

1 medium avocado	1½ lbs. ground beef
1 tblsp. lemon juice	Salt
1 tblsp. finely chopped	Pepper
onion	6 hamburger buns, split
½ tsp. salt	and toasted
¼ tsp. bottled hot pepper	6 slices tomato
sauce	1 c. shredded lettuce

Mash avocado in small bowl. Stir in lemon juice, onion, ½ tsp. salt and hot pepper sauce.

Form ground beef into 6 patties. Pan-broil on both sides or broil in oven. Sprinkle with salt and pepper to taste. Place each patty on bun half. Top with tomato slice, avocado mixture, lettuce and bun top. Makes 6 servings.

CHICKEN TOSTADAS

If you are looking for something different to serve for supper or a snack, consider Chicken Tostadas, an old-time Mexican favorite. Although Southwesterners have naturalized it somewhat, it quite closely resembles the tostadas sold at school festivals and outside the church at semireligious fiestas in Mexico.

Our Chicken Tostadas start with tortillas quickly fried in shallow fat until crisp, then layered with food. Refried Beans (see Index) sprinkled with shredded cheese form the first layer. This is topped with cubes of cooked chicken, then with chopped tomatoes and shredded lettuce. Strips of avocado or mashed and seasoned avocado (guacamole), preferred in Mexico, garnish the top.

We suggest passing bottled taco sauce to drizzle over Chicken Tostadas, if desired. Mexicans often use a combination of vinegar and oil instead of the sauce.

CHICKEN TOSTADAS

Leftover turkey can also be used in this tasty recipe

12 corn tortillas, canned or
  frozen and thawed
Cooking oil
4 c. Refried Beans (see
  Index) or 2 (15½ oz.)
  cans refried beans
2 c. shredded Monterey
  Jack cheese (8 oz.)

2 c. cubed, cooked chicken
3 c. shredded lettuce
2 medium tomatoes,
  chopped
1 avocado, cut in 12 slices
Bottled or canned taco
  sauce

Fry tortillas in ½" hot oil in 8" skillet until crisp and golden brown, about 3 seconds. Hold top side of tortilla under fat with spatula during cooking. Drain on paper towels. (Tortillas can be fried in advance, stored airtight and heated in oven just before using.)

Heat beans. Spread ⅓ c. beans over each fried tortilla. Sprinkle with cheese, chicken, lettuce and tomatoes. Garnish each with strip of avocado. Pass taco sauce. Makes 6 servings.

PAELLA VALENCIANA

In Spain there are hundreds of "authentic" recipes for p...
It can be made with seafood only or meat or chicken. The green
vegetable may be peas, beans, lima beans or artichoke hearts.
There are basic rules for true Spanish paella however. It must
always be made with olive oil and saffron must always be added
to the rice to give it golden color. All ingredients are cooked
together in a large shallow paella pan. We present our adaptation
of Paella Valenciana. If you do not have a paella pan, cook the
ingredients together in a skillet and transfer to a large casserole
and finish baking in the oven.

PAELLA VALENCIANA

Accent this flavorful Spanish main dish with a crisp, green salad

4 chicken breasts, halved
Salt
Pepper
¼ c. butter or regular
  margarine, melted
Paprika
⅓ c. sherry (optional)
2 cloves garlic, minced
1 medium onion, chopped
1½ c. regular rice
⅓ c. olive oil
1 green pepper, chopped

2 c. clam broth plus 1 c.
  chicken broth (or 3 c.
  chicken broth)
1 (1 lb.) can tomatoes
1 tsp. salt
1 tsp. sugar
1 lb. frozen or fresh raw
  shrimp, shelled and
  deveined
⅛ tsp. red pepper
¾ c. pimiento-stuffed green
  olives, halved

Place chicken breasts, skin side up in greased 13×9×2" baking pan. Season with salt and pepper; brush with melted butter.
Sprinkle with paprika.

Cover with aluminum foil. Bake in 350° oven for 40 minutes.
Uncover; pour sherry over chicken. Continue baking 20 minutes
or until tender and nicely browned. Baste chicken occasionally
with drippings from pan.

Cook garlic, onion and rice in hot oil in large skillet until golden, stirring constantly. Add green pepper, broth, tomatoes, 1 tsp. salt and sugar. Cover; boil gently for 20 minutes or until rice is tender. Stir occasionally.

Stir in shrimp, red pepper and olives. Cover and continue cooking for about 5 minutes or until shrimp is cooked and liquid is absorbed.

Spoon rice onto large platter or pan. Arrange chicken on rice. Makes 8 servings.

REFRIED BEANS

In the Old World, before Columbus discovered America, only soy and fava beans were known. Spanish conquistadors and early English colonists alike found Indians growing, cooking and eating many kinds of beans throughout the New World—from Cape Cod to the Andean heights thousands of miles apart.

The pre-Incas of Peru cultivated and developed most of the New World beans. Later the Mayas, Aztecs and other Indians in Central America and Mexico grew them. Refried Beans developed after the Spanish introduced hogs to Mexico and lard became available; heating the cooked vegetable in lard was a logical development.

Potato mashers are used more on beans than potatoes in the southwestern homes where Refried Beans are standard fare. (In Mexico "re" does not mean "again," but "thoroughly"—the beans are not "fried" a second time, but they are mashed thoroughly.) Frequently they accompany chili con carne; sometimes they are an ingredient in other Spanish-American dishes, such as Chicken Tostadas (see Index).

REFRIED BEANS

For a special treat, fold a little shredded Monterey Jack or Muenster cheese into beans 3 minutes before removing from heat

1 lb. dry pinto or red beans	½ c. bacon fat or lard
6 c. water	Salt
1 c. chopped onion	

Wash beans. Combine with water in Dutch oven. Bring to a boil; boil 2 minutes. Remove from heat; cover and let stand 1 hour. (Or soak beans overnight.) Add onion. Bring to a boil. Reduce heat and simmer 2½ to 3 hours or until beans are very tender. Stir occasionally the last 30 minutes so beans do not stick.

Mash beans with a potato masher. Add bacon fat. Continue cooking over low heat, stirring frequently, until beans are thickened and fat is absorbed. Add salt to taste. Makes 8 servings.

RANCH-HAND BEANS

Dry beans cooked with ham hocks are country food as American as the Fourth of July. This combination of farm favorites traveled West with pioneers. In the Southwest, they added seasonings reflecting the influence of Mexican kitchens.

Ranch-hand Beans are seasoned with garlic, tomatoes, onions, chili powder, cumin and marjoram.

Substantial bean and ham dishes rated high in the Old West around campfires and chuck wagons where cowboys gathered at mealtime. Today these dishes score equal success at picnics, community gatherings and family meals.

RANCH-HAND BEANS

Serve with corn sticks, Sour Cream Coleslaw or Wilted Spinach Salad (see Index)

1 lb. dry pinto or red beans	1 tblsp. chili powder
6 c. water	1 tsp. salt
1 tsp. salt	½ tsp. ground cumin
2 c. chopped onion	½ tsp. dried marjoram
1 large clove garlic, minced	leaves
1 lb. ham hocks	
1 (1 lb. 12 oz.) can tomatoes, cut up	

Wash beans. Combine beans and water in Dutch oven. Bring to a boil; boil 2 minutes. Remove from heat; cover and let stand 1 hour. (Or soak beans overnight.)

Add 1 tsp. salt, onion, garlic and ham hocks. Bring to a boil. Reduce heat; cover and simmer about 2 hours or until beans are tender. Remove ham hocks. Cut in small pieces, discarding bones and skin. Drain beans, reserving 1 c. liquid.

Return beans and ham to Dutch oven. Add tomatoes, chili powder, 1 tsp. salt, cumin and marjoram. Stir in reserved bean liquid. Bring to a boil. Reduce heat; simmer uncovered 30 minutes, stirring occasionally. Makes 6 to 8 servings.

TEXAS BEANS AND HOMINY

Four native Mexican foods savored for centuries combine in Texas Beans and Hominy, a great side dish to serve with hamburgers, hot dogs, steaks or other meat grilled over coals. To the basic four—kidney beans, hominy, tomatoes (in sauce) and green chili peppers—Texans add vinegar, mustard and Worcestershire sauce.

For a summer evening meal bring Texas Beans and Hominy from the oven just as the sizzling steaks come off the grill. Set out a big bowl of tossed green salad. Pass crusty bread. Serve melon or sherbet for dessert.

TEXAS BEANS AND HOMINY

The earthy character and flavor especially delight most men

3 slices bacon, diced	1 (8 oz.) can tomato sauce
¾ c. chopped onion	1 to 2 tblsp. chopped,
1 (1 lb.) can hominy,	canned green chilies
drained	1 tblsp. vinegar
1 (15 oz.) can kidney beans,	1 tsp. prepared mustard
drained	1 tsp. Worcestershire sauce

Cook bacon in skillet until crisp. Remove from skillet and drain on paper towels. Drain off all but 1 tblsp. drippings.

Sauté onion in 1 tblsp. bacon drippings until soft. Add hominy, kidney beans, tomato sauce, chilies, vinegar, mustard and Worcestershire sauce. Turn into greased 1½-qt. casserole. Sprinkle bacon over top.

Cover and bake in 350° oven 1 hour or until hot and bubbly. Makes 6 servings.

PUEBLO GREENS AND BEANS

Although Pueblo Indians now have electricity, modern ranges and other conveniences, they continue to prepare many of the foods of their ancestors. Some of the dishes were influenced by the Spanish colonists, who settled in New Mexico in the 16th century, years before the *Mayflower* crossed the Atlantic Ocean.

Pueblo dishes also found their way into southwest kitchens. In Montezuma County, Colorado, where more than 6000 ruins of pueblos have been recorded, you still see fields of pinto beans as you drive through the area in summer.

In Pueblo Greens and Beans, frozen spinach substitutes for the spring greens Indians gathered and the beans come from cans. This makes it an easy all-American dish, but the seasonings have much to do with the success of the vegetable combination.

PUEBLO GREENS AND BEANS

A tasty New Mexican dish patterned after an old Indian favorite

6 slices bacon, chopped	½ tsp. salt
2 (10 oz.) pkgs. frozen	¼ tsp. pepper
chopped spinach	⅛ tsp. dried oregano leaves
¼ c. chopped onion	1 (15 oz.) can pinto or red
1 clove garlic, minced	beans, drained
¼ c. water	

Cook bacon in large saucepan until crisp. Drain on paper towels. Pour off all but 2 tblsp. bacon drippings. Add spinach, onion, garlic, water, salt, pepper and oregano to saucepan. Cover and simmer until spinach is cooked, stirring occasionally to break up spinach blocks. Add beans and bacon, and heat thoroughly. Makes 8 servings.

RANCHERO CHILI CORN

Chili, corn and cheese dishes are among the tasty Mexican favorites. Many of them also contain slightly sour cream, which is made in home kitchens by adding a little buttermilk to cream. Americans usually omit the cream and make their dish with canned chilies and corn; they use Monterey Jack cheese, a California original that went national in 1960. Some people consider it the American mozzarella.

RANCHERO CHILI CORN

The combination of flavors is rewarding and easy to make

½ c. chopped onion
1 clove garlic, minced
2 tblsp. melted butter or
    regular margarine
2 (12 oz.) cans whole kernel
    corn, drained

2 tblsp. chopped, canned
    green chilies
½ tsp. salt
½ c. shredded Monterey
    Jack cheese (2 oz.)

Sauté onion and garlic in melted butter in 2-qt. saucepan until tender. Add corn, chilies and salt; heat thoroughly, stirring occasionally. Sprinkle with cheese. Makes 6 servings.

FOUR-SEASON SUCCOTASH

American Indians, the people who first put corn and lima beans in a cooking pot together, used corn cut from cobs and fresh-shelled lima beans in summer, dried corn and dried beans the remainder of the year. Early colonists gratefully adopted and liked both kinds. This adapted Four-season Succotash uses frozen corn and dry beans, both available throughout the year.

All Indian tribes made succotash, but the dish varied from one region, as well as from one season, to another. For instance, bear fat, when available, often enriched it. In Four-season Succotash dairy half-and-half is used but you can substitute light cream if you prefer. And instead of dry red beans, you may wish to choose dry cranberry, pinto or kidney beans.

FOUR-SEASON SUCCOTASH

For a good, old-fashioned dinner, serve with roast pork or ham

1 c. dry pinto or red beans	½ c. dairy half-and-half
4 c. water	2 tblsp. butter or regular
1 tsp. salt	margarine
1 c. chopped onion	¼ tsp. pepper
2 c. frozen corn, thawed	

Wash beans. Combine beans and water in large saucepan. Bring to a boil; boil 2 minutes. Remove from heat; cover and let stand 1 hour. (Or soak beans overnight.)

Add salt and onion; simmer 1½ to 2 hours or until beans are tender. Pour off liquid.

Add corn and dairy half-and-half. Bring to a boil. Reduce heat and simmer about 3 minutes or until corn is tender. Add butter and pepper. Simmer, stirring, until butter is melted. Makes 8 servings.

PUEBLO SUCCOTASH

This corn-bean dish is somewhat different from that served in the Thirteen Original States (see Index for Winter Succotash and Ham Succotash Supper). Ground beef, tomato sauce and chili powder combine with green beans, but the surprise ingredient is sunflower seeds, toasted and salted, and added just before serving to keep them crisp. Early Pueblo Indians ate the native sunflower seeds raw or roasted; they also pounded them into meal, shaped into cakes and cooked them or served them as cereal. Many supermarkets and almost all health food stores carry sunflower seeds.

PUEBLO SUCCOTASH

The sunflower seeds make this a southwestern special

1 lb. ground beef	¼ tsp. pepper
1 c. chopped onion	1 (10 oz.) pkg. frozen green
1 (8 oz.) can tomato sauce	beans
2 tblsp. water	1 (10 oz.) pkg. frozen corn
1 tsp. salt	½ c. toasted salted sunflower
½ tsp. chili powder	seeds

Cook ground beef and onion in skillet until beef is browned. Add tomato sauce, water, salt, chili powder and pepper. Cover and simmer 5 minutes.

Add beans and corn. Cover and continue simmering about 10 minutes or until vegetables are tender. Add sunflower seeds. Heat thoroughly. Makes 6 servings.

INDIAN VEGETABLE SCALLOP

Indian Vegetable Scallop is a modern New Mexican dish that makes it easy for children to eat their share of vegetables at a meal. It is akin to dishes Indians put together over many years with sweet corn, yellow or green squash and juicy, red tomatoes.

INDIAN VEGETABLE SCALLOP

Good with cold cuts, hamburgers, fried chicken, meat loaves

¼ c. butter or regular	3 tomatoes, peeled and
margarine	chopped
4 small summer squash	½ c. chopped onion
(zucchini or yellow),	1 tsp. salt
sliced	¼ tsp. pepper
4 ears corn	

Melt butter in 3-qt. saucepan. Add squash, corn, cut from cob, tomatoes, onion, salt and pepper. Cover and cook over low heat, stirring occasionally, about 30 minutes or until tender. Makes 6 servings.

CALIFORNIA BAKED TOMATOES

Red, ripe, white-capped tomato halves add a decorative note to meals and it takes little work and time to prepare them. Top the cut surface of the tomatoes with a fluffy dressing made by combining mayonnaise and sour cream seasoned with basil, and put them in the oven to heat thoroughly, or for about 15 minutes. They are a great companion for grilled meats, such as steaks, beef patties and liver; they are equally at home with baked beans.

CALIFORNIA BAKED TOMATOES

Speedy special guaranteed to give both flavor and eye appeal

6 medium tomatoes	**¼ c. mayonnaise or salad**
¾ tsp. seasoned salt	**dressing**
½ c. dairy sour cream	**¼ tsp. dried basil leaves**

Remove stems from tomatoes. Cut in crosswise halves; place in 15½ ×10½ ×1″ jelly roll pan. Sprinkle with seasoned salt.

Stir together sour cream, mayonnaise and basil. Spread over cut surface of tomatoes.

Bake in 375° oven about 15 minutes or until tender. Makes 6 servings.

ZUNI VEGETABLE RELISH

Chili powder and dried oregano, a wild marjoram, are used to turn a commonplace dish into something special in the Southwest. These favorite seasonings, sparingly used, give Zuni Vegetable Relish its distinctive taste.

Chili powder, made from dried chili peppers with spices added, did not appear on the market until around 1900. Before then families made their own. Chili peppers are difficult to grow unless the climate is just right. The pods grow points down—the cup around the stems catches rain and excess moisture ruins peppers. They thrive successfully on some California coastal plains and in the arid, mountainous regions of interior Mexico.

ZUNI VEGETABLE RELISH

Make this a day ahead and chill to blend flavors—great served with fried fish or chicken

2 c. finely shredded cabbage	2 tblsp. sugar
½ c. grated peeled carrot	2 tsp. salt
½ c. chopped onion	⅛ tsp. dried oregano leaves
½ c. chopped green pepper	¼ tsp. chili powder
1 medium tomato, diced	¼ c. vinegar

Combine all ingredients. Cover and refrigerate at least 4 hours, or overnight. Stir occasionally. Makes 6 servings.

MEXICAN RICE

Mexican Rice, like many a southwestern dish, has a base of tomatoes, onion and green peppers. It takes the place of potatoes when served with hamburgers, pork chops or chicken.

Our recipe calls for bacon drippings, which have a way of accumulating in country kitchens. Chili powder, tomatoes, onion and green pepper and the drippings season the rice so successfully that people who usually do not care for rice enjoy this version adapted from Mexico.

MEXICAN RICE

Garnish the top of this rice dish with chopped green pepper

1 c. chopped onion	1 c. water
1 c. chopped green pepper	1½ c. uncooked rice
¼ c. bacon drippings	2 tsp. salt
1 (1 lb.) can tomatoes, cut up	1 tsp. chili powder

Sauté onion and chopped green pepper in bacon drippings in 3-qt. saucepan until soft. Add tomatoes, water, rice, salt and chili powder. Bring to a boil. Reduce heat; cover and simmer 20 minutes. Serve garnished with chopped fresh tomato and green pepper, if desired. Makes 6 to 8 servings.

BEEF/VEGETABLE STEW SAN JUAN

This meal-in-a-dish is strictly for the season when gardens supply vegetables at their succulent best. Select tiny squash—zucchini, pattypan or yellow crookneck or straightneck. All you have to do to prepare them for cooking is to remove stem ends, wash and slice. Use tender green beans.

Make this dish with sweet corn at its flavor peak. Husk, remove silks and instead of cutting the kernels from the cobs, do as many Mexicans do: Cut through the ears to divide them in 2-inch lengths. The corn, seasoned in the stew, can be eaten like corn on the cob.

While early Europeans in the eastern colonies did not praise the primitive stews the Indians there made with corn, beans and squash, people south of the border developed the dish so that it now is a favorite in the Southwest. Beef, ripe tomatoes and green onions touched with chili powder turn this stew into something very tasty.

BEEF/VEGETABLE STEW SAN JUAN

Serve for supper with crusty bread and chilled watermelon

2 lbs. stewing beef	2 tomatoes, peeled and
2 tblsp. cooking oil	chopped
4 c. water	¼ c. sliced green onions and
1 tblsp. salt	tops
½ tsp. chili powder	4 small zucchini, sliced
¼ tsp. pepper	3 ears corn, cut in 2″ pieces
½ lb. green beans, cut in	¼ c. sliced green onions and
pieces	tops

Brown meat in oil in Dutch oven. Add water, salt, chili powder and pepper. Cover and simmer 1½ to 2 hours or until tender. Skim off excess fat.

Add beans, tomatoes and ¼ c. green onions. Cover and simmer 20 minutes.

Add zucchini and corn; continue to simmer about 20 minutes or until all vegetables are tender. Sprinkle with ¼ c. green onions. Makes 6 servings.

TOMATO/CORN SOUP

For a quick and easy soup, try this southwestern favorite on a chilly day. Serve it with cheese sandwiches or hamburgers for a lunch or supper that usually satisfies even the hungriest men and boys. Round out the meal with crisp relishes and a chocolate dessert. For a lighter dessert, serve pink grapefruit for which the American side of the Rio Grande is now famous.

TOMATO/CORN SOUP

You can make this vegetable soup in less than 20 minutes

2 (13¾ oz.) cans chicken
  broth
1 (1 lb.) can tomatoes, cut
  up
1 (12 oz.) can whole kernel
  corn

¼ tsp. dried oregano leaves
¼ tsp. salt
⅛ tsp. pepper

Combine all ingredients in large saucepan. Bring to a boil. Reduce heat; cover and simmer 10 minutes. Makes about 2 quarts.

ESPAÑOLA VALLEY SOUP

Kitchens of families living in the green Española Valley between Taos and Santa Fe, New Mexico, turn out wonderful food that reflects three cultures—Indian, Spanish and American. Some of the dishes, adapted to changing times, have been enjoyed in this oasis since 1598 when a Spaniard at San Juan de Los Canalleros established the capital of New Spain. Social life has quickened in the valley since the Los Alamos project has brought many new residents. Buffet suppers now frequently take the place of sit-down dinners.

Española Valley Soup, a popular dish served from a tureen or bowl on the buffet, is worthy of duplication anywhere. Flanked by smaller bowls of soup toppings, such as shredded carrots, chopped lettuce, sliced radishes, avocado cubes and shredded Monterey Jack or Muenster cheese, the service is colorful and inviting. The taste of the soup lives up to its good looks.

ESPAÑOLA VALLEY SOUP

Serve with hot corn sticks or muffins or with crusty rolls

3 lbs. fresh pork hocks
3 qts. water
1 (1 lb.) can tomatoes, cut up
2 c. chopped onion
1 clove garlic, minced
5 tsp. salt
1 tblsp. chili powder
2 (1 lb.) cans whole kernel corn or hominy

1 (10 oz.) pkg. frozen lima beans
Chopped fresh parsley
Assorted toppings: shredded carrots, chopped lettuce, sliced radishes, sliced green onions, avocado cubes and shredded Monterey Jack or Muenster cheese

Combine pork hocks, water, tomatoes, onion, garlic, salt and chili powder in 8-qt. kettle. Cover and bring mixture to a boil. Reduce heat and simmer 1½ hours or until pork is tender. Remove pork. Cut up meat and return to broth; discard fat and bones. Cool broth. Refrigerate.

Skim off fat from broth. Add corn and lima beans to broth in kettle. Bring to a boil. Reduce heat and simmer 15 minutes or until beans are tender.

Garnish bowls of soup with parsley. Pass several bowls of the assorted toppings to spoon on soup. Makes about 4 quarts or 12 servings.

POTATO SALAD FRANCISCAN

For a distinctive potato salad to serve on special occasions, try Potato Salad Franciscan. Unusual ingredients are tiny cheese cubes and mashed, seasoned avocado, which contrast with the darker greens of chopped parsley and peppers.

POTATO SALAD FRANCISCAN

A delicious salad that contributes eye appeal to a buffet

4 c. hot, diced, cooked
  potatoes
1 tsp. salt
⅛ tsp. pepper
2 tblsp. salad oil
2 tblsp. vinegar
½ c. chopped celery
½ c. small cubes Monterey
  Jack cheese
2 tblsp. finely chopped green
  pepper
2 tblsp. finely chopped
  onion

⅓ c. mayonnaise or salad
  dressing
1 tsp. prepared mustard
1 large avocado
½ c. dairy sour cream
1 tblsp. chopped fresh
  parsley
1 tblsp. chopped green
  pepper
2 tsp. lemon juice
¼ tsp. salt

Sprinkle hot potatoes with 1 tsp. salt and pepper. Add oil and vinegar and toss gently. Cool. Add celery, cheese, 2 tblsp. chopped green pepper and onion.

Blend together mayonnaise and mustard. Fold into salad mixture. Chill in shallow serving bowl.

Shortly before serving, mash avocado. Stir in sour cream, parsley, 1 tblsp. chopped green pepper, lemon juice and ¼ tsp. salt. Spread mixture completely over potato salad. Makes 6 servings.

SANTA CLARA TWO-BEAN SALAD

Pueblo Indian women, years before Europeans built homes in America, earned an enviable reputation for the clever ways they prepared vegetables. These were the women who created the basic cookery of the Southwest. Many foods served daily on our tables were first enjoyed in Pueblo country.

Santa Clara Two-bean Salad is a classic example. Canned red or pinto and cut green beans are the mainstays, with bits of green pepper and mild, not fiery, seasoning of chili powder.

Many menu planners rely on salads made with two or more kinds of canned beans to introduce variety, tastiness and protein to meals. Most everyone likes them, and busy women know such salads may be kept in the refrigerator a few days, ready to serve on short notice.

SANTA CLARA TWO-BEAN SALAD

Excellent for barbecues, good with grilled cheese sandwiches

1 (15 oz.) can pinto or red beans, drained and rinsed
1 (1 lb.) can cut green beans, drained
¼ c. chopped onion
¼ c. chopped green pepper
1 tblsp. sugar
½ tsp. chili powder
¼ tsp. salt
¼ c. vinegar
¼ c. salad oil

Combine all ingredients. Cover and refrigerate overnight. Drain before serving. Makes 6 servings.

OFF-THE-SHELF RANCHO SALAD

In this salad, pinto or kidney beans team with chick-peas, one of the oldest vegetables in the world. This legume has been cultivated in the Mideast from earliest biblical times. Spaniards brought it to Mexico more than 300 years ago and from there they came to the American Southwest where they are often called by their Spanish name, *garbanzos*. They now are available in supermarkets from coast to coast.

A mixture of lemon juice, vinegar and salad oil and seasoning make a delicious dressing for this Off-the-Shelf Rancho Salad. To develop the flavors, cover and chill the salad several hours or overnight, stirring occasionally.

OFF-THE-SHELF RANCHO SALAD

Proof that not all southwestern salads with chili powder are hot

1 (15 oz.) can kidney beans, drained and rinsed	¼ c. chopped green pepper
	⅓ c. salad oil
1 (15 oz.) can garbanzos (chick-peas), drained and rinsed	¼ c. lemon juice
	2 tblsp. wine vinegar
1 c. chopped celery	1 tsp. garlic salt
¼ c. chopped onion	¼ tsp. pepper

Combine all ingredients. Cover and refrigerate at least 4 hours. Stir occasionally. Makes 6 servings.

CHRISTMAS EVE SALAD

Americans who have sat in a sidewalk restaurant in Oaxaca, Mexico, on Christmas Eve, were as enchanted by the traditional Christmas Eve Salad served for supper as by the fireworks that lighted the skies. Many hostesses in the Southwest serve their version of the beautiful vegetable-fruit salad sometime during the holiday season. In our recipe apples substitute for *jacamas,* the bulbous roots of a plant native to Mexico. The vegetable is now appearing in some markets across the United States, however. To use jacamas, peel off the thin, light brown skin with a potato peeler and cut into thin slices—as crisp as spring radishes.

The traditional dressing for the salad is made with lime juice and oil; it provides delightful flavor to the vegetables and fruits, but you may use vinegar. Pomegranate seeds contribute color, and scattering peanuts over the salad is authentic.

The salad is a fine selection for a menu in which a Mexican-type main dish is chosen. This might be American Chili, Southwestern Beef Enchiladas or Beef Tamale Pie Arizona and Refried Beans (see Index) in the meal.

CHRISTMAS EVE SALAD

Color, texture and flavor contrasts make this salad memorable

1 head romaine, torn in
bite-size pieces (about
6 c.)
1 (13¼ oz.) can pineapple
chunks, chilled
2 unpared apples, cored and
sliced
2 bananas, sliced
2 oranges, peeled and sliced
1 (8 oz.) can whole beets,
chilled, drained and
sliced

¾ c. coarsely chopped
peanuts
Seeds from 1 pomegranate
½ c. salad oil
3 tblsp. lime juice or
vinegar
½ tsp. sugar
¼ tsp. salt

Place romaine in salad bowl.

Drain pineapple, reserving juice. Dip apple and banana slices in pineapple juice to prevent darkening. Arrange pineapple chunks, apple, banana, orange and beet slices on top of romaine. Sprinkle with peanuts and pomegranate seeds.

Shake together oil, lime juice, sugar and salt. Pour over salad and toss gently. Makes 8 servings.

MEXICAN SALAD BOWL

The avocado is at home in Mexican meals, for the trees that produce it have been cultivated there for centuries. The fruit is depicted on the ancient pottery and sculptures of such countries as Peru, Guatemala and Mexico (especially Yucatan). While avocados have many uses in Mexican meals, in the United States we use them mainly in salads and dips.

Avocado dressing is a California offshoot of guacamole. It is the perfect touch for Mexican Salad Bowl, which combines such foods as mixed greens, onion, green pepper, tomatoes, cheese and ripe olives. Crisp corn chips are a pleasing addition.

MEXICAN SALAD BOWL

Mexican-American variation of familiar tossed salads

2 qts. mixed greens	¼ c. shredded Cheddar
¼ c. chopped green onion	cheese
¼ c. chopped green pepper	1 c. coarsely crushed corn
¼ c. sliced, pitted ripe	chips
olives	Avocado Salad Dressing
2 tomatoes, cut in wedges	(recipe follows)

Combine greens, onion, green pepper, olives and tomatoes in salad bowl. Sprinkle with cheese, then corn chips. Top with Avocado Salad Dressing and toss lightly. Makes 6 to 8 servings.

Avocado Salad Dressing: Mash 1 avocado with 2 tblsp. lemon juice. Combine with ½ c. dairy sour cream, ¼ c. salad oil, 1 tsp. seasoned salt and ¼ tsp. chili powder. Cover and refrigerate several hours.

QUICK-AND-EASY BARBECUE SAUCE

In some sections of the Southwest the season for outdoor cooking over coals is longer than in other places in America. Barbecue sauces for basting the meat, fish and chicken are a year-round staple in these areas.

All the makings for Quick-and-Easy Barbecue Sauce may be kept on the shelf ready to use. Especially good with fish and chicken, but also on ground beef patties and other meats. And there is no law against adding more seasonings to meet personal tastes.

QUICK-AND-EASY BARBECUE SAUCE

Add a few extra drops of hot pepper sauce for more flavor

1 (8 oz.) can tomato sauce	2 tsp. instant minced onion
¼ c. wine vinegar	¼ tsp. bottled hot pepper
2 tblsp. brown sugar, firmly	sauce
packed	
1 tblsp. Worcestershire	
sauce	

Combine all ingredients in small saucepan. Bring to a boil. Reduce heat and simmer uncovered 5 minutes. Makes 1¼ cups.

INDIAN SUN BREAD

Anyone who has eaten Indian bread baked in adobe ovens, shaped like beehives, knows how wonderful it tastes. People in Santa Fe, New Mexico, frequently buy more than one loaf of the crusty bread sold by Indians on the sidewalk by the Governor's Palace. They like to have an extra loaf or two to store in their freezers for special occasions. Tourists in the fascinating old city buy a loaf to snack on in their motel rooms.

Indian Sun Bread has a distinctive shape, which honors the sun god. After the dough has risen and is light, it is rolled into a circle and one half is folded on top of the other half. Then it is cut in several places from the circular edge about two thirds of the way inward to the folded edge. The strips of dough are separated so they do not touch in baking and when the loaf comes from the oven, they resemble the rays of the sun. The texture and crust are not quite the same as loaves baked in beehive ovens, but no one will complain.

INDIAN SUN BREAD

This loaf of homemade bread will be the talk of any party

2 pkgs. active dry yeast	3 tblsp. shortening
6 to 6½ c. sifted flour	1 tblsp. sugar
2 c. water	1 tblsp. salt

Combine yeast and 2¼ c. flour in large mixer bowl.

Heat water, shortening, sugar and salt just until warm, stirring occasionally, to melt shortening. Add to flour mixture. Beat at low speed 30 seconds, scraping sides of bowl constantly. Beat 3 minutes at high speed, scraping bowl occasionally. By hand, add enough remaining flour to make a soft dough. Turn out on lightly floured board and knead until smooth and elastic, about 5 minutes. Place in large, greased bowl; turn dough over to grease top. Cover and let rise in warm place until double, about 1 hour.

Punch dough down. Divide in thirds. Shape each third into a ball. Cover and let rest 10 minutes. On lightly floured surface roll each ball into a 9″ circle. Fold each circle almost in half so that top circular edge is about ½″ from bottom circular edge. Place on greased baking sheets. Make 6 gashes in dough with kitchen scissors, cutting circular edges about two thirds of the way inward to the folded edges. Spread the strips of dough apart so they will not touch during baking. Let rise in warm place until double, about 45 minutes.

Bake in 350° oven 45 to 50 minutes or until loaves sound hollow when tapped. Remove from baking sheet. Cool on racks. Makes 3 loaves.

ALAMOSA CORN MUFFINS

Canned green chili peppers enhance dishes containing corn in some form. They are appearing more frequently on supermarket shelves elsewhere than in the Southwest.

This recipe was developed by an Iowa home economist after tasting a similar hot bread while visiting in southwestern Colorado. The small muffins have the texture and consistency of corn bread made without the addition of flour. They are tender, but not light.

ALAMOSA CORN MUFFINS

Delicious when served hot from the oven

1½ c. yellow cornmeal	1 c. dairy sour cream
3 tsp. baking powder	1 (8¾ oz.) can cream-style
½ tsp. salt	corn
½ c. shortening	⅓ c. chopped, canned
2 eggs	green chilies

Sift together cornmeal, baking powder and salt in a large mixing bowl. Cut in shortening until crumbly. Beat in eggs and sour cream until well blended. Stir in corn and chilies. Spoon into greased 2½″ muffin-pan cups, filling two-thirds full.

Bake in 450° oven 12 to 15 minutes or until golden brown. Makes 18 muffins.

MEXICAN FLAG DESSERT

Southwesterners commonly call this the Mexican Flag Dessert, even though one layer of the gelatin mixture is tinted pink, rather than the red of the Mexican flag. One advantage of this dessert is that it is made ahead and chilled. Only the whipped cream needs to be folded into the velvety custard sauce at serving time.

MEXICAN FLAG DESSERT

An ideal light dessert in meals featuring Mexican-type foods

1 c. sugar	1 c. chopped, blanched
1 envelope unflavored	almonds
gelatin	Red food color
1¼ c. water	Green food color
5 eggs whites	Custard Sauce (recipe
¼ tsp. cream of tartar	follows)
¼ tsp. almond extract	

Stir together sugar and gelatin in medium saucepan; blend in water. Cook, stirring constantly, until gelatin dissolves. Chill until partially set.

Beat egg whites with cream of tartar and almond extract until stiff peaks form.

Beat gelatin mixture until frothy. Fold egg whites into gelatin mixture. Gently fold in almonds. Divide mixture equally in three bowls. Tint one pink and another pale green with food color; leave one mixture plain. Turn pink mixture into 1½-qt. mold or 9×5×3" loaf pan. Top with plain mixture, then green mixture. Chill until firm. Serve with Custard Sauce. Makes 8 servings.

Custard Sauce: Beat 3 egg yolks slightly. Combine with 2 tblsp. sugar and dash of salt in heavy saucepan. Gradually stir in 1 c. milk. Cook over low heat, stirring constantly, until mixture thickens and coats a metal spoon. Remove from heat and pour into bowl. Stir in ½ tsp. vanilla; chill. Fold in ½ c. heavy cream, whipped. Makes about 2 cups.

MEXICAN COOKIE RINGS

No matter how many other cookies are on the tray at the tea or coffee party or packed in the gift Christmas box, Mexican Cookie Rings will win compliments. And they don't take hours to make.

MEXICAN COOKIE RINGS

Twice as easy to shape as cookies made with a cookie press

1½ c. sifted flour	3 egg yolks
½ tsp. baking powder	1 tsp. vanilla
½ tsp. salt	5 tblsp. tiny multicolored
½ c. butter	decorating candies
⅔ c. sugar	

Sift together flour, baking powder and salt.

Cream together butter and sugar. Add egg yolks and vanilla; beat until light and fluffy. Mix in sifted dry ingredients. Shape into 1" balls. Push your thumb through center of each ball and shape dough into a ring. Dip top of each ring in decorating candies. Place on lightly greased baking sheets.

Bake in 375° oven 10 to 12 minutes or until golden brown. Remove from baking sheets and cool on racks. Makes 2 dozen.

BUTTERMILK PRALINES

When in doubt about what to serve for dessert to end a Mexican-type meal, borrow an old custom of theirs and serve candy. The dividing line between desserts and candies in Mexico is indistinct. Some Texans pass a plate of pralines to top off such dinners. One advantage of candy is that everyone can take one or more pieces, depending on his appetite.

Buttermilk Pralines differ from both the sugary, brittle pecan candy originated in New Orleans during the French and Spanish colonial period, and also from the chewy Texan pralines that resemble soft caramels. They are the first choice of a rancher's wife, a sixth-generation American of Mexican descent, who lives in Colorado's San Luis Valley.

BUTTERMILK PRALINES

The unusual ingredient is buttermilk; candy discs are delicious

2 c. sugar	2 tblsp. butter or regular
1 tsp. baking soda	margarine
⅛ tsp. salt	1½ c. pecan halves
1 c. buttermilk	

Combine sugar, baking soda, salt and buttermilk in heavy 5-qt. Dutch oven. Cook over high heat to 210° on candy thermometer, about 5 minutes. Stir frequently, scraping sides and bottom of pan. Add butter and pecans. Cook, stirring constantly, to very soft ball stage, 230° on candy thermometer. Remove from heat; cool 2 minutes. Beat until thickened and creamy. Drop by tablespoonfuls onto waxed paper. Makes 15 (2½") pralines.

MEXICAN CHOCOLATE

When conquering the Aztecs, Cortez and his soldiers were amazed at the quantities of a strange hot beverage, *cacaoquahitl,* the Emperor Montezuma drank—legend says as many as fifty cups a day. Indians made the beverage by boiling dried and cured cacao seeds in water. They also enjoyed a thicker chocolate drink, sweetened with honey and flavored with vanilla and spices. They called it *chocolatl*—this the Spaniards liked from the start. They called the beverages cacao and chocolate.

Pizarro found Incas in South America drinking a chocolate beverage which they called *cacahua.* Many years later in Peruvian archaeological excavations a ceramic chocolate cup was found. The design on it was of a man holding cacao seed pods.

Mexicans drink lots of hot chocolate, sweetened and flavored with cinnamon and vanilla. Southwesterners also make this beverage using commercial cocoa and the Mexican seasonings. Mexicans use a lovely, carved tool, *molinillos,* to whirl in the hot drink to make a frothy top. In this country, a rotary beater is used to make the chocolate foamy.

MEXICAN CHOCOLATE

If you have an antique chocolate set, use it to serve this drink

½ c. sugar	Dash of salt
¼ c. baking cocoa	4 c. milk
2 tsp. instant coffee	1 tsp. vanilla
¾ tsp. ground cinnamon	

Combine sugar, cocoa, instant coffee, cinnamon and salt in heavy saucepan. Gradually add 1 c. milk, beating with wire whisk or rotary beater until smooth. Bring to a boil over low heat, stirring constantly. Add remaining milk; bring to a boil, stirring frequently. Add vanilla. Beat with rotary beater until frothy before serving. Makes 6 servings.

MEXICAN CHOCOLATE CAKE

Seeing cacao trees in bloom for the first time is a sight never forgotten. The tiny, pale pink flowers sprout directly from the bark of tree trunks and limbs. Large, rough pods develop—they are filled with a sticky mixture enclosing big, soft seeds called cacao beans, the source of chocolate. Indians crushed the seeds with grinding stones; efficient machinery does the work today.

Cacao trees now grow around the world, especially in Africa, but they originated in the Americas. Like many foods, they reached Europe through Spain. Chocolate cake is almost a universal favorite.

Mexican Chocolate Cake has an enthusiastic following in the Southwest. It combines cinnamon and vanilla with chocolate.

MEXICAN CHOCOLATE CAKE

Originally made in ranch kitchens with sour milk, but buttermilk is now more available

2 c. sifted flour
2 c. sugar
1 tsp. baking soda
1 tsp. salt
1½ tsp. ground cinnamon
½ tsp. baking powder
¾ c. water
¾ c. buttermilk

½ c. shortening
2 eggs
4 squares unsweetened chocolate, melted
1 tsp. vanilla
Chocolate Frosting (recipe follows)

Sift together flour, sugar, soda, salt, cinnamon and baking powder into large mixer bowl. Add water, buttermilk, shortening, eggs, melted chocolate and vanilla. Blend 30 seconds at low speed, scraping sides and bottom of bowl constantly. Beat at high speed 3 minutes, scraping bowl occasionally. Spread batter evenly in greased and floured 13×9×2″ pan or two 9″ round layer cake pans.

Bake in 350° oven 40 to 45 minutes for large pan, 30 to 35

minutes for layer pans. Cool on rack. Spread cooled cake with Chocolate frosting. Makes 12 servings.

Chocolate Frosting: Combine ½ c. butter or regular margarine, 2 squares unsweetened chocolate and ¼ c. milk in saucepan. Heat until bubbles form around edge of pan, stirring occasionally. Remove from heat. Add 1 lb. box confectioners sugar, sifted (about 4¾ c.), 1 tsp. vanilla and ½ c. chopped pecans. Beat until of spreading consistency. If necessary, add 1 to 2 tblsp. milk.

CARAMEL/PUMPKIN RING

Suggesting a pumpkin dessert other than pie for the Thanksgiving and Christmas seasons receives at best a lukewarm reception. Pumpkin pie is traditional, it tastes wonderful and almost everyone likes it. So why change? Caramel/Pumpkin Ring is a good reason. Caramel and pumpkin combinations long have been favorites in Mexico.

Caramel/Pumpkin Ring is an adaptation which consists of caramel custard with pumpkin added and baked in a ring mold. Since thorough chilling is desirable, it is a good idea to make the dessert a day ahead, cover the mold with foil and store it in the refrigerator. When ready to serve turn out on a plate and fill the opening in the center with whipped cream or whipped dessert topping.

CARAMEL/PUMPKIN RING

Spicy pumpkin taste with rich caramel overtones—delicious

½ c. sugar
1 c. canned pumpkin
¾ c. sugar
½ tsp. salt
½ tsp. ground cinnamon
¼ tsp. ground ginger
¼ tsp. ground nutmeg

5 eggs, slightly beaten
1 (14½ oz.) can evaporated milk
1 tsp. vanilla
Whipped cream or whipped dessert topping (optional)

Melt ½ c. sugar in skillet over low heat until a golden syrup is formed, stirring constantly to prevent burning. Immediately pour into a 5-c. ring mold, turning and rolling from side to side to coat with sugar syrup. Set aside.

Stir together pumpkin, ¾ c. sugar, salt and spices. Blend in eggs. Stir in evaporated milk and vanilla. Pour into mold. Place in pan of hot water and bake in 350° oven about 1 hour or until knife inserted halfway between center and outer edge comes out clean. Cool, then chill thoroughly. To serve, run knife around sides of pan. Invert on serving plate. Serve with whipped cream, if desired. Makes 8 servings.

MEXICAN PRUNE CANDY

Many women in Mexico treasure candy recipes that have been handed down from one generation to another. One characteristic of many of their sweets is caramel flavor. In Mexican Prune Candy caramel and orange flavors blend delightfully with the prunes and nuts. Mexican Prune Candy is popular in our Southwest, especially in California, an important prune and walnut growing area.

MEXICAN PRUNE CANDY

Exceptionally easy to make but stuffing the prunes will take time

½ c. butter or regular margarine	2 tsp. grated orange peel
1 c. brown sugar, firmly packed	1 tsp. vanilla
	1 c. chopped walnuts
½ c. orange juice	2 (12 oz.) pkgs. pitted prunes
2 c. sifted confectioners sugar	

Melt butter in heavy saucepan. Add brown sugar and cook, stirring constantly, until mixture is bubbly. Stir in orange juice. Cook over low heat without stirring to the soft ball stage, 234°

on candy thermometer. Remove from heat and cool to lukewarm (110°) without stirring.

Add confectioners sugar and beat until mixture loses its gloss. Beat in orange peel and vanilla. Stir in nuts.

Meanwhile, prepare prunes. If necessary to soften, pour boiling water over them and let stand 5 to 10 minutes. Cut opening in prunes. Stuff with candy. Makes about 6½ dozen small stuffed prunes.

Part II

FROM THE OLD COUNTRY TO THE NEW LAND

INTRODUCTION

Immigrants came to America in waves from all over the European continent. A large migration to this country began in 1830 and continued through 1860. These were mostly people from Germany, Ireland, Scotland and Wales. Norwegian-Americans observed their Sesquicentennial in 1975—the 150th anniversary of their first migration.

But the largest group of Scandinavians immigrated from 1860 to 1890 along with Bohemians and Germans. Over 17 million came to find a new life within a 25-year period.

Packed into ships these brave people endured rough, stormy crossings and they were homesick for the relatives they had left behind. But they were sustained by the promise of this rich new land with its opportunities for those willing to work hard.

Our great-great-grandmothers labored in primitive surroundings from dawn until long after the sun had set. They worked as hard if not harder than the men. They corned beef, salted pork, grew and killed chickens, boiled calves feet to extract the gelatin, preserved and dried fruits and vegetables in readiness for the long winters ahead.

The family garden supplied the family with vegetables. Root vegetables were stored in the cellar or sometimes in a separate cellar dug nearby the house. Ham and bacon hung from rafters. Staples such as flour, sugar and salt were obtained in exchange for chicken and eggs.

Our pioneer women brought recipes from their home countries; often carried in their heads or written down hastily. They made do with what they had and turned out comforting and nourishing fare for the family. It might be a simple pudding of buttered bread and sour cherries stewed in a bit of sugar and water. After the mixture was cooked the deep stoneware was set out in the snow until the mixture half-froze into thick jelly, then served with custard sauce made from eggs and milk. This was the end of a hearty meal of smoked ham and tangy sauerkraut.

These women cooked as their mothers had done—by the feel and the look of the recipe. In those early days flour often was not listed as an ingredient—you simply remembered that it was added until the batter or dough felt right. Cookies were made by the tubful, with just enough flour so that the dough rolled easily. Baking day was Saturday in most households and the kitchen was a beehive of activity, producing cakes, tubs of cookies, batches of doughnuts and homemade, crusty bread.

At first the ethnic groups clung together and formed a tightly knit family. They cooked their recipes from the "old country" to help ease the pangs of homesickness. Then neighborhood and community husking bees and church suppers sprang up and brought the different nationalities together. And as women have done for generations, they compared, swapped and shared recipes. Soon a Yankee housewife, who had left her New England life to homestead in the Middle West, was serving her family her neighbor's Swedish meatballs while a German family was eating corn bread along with their own sauerbraten.

Our ancestors not only had the expertise to turn out a perfect meal, they had the ingenuity and skill of using what they had on hand to make their family's treasured dishes. The inspiration for many of our recipes arrived with the immigrants from Europe. Many survive in their original form while others have taken on the stamp of the American kitchen.

Chapter 1

THE HERITAGE
OF ENGLISH
COOKING

Our English ancestors combined their simple foods with a flourish of creativity and these dishes were brought with them when they came to this country and have lasted through the generations.

Our American favorites, apple crisp and baked apples filled with raisins and nuts then sweetened with sugar and dashed with cinnamon, are heirlooms from our English relatives.

The English were proud of their puddings. Every home had their special recipe for plum pudding. Even when times were hard and the larder was almost depleted, the English homemaker would combine flour, syrup, a few raisins and mix it with water and a bit of baking soda until a heavy dough was formed. Then she wrapped the dough in a floured cloth and boiled the mixture for hours. Served with a trickle of treacle, this makeshift sweet did wonders to cheer the family's spirits. These puddings were brought to America and through the years became our steamed puddings.

The early English farmers slaughtered their own pigs and cured their bacon. Every family had a pig—each farmer had his own formula for curing. Some used the simplest method, that of rubbing the hams thoroughly with salt and then covering them completely with salt for several days. Others were a little more inventive and devised their own pickling brew. The recipes also varied from area to area. In some regions saltpeter, coarse brown sugar, black treacle and vinegar were added to the salt. The hams were soaked in the pickling brine for several weeks, hung up to dry, and then smoked. Most of the English hams were delicately flavored and the recipes for proper curing were handed down through many generations. These techniques were brought to this country by the early settlers.

The hot mince pies, rich dark fruitcakes and flaming plum puddings that we prepare and are a part of our Christmas holidays are all of English origin. In northern England the fruitcakes were decorated with almonds and holly and in the south of England they were frosted with a thick white icing that had been swirled into many little peaks to simulate a mountain of snow. Today in our test kitchens we have many recipes from our farm women for fruitcakes and some are iced and others are simply decorated with cherries and nuts.

English farm cooks have always had a reputation for thrift. They invented some clever ways to use up Sunday's roast beef. The names were imaginative, too. Bubble and Squeak is one leftover that youngsters loved. The original recipe was simply a layer of cold meat covered with a layer of cabbage and onion. This was all stirred together until crusty and browned. As it cooked, it bubbled and squeaked. To this day every English household has their version of this easy leftover dish. Essentially though, it is chopped, leftover roast, potatoes and Sunday's leftover vegetables. When the immigrants brought it to this country, it became American hash. Two other leftover recipes are shepherd's pie and Toad-in-the-Hole. The shepherd's pie is a tasty combination of minced, cooked meat, onions, potatoes and gravy turned into a casserole, blanketed with fluffy mashed potatoes and baked. Toad-in-the-Hole (see Index) is simply sausages covered with a batter and baked until high and golden. Both these recipes have been passed down through English descendants in our country.

ENGLISH FISH AND CHIPS

Fish and chips run a close second to roast beef in popularity in England. Potatoes and fish are abundant in England so it's a natural combination.

Fish is coated with a batter of flour, eggs and milk and plunged into the sputtering hot fat. Then it emerges in a crisp golden jacket. The fried potatoes (chips) and fish are wrapped in a cornucopia of newspaper. A generous shake of salt and several dashes of vinegar and they're ready to eat. We give you a traditional fish and chips recipe but omit the newspaper!

ENGLISH FISH AND CHIPS

A very special treat . . . golden fries and batter-fried fish

3 lbs. potatoes, pared	6 tblsp. milk
Cooking oil	6 tblsp. water
2 c. sifted flour	2 lbs. white fish fillets, such
2 eggs, separated	as haddock, sole or
¼ c. beer	flounder
½ tsp. salt	Salt

Several hours before serving, cut potatoes in ⅜″ slices and then in lengthwise strips ⅜″ wide. Wash in very cold water; dry well between paper towels. Fry in deep, hot oil (370°) until tender but not brown, about 5 minutes. Drain on paper towels in baking pan. Cover with waxed paper; set aside until just before mealtime.

Combine flour, egg yolks, beer and ½ tsp. salt; mix well. Gradually add milk and water; stir until batter is smooth. Let stand 30 minutes.

Beat egg whites until stiff peaks form. Fold into batter.

Cut fish fillets into 5×3″ pieces. Coat fish with batter. Fry several pieces at a time in deep, hot oil (375°) until golden brown and tender, about 5 minutes. Turn fillets frequently to keep them from sticking. Drain on paper towels. Keep warm in 300° oven.

Brown precooked potatoes in deep, hot oil (390°) until crisp and brown. Drain on paper towels; sprinkle with salt. Keep warm in 300° oven. Makes 6 servings.

STEAK AND ONION PIE

A basic stew with a pleasant snap of spices and onion baked under a blanket of flaky pastry. An English recipe that originally had beef kidneys as an ingredient. But as it passed down through the families in America, round steak was substituted for kidneys.

A substantial meal to serve a hungry family and field crew. Toss a green salad, and end the meal with hot gingerbread topped with warm applesauce.

STEAK AND ONION PIE

Every "meat and potatoes" man will like this hearty main dish

3 tblsp. flour	4 c. beef broth
1 tsp. salt	2 c. sliced pared potatoes
½ tsp. paprika	(⅛" thick)
⅛ tsp. pepper	2 tblsp. flour
⅛ tsp. ground ginger	3 tblsp. water
⅛ tsp. ground allspice	1 c. sifted flour
1 lb. round steak, cut in	¼ tsp. salt
½" cubes	⅓ c. shortening
⅓ c. cooking oil	1 egg
2 c. chopped onion	

Combine 3 tblsp. flour, 1 tsp. salt, paprika, pepper, ginger and allspice. Coat beef cubes with flour mixture.

Cook beef cubes in hot oil in Dutch oven, stirring frequently. When beef begins to change color; add onion and sauté until mixture is well browned. Add beef broth. Cover. Bring to a boil; reduce heat and simmer 1 hour or until meat is tender. Add potatoes and cook 20 more minutes or until tender.

Combine 2 tblsp. flour and water. Gradually stir into meat mixture. Cook, stirring constantly, until mixture thickens.

Meanwhile, prepare pastry dough. Combine 1 c. flour and ¼ tsp. salt in bowl. Cut in shortening with pastry blender or two knives until mixture resembles coarse meal. Add egg; toss lightly to mix. Knead lightly until mixture holds together.

Roll dough on floured surface to 10″ circle.

Pour hot meat mixture into 2-qt. casserole. Top with dough. Seal edges and cut vents for steam.

Bake in 425° oven 25 minutes or until golden brown. Makes 6 servings.

WELSH RAREBIT

Creamy, tangy Leicester is a favorite English cheese for Welsh rarebit. Depending on how sharp you prefer your rarebit any of our cheeses will do. The original name, "rabbit," it is said comes from a Welsh joke. Cheese was often plentiful when rabbits were not so they called it rabbit. In the 18th century it becomes rarebit, but rabbit is the original name.

This nippy rarebit is a protein-rich nourishing supper. It's a great dish to make when unexpected guests arrive. Serve with frosty cold glasses of milk or a pitcher of chilled cider. A dish of fruit completes the meal.

WELSH RAREBIT

Also good served over toasted English muffins with tomato slices

1 lb. shredded, sharp Cheddar cheese	**2 tsp. Worcestershire sauce**
2 tblsp. flour	**1 tsp. dry mustard**
1 c. beer	**¼ tsp. cayenne pepper**
2 tblsp. butter or regular margarine	**12 slices bread, toasted and cut in triangles**

Combine cheese with flour in heavy 2-qt. saucepan. Add beer, butter, Worcestershire sauce, mustard and cayenne pepper; mix well. Cook over medium heat, stirring constantly, until cheese is completely melted and mixture is smooth (about 15 minutes).

Pour cheese sauce over hot toast, allowing 2 slices of toast per serving. If you wish, you can place Welsh rarebit under the broiler before serving. Place 2 slices toast in each ovenproof shallow baking dish or 8" pie plate. Pour cheese sauce over all. Place under broiler, 4" from source of heat, and broil 1½ minutes or until top is lightly browned and cheese is bubbly. Makes 6 servings.

CORNISH PASTIES

A Michigan farm woman shares her English recipe for meat and vegetable pasties. The miners in England carried them in their lunch pails wrapped in layers of newspaper. They kept warm for hours.

When the family heads for a football game, she has a triple batch of pasties ready for them. They are popular at picnics and family reunions, too.

CORNISH PASTIES

These flaky, individual meat pies are also good served cold

1 lb. stewing beef, minced	⅛ tsp. pepper
2 c. diced pared potatoes	3 c. sifted flour
1½ c. chopped onion	1½ tsp. salt
1 tblsp. Worcestershire	1 c. lard
sauce	4 to 5 tblsp. cold water
2 tsp. salt	1 egg, beaten

Combine beef, potatoes, onion, Worcestershire sauce, 2 tsp. salt and pepper; mix lightly. Set aside.

Sift together flour and 1½ tsp. salt into bowl. Cut in lard with pastry blender or two knives until mixture is like coarse cornmeal. Sprinkle with cold water, 1 tblsp. at a time, tossing lightly. (Mixture should be moist enough to hold together.)

Divide dough into 6 parts. Roll each part into a 7" round. Place ⅙ of meat mixture on half of round. Fold other half over meat mixture; press edges together to seal. Cut slits in top of pastry. Place on ungreased baking sheet. Brush with beaten egg. Repeat with remaining dough.

Bake in 350° oven 45 minutes or until golden brown and meat mixture is tender. Makes 6 servings.

YORKSHIRE PUDDING

In an English family Yorkshire pudding is a must with a roast beef. Egg and milk batter is poured over the meat drippings and rises to a high, puffy crust. One of the secrets for a perfect Yorkshire pudding is a hot oven.

This recipe comes from a Nebraska homemaker; it is her husband's favorite and dates back to his great-grandmother. Every successive daughter-in-law was taught to make this crispy accompaniment to the roast. Half the family prefers the pudding slathered with softened butter, and the other half pour on a generous ladling of rich brown gravy.

YORKSHIRE PUDDING

Tastes like a huge popover . . . crusty brown with a moist center

¼ c. cooking oil or pan drippings from roast beef	1 c. milk
	1 c. sifted flour
	2 tsp. baking powder
2 eggs	½ tsp. salt

Pour oil into 9″ square baking pan. Heat in 425° oven 5 minutes.

Beat eggs until frothy with rotary beater. Add milk; blend well. Add flour, baking powder and salt. Beat until smooth. Pour batter into hot 9″ square baking pan.

Bake in 425° oven 35 to 40 minutes or until pudding is golden brown and puffy. Edges should be crusty. Serve hot with roast beef. (Pudding will fall in the middle as it cools.) Makes 6 servings.

TOAD-IN-THE-HOLE

Tastes like a popover. Crusty and golden brown on the outside and moist inside. Youngsters love to peer through the glass door of the oven and watch the batter climb against the sides of the pan while the sausages nestle in pockets of dough.

This is an economical, nourishing supper. Serve with fresh green beans and thick slices of tomato. A quick and easy meal.

TOAD-IN-THE-HOLE

Delight your family with this nourishing English supper dish

1 lb. small, fresh pork sausage links	1 c. milk
2 tblsp. water	1 c. sifted flour
2 eggs	½ tsp. salt
	⅛ tsp. pepper

Place sausages and water in 10″ skillet. Cover and cook over low heat 3 minutes. Remove cover; increase heat to medium. Continue cooking sausages, turning them frequently until the water evaporates and sausages begin to brown.

Meanwhile, prepare batter. Beat eggs with rotary beater. Add milk; blend well. Add flour, salt and pepper, beating until batter is smooth.

Pour ¼ c. sausage drippings in bottom of 11×7×1½″ baking dish. Arrange sausage links in bottom of dish. Pour batter over all.

Bake in 425° oven 30 minutes. Makes 6 servings.

ST. JAMES COFFEE CAKE

An Indiana woman sent us her recipe for St. James Coffee Cake that came from England. She has found this is a versatile coffee cake, inexpensive to make and a good keeper. When there is a church supper she makes several. She always greets a new neighbor with a warm hello and her special coffee cake. Everyone that tastes it asks for the recipe.

ʋ1. JAMES COFFEE CAKE

An old-fashioned coffee cake that is great for Sunday breakfast

3 c. sifted flour	2 c. sour milk
2 c. sugar	1 tsp. baking soda
½ tsp. ground cinnamon	1 egg, beaten
½ tsp. ground cloves	1 c. raisins
½ tsp. ground nutmeg	1 c. chopped walnuts
¾ c. butter or regular	1 tblsp. flour
margarine	

Sift together 3 c. flour, sugar, cinnamon, cloves and nutmeg into bowl. Cut in butter until mixture resembles coarse meal. Reserve ½ c. crumbs; set aside.

Combine sour milk and baking soda. Add egg and milk mixture to remaining crumb mixture, beating well.

Combine raisins, walnuts and 1 tblsp. flour. Stir into batter. Spread batter in greased and floured 13×9×2″ cake pan. Sprinkle with reserved ½ c. crumbs.

Bake in 350° oven 55 minutes or until done. Serve warm or cold. Makes 16 servings.

ENGLISH SHORTBREAD

Perfect with a cup of scalding hot tea. The English and Scots are famous for their shortbreads. Some are richer than others— this one is not as rich as some, but flaky with a subtle flavor.

ENGLISH SHORTBREAD

The perfect choice for those who prefer a plain butter cookie

1 c. butter or regular	1 egg
margarine	3 c. sifted flour
½ c. sugar	1 tsp. baking powder

Cream together butter and sugar until light and fluffy. Beat in egg.

Sift together flour and baking powder. Add dry ingredients to creamed mixture, stirring well to blend. Knead dough lightly until it holds together.

Roll dough on floured surface to 14″ square. Cut into 49 (2″) squares. Place squares about 2″ apart on ungreased baking sheet. Prick each with fork.

Bake in 325° oven 12 minutes or until lightly browned. Remove from baking sheets; cool on racks. Makes 49 squares.

UNCLE JIM'S OATMEAL COOKIES

This old Welsh recipe written in a thin and spidery hand on yellowed paper has lasted through several generations. A Wisconsin farm woman makes a batch a week of these crisp-edged cookies that were a favorite of her great-great uncle. No temperature or baking time was given—after trial and error she perfected the recipe.

UNCLE JIM'S OATMEAL COOKIES

Good, basic oatmeal cookie to pack in children's lunch boxes

¾ c. butter or regular margarine	¾ tsp. baking soda
1 c. sugar	½ tsp. baking powder
2 eggs, beaten	½ tsp salt
2 tblsp. molasses	3 tblsp. sour milk
1½ c. sifted flour	3 c. rolled oats
1 tsp. ground cinnamon	½ c. raisins

Cream together butter and sugar until light and fluffy. Add eggs, one at a time, beating well after each addition. Beat in molasses.

Sift together flour, cinnamon, baking soda, baking powder and salt. Add dry ingredients alternately with sour milk to creamed mixture, mixing well after each addition. Stir in oats and raisins. Drop mixture by teaspoonfuls about 2″ apart on greased baking sheet.

Bake in 350° oven 10 to 12 minutes or until golden brown. Remove from baking sheets; cool on racks. Makes 6 dozen.

ENGLISH SCONES

Whenever she visited her grandmother, a South Carolina farm woman knew she would have a special treat awaiting . . . scones with lots of butter and three kinds of jam. They were rich and crumbly, not too sweet and not too hearty.

As she sipped her tea that was half-tea half-milk, her grandmother would tell her that her great-grandmother had brought the recipe from England.

ENGLISH SCONES

Like our American baking powder biscuits but not as flaky

2 c. sifted flour	¼ c. currants or chopped
3 tblsp. sugar	raisins
3 tsp. baking powder	2 eggs, beaten
1 tsp. salt	½ c. light cream
¼ c. butter or regular	1 egg white
margarine	

Sift together flour, sugar, baking powder and salt into bowl. Cut in butter until mixture is crumbly. Add currants.

Combine eggs and cream. Add to crumb mixture all at once, stirring just enough with fork to mix.

Roll dough on floured surface to ½″ thickness. Cut with floured 2″ cutter and place about 1″ apart on greased baking sheet.

Beat egg white until frothy and brush tops of scones.

Bake in 375° oven 15 minutes or until golden. Makes 24.

CHEESE STRAWS

This English recipe that is popular at teatime makes a buttery-crisp pastry stick with a good cheese flavor. We suggest serving with chilled tomato juice spiked with lemon as an appetizer for a company meal. These would make a delightful Christmas gift, packed carefully in a pretty tin box.

CHEESE STRAWS

Make ahead to serve drop-in guests with an icy cold soft drink

¾ c. sifted flour
¼ tsp. salt
⅛ tsp. cayenne pepper
¼ c. finely shredded, sharp
  Cheddar cheese

¼ c. butter or regular
  margarine
1 egg yolk, beaten
2 tblsp. ice water

Sift together flour, salt and cayenne pepper into bowl. Mix in cheese. Cut in butter with pastry blender or two knives until mixture resembles coarse meal. Combine egg yolk and ice water. Sprinkle over mixture. Toss lightly until mixed. Shape into ball. Dust lightly with flour. Cover with plastic wrap. Chill in refrigerator at least 1 hour.

Roll dough on floured surface to 14×4″ rectangle. Cut into 28 strips, 4″ long and ½″ wide. Place strips about 1″ apart on ungreased baking sheet.

Bake in 400° oven 10 minutes or until straws are firm and light-colored. Remove from baking sheet; cool on racks. Cheese straws will keep up to two weeks in a tightly covered container. Makes 28 straws.

DUNDEE CAKE

Bring this out on your prettiest cake plate during the holidays. Studded with raisins, currants, candied peel, cherries—the batter is rich in eggs. Blanched, whole almonds form a pattern on top of the cake. This cake needs no glaze—it's handsome as it is. Make several and freeze ahead for the holidays.

DUNDEE CAKE

Serve wedges of this with coffee during the Christmas holidays

1 c. butter or regular margarine	¾ c. raisins
1 c. sugar	¾ c. chopped, mixed candied fruit
5 eggs	8 red candied cherries, cut in half
1 tsp. baking soda	
1 tsp. milk	½ c. ground almonds
2½ c. sifted flour	2 tblsp. grated orange peel
⅛ tsp. salt	⅓ c. whole, blanched almonds
¾ c. currants	

Cream together butter and sugar until light and fluffy. Add eggs, one at a time, beating well after each addition.

Dissolve baking soda in milk; add to creamed mixture.

Sift together flour and salt; reserve 1 tblsp. Gradually add dry ingredients to creamed mixture, blending well after each addition.

Combine currants, raisins, candied fruit, candied cherries, ground almonds, orange peel and reserved 1 tblsp. flour; mix well. Stir into batter. Spread batter in greased and floured 8" springform pan. Arrange whole almonds in concentric circles on top of batter.

Bake in 300° oven 1 hour 30 minutes or until cake tests done. Cool in pan on rack 5 minutes. Remove outer rim and cool completely. Makes 12 servings.

ENGLISH TRIFLE

English trifle can be made with leftover stale cake, the last of the jam and smidgens of leftover fruit. Combined with a creamy custard it tastes elegant.

You can also start with fresh cake and a lovely jar of home-made jam, lots of heavy cream and turn out a sublime dessert. A sweet finale that will bring accolades from guests.

ENGLISH TRIFLE

You can substitute a purchased spongecake for the jelly roll

5 eggs	**1 egg**
¾ c. sugar	**2 eggs, separated**
½ tsp. almond extract	**1 tblsp. sugar**
¾ c. sifted cake flour	**2 c. milk, scalded**
¾ tsp. baking powder	**1 c. heavy cream**
¼ tsp. salt	**1 tblsp. sugar**
1 c. red raspberry jam	**½ c. toasted, sliced almonds**
½ c. cream sherry	

Beat 5 eggs, ¾ c. sugar and almond extract until thick and lemon-colored, about 5 minutes.

Sift together cake flour, baking powder and salt. Fold dry ingredients into egg mixture. Spread batter in greased and waxed-paper-lined 15½ ×10½ ×1″ jelly roll pan.

Bake in 350° oven 20 minutes or until cake tests done. Loosen cake around edges. Turn out on rack to cool.

Divide cooled spongecake into fourths. Spread each quarter with ¼ c. jam. Cut each into 8 pieces. Place 8 pieces in bottom of 3-qt. serving bowl. Sprinkle with ¼ of sherry. Repeat layers. Cover with plastic wrap and let stand 1 hour at room temperature.

Combine 1 egg, 2 egg yolks and 1 tblsp. sugar in double boiler top. Beat well with rotary beater. Slowly beat in scalded milk. Cook over simmering water, stirring occasionally, until it begins to thicken (about 15 minutes). Remove from heat; cool 5 minutes. Pour warm custard over cake. Chill in refrigerator 1 hour.

Beat 2 egg whites until soft peaks form. Whip heavy cream until it begins to thicken. Slowly beat in 1 tblsp. sugar. Beat until soft peaks form. Fold egg whites into beaten cream. Spoon over top of trifle. Decorate with sliced almonds. Chill until serving time. Makes 8 servings.

BLACKBERRY JAM CAKE

Solid and moist with blackberry jam, this is a truly English cake and special company cake for an Ohio family. It can be made several days before eating as it improves with aging. Cut in small wedges as it is a rich cake—has a subtle, spicy flavor.

BLACKBERRY JAM CAKE

Also luscious if made with strawberry or raspberry jam

1 c. butter or regular margarine	1 tsp. baking powder
1 c. sugar	1 tsp. ground cinnamon
4 eggs	1 tsp. ground nutmeg
1 c. blackberry jam	1 tsp. ground allspice
3¼ c. sifted flour	¾ tsp. salt
1 tsp. baking soda	1 c. buttermilk
	1⅓ c. chopped walnuts

Cream together butter and sugar until light and fluffy. Add eggs, one at a time, beating well after each addition. Beat in jam.

Sift together flour, baking soda, baking powder, cinnamon, nutmeg, allspice and salt. Add dry ingredients alternately with buttermilk, beating well after each addition. Stir in walnuts. Spread batter in greased and waxed-paper-lined 9" tube pan.

Bake in 325° oven 1 hour 30 minutes or until cake tests done. Makes 10 servings.

LEMON CAKE ROLL

This dessert looks and tastes like spring—a superb dessert to end an Easter dinner. The light, tender spongecake filled with a zingy lemon curd came to the United States from England and is a truly elegant English dessert.

LEMON CAKE ROLL

This delicate sponge roll makes a lovely last-minute dessert

3 eggs	Confectioners sugar
1 c. sugar	¼ c. butter or regular
¼ c. water	margarine
1 tblsp. lemon juice	⅔ c. sugar
1 tsp. grated lemon peel	3 tblsp. lemon juice
1 c. sifted cake flour	3 tblsp. water
1 tsp. baking powder	3 egg yolks, slightly beaten
¼ tsp. salt	1 tsp. grated lemon peel

Beat eggs at high speed until thick and lemon-colored, about 3 minutes. Gradually beat in 1 c. sugar. Continue beating until very thick. Blend in ¼ c. water, 1 tblsp. lemon juice and 1 tsp. lemon peel.

Sift together cake flour, baking powder and salt. Gently fold dry ingredients into egg mixture. Spread batter in greased and waxed-paper-lined 15½ × 10½ × 1″ jelly roll pan.

Bake in 375° oven 14 minutes or until cake tests done. Loosen edges of cake; turn out on towel dusted with confectioners sugar. Peel off paper carefully. Cut off browned edges of cake. Roll cake up in towel, starting from narrow side. Cool on rack.

Combine butter, ⅔ c. sugar, 3 tblsp. lemon juice, 3 tblsp. water and egg yolks in double boiler top; mix well. Cook over simmering water, stirring constantly, until mixture coats a spoon. Remove from heat. Pour into bowl. Stir in 1 tsp. lemon peel. Cover with plastic wrap and cool completely.

Unroll cake roll. Spread with cooled lemon curd. Refrigerate until serving time. Makes 8 servings.

OLD-FASHIONED SUET PUDDING

The English love their puddings as much now as they did generations ago. The recipes for suet pudding number in the hundreds, some plain and some fancier. This third-generation suet pudding is a hearty one that's served on cold winter days in a Wisconsin farm home. Everyone looks forward to Great-grandma's pudding.

The Wisconsin farm wife told us that when, for a change, she made a fancy custard sauce instead of the usual Nutmeg Sauce, everyone was disappointed. They all said that the Nutmeg Sauce belonged with the pudding—it just wasn't the same.

OLD-FASHIONED SUET PUDDING

A simple, hearty pudding with a sauce flavored with nutmeg

1 c. ground beef suet	¼ tsp. salt
1 c. sugar	1¼ c. milk
2 eggs	1 c. raisins
3 c. sifted flour	Nutmeg Sauce (recipe
3 tsp. baking powder	follows)

Mix together suet and sugar until well blended. Add eggs, one at a time, mixing well after each addition with spoon.

Sift together flour, baking powder and salt. Add dry ingredients alternately with milk to suet mixture, stirring well after each addition. Stir in raisins. Turn into greased 2-qt. ring mold. Cover with aluminum foil.

Place cooling rack or trivet in bottom of large kettle. Add 2″ boiling water. Place mold in kettle. Cover and steam 1½ hours or until pudding tests done. Add more boiling water if necessary.

Remove mold from kettle. Let stand 2 minutes. Turn pudding out of mold onto serving plate. Serve pudding hot with Nutmeg Sauce. Makes 10 servings.

Nutmeg Sauce: Combine ½ c. sugar, 2 tblsp. cornstarch and ⅛ tsp. salt in 2-qt. saucepan. Gradually stir in 2 c. boiling water. Add 3 tblsp. butter or regular margarine. Cook over medium heat, stirring constantly, until thick and clear. Remove from heat. Stir in ¼ tsp. ground nutmeg and 1 tsp. vanilla.

SPICY SUET PUDDING

A treasured recipe that has been handed down through the family.

A Nebraska farm woman remembers her Christmas holiday as a child. Her mother would be up before dawn on Christmas morning to prepare suet pudding. Now all children fix the same pudding on Christmas day.

A solid pudding, rich in spices served with a warm Vanilla Sauce.

SPICY SUET PUDDING

A 2-qt. ring mold can also be used . . . just cover with foil

1 c. ground beef suet	1/8 tsp. salt
1 c. sugar	1 c. sour milk
2¼ c. sifted flour	1 c. raisins
½ tsp. ground cinnamon	Vanilla Sauce (recipe
½ tsp. ground cloves	follows)
½ tsp. baking soda	

Mix together suet and sugar until well blended.

Sift together flour, cinnamon, cloves, baking soda and salt. Add dry ingredients alternately with sour milk to suet mixture, stirring well after each addition. Stir in raisins. Turn into greased 2-qt. pudding mold. Cover.

Place cooling rack or trivet in bottom of large kettle. Add 2" boiling water. Place mold in kettle. Cover and steam 3 hours or until pudding tests done. Add more boiling water if necessary.

Remove mold from kettle. Let stand 2 minutes. Turn pudding out of mold onto serving plate. Serve pudding hot with Vanilla Sauce. Makes 10 servings.

Vanilla Sauce: Combine ½ c. sugar, 2 tblsp. cornstarch and ¼ tsp. salt in 2-qt. saucepan. Gradually stir in 2 c. boiling water. Cook over medium heat, stirring constantly, until it comes to a boil. Boil 5 minutes. Remove from heat. Stir in

¼ c. butter or regular margarine, 2 tsp. vanilla and ⅛ tsp. ground nutmeg; mix well.

STEAMED CHRISTMAS PUDDING

Rich in molasses, nuts, spices and raisins, this pudding stands 4 inches tall. The recipe is now in the files of a Nebraska farm woman descended from early English colonists. Always served during the holidays, this pudding is a favorite company dessert in the cold weather months. We suggest a cold Custard Sauce or a buttery hard sauce to go along with the pudding.

STEAMED CHRISTMAS PUDDING

Gently spiced and served with a pour of velvety sauce

1 c. ground beef suet	**1 c. milk**
½ c. sugar	**½ c. chopped, mixed**
1 egg	**candied fruit**
½ c. molasses	**½ c. chopped walnuts**
2 c. sifted flour	**½ c. raisins**
1 tsp. baking soda	**1 tblsp. flour**
½ tsp. ground cinnamon	**Custard Sauce (recipe**
½ tsp. ground cloves	**follows)**
½ tsp. ground nutmeg	

Cream together suet and sugar until well blended. Add egg and molasses, beating well.

Sift together 2 c. flour, baking soda, cinnamon, cloves and nutmeg. Add dry ingredients alternately with milk to suet mixture, beating well after each addition.

Combine candied fruit, walnuts, raisins and 1 tblsp. flour; mix well. Stir into mixture. Turn into greased 2-qt. pudding mold. Cover.

Place cooling rack or trivet in bottom of large kettle. Add 2″ boiling water. Place mold in kettle. Cover and steam 3 hours or until pudding tests done. Add more boiling water if necessary.

Remove mold from kettle. Let stand 2 minutes. Turn pudding out of mold onto serving plate. Serve pudding hot with Custard Sauce. Makes 10 servings.

Custard Sauce: Combine 1 (3¼ oz.) pkg. vanilla pudding and pie filling and 2¾ c. milk in medium saucepan. Bring mixture to a boil, stirring constantly. Remove from heat. Stir in ½ tsp. vanilla. Cool slightly.

STEAMED CARROT PUDDING

English cooks were famous for their steamed puddings. When they came to this country, they brought their recipes with them. Carrots and potatoes were plentiful in their new land. Before long, steamed puddings were made using these two vegetables.

Grated potatoes and carrots, mixed with spices, raisins and nuts, steam to moist perfection. A Utah homemaker makes this heirloom recipe in 3-pound shortening cans and gives them to neighbors during the holidays. She often adds a small crock of Hard Sauce, too. Flecked with bits of bright orange carrots, this golden brown pudding makes a great homemade gift.

STEAMED CARROT PUDDING

So tender and moist, a lovely choice for a holiday dessert

¾ c. butter or regular margarine	½ tsp. ground nutmeg
1 c. sugar	¾ c. sour milk
2 eggs	1 c. grated carrots
2 c. sifted flour	1 c. grated pared potatoes
2 tsp. ground cinnamon	1 c. currants
1 tsp. baking powder	½ c. chopped walnuts
½ tsp. baking soda	1 tblsp. flour
½ tsp. ground allspice	Hard Sauce (recipe follows)

Cream together butter and sugar until light and fluffy. Add eggs, one at a time, beating well after each addition.

Sift together 2 c. flour, cinnamon, baking powder, baking soda, allspice and nutmeg. Add dry ingredients alternately with sour milk to creamed mixture, stirring well after each addition.

Combine carrots, potatoes, currants, walnuts and 1 tblsp. flour; mix well. Stir into batter. Turn into greased 2-qt. pudding mold. Cover. Place cooling rack or trivet in bottom of large kettle. Add 2" boiling water. Place mold in kettle. Cover and steam 2 hours or until pudding tests done. Add more boiling water if necessary.

Remove mold from kettle. Let stand 2 minutes. Turn pudding out of mold onto serving plate. Serve pudding hot with Hard Sauce. Makes 10 servings.

Hard Sauce: Beat ½ c. butter or regular margarine and 1 c. sifted confectioners sugar until light and fluffy. Beat in ½ tsp. vanilla. Spoon into serving dish. Top with grated orange peel, if you wish. Refrigerate until firm.

STEAMED CHERRY PUDDING

Light, fine-textured cakes form the base for this heirloom pudding, a versatile dessert that can be served year round. While the pudding steams, make the bright red sauce to trickle over each individual cherry-studded pudding.

A favorite menu with an Iowa family is baked pork chops and scalloped potato, buttered carrots and their treasured Cherry Pudding. The children call them Cherry Puffs.

BLAZING PLUM PUDDING IS SYNONYMOUS WITH ENGLAND. On Christmas Day this rich pudding wreathed with holly is brought to the table in flaming beauty. *Steamed Christmas Pudding* (page 182) reflects English heritage.

OLIEBOLLEN, HOLLAND'S NEW YEAR'S EVE DOUGHNUT. Dutch descendants in our country make these raisin-filled yeast doughnuts (*Oliebollen* page 225) all year round to serve warm with a pot of well-brewed coffee.

BRAISED MEAT, VEGETABLES . . . STAPLE FARE IN GERMANY. *Pork Chop Skillet Dinner* (page 191) is a mouth-watering combination of pork chops, cabbage, potatoes and carrots—favorites in families of German descent.

FATTIGMAN, NORWAY'S FAMED CHRISTMAS COOKIE. This light crisp cookie (*Fattigman* page 239) handed down by Norwegian-Americans is served in Scandinavian homes all over the U.S.A. during the holiday season.

STEAMED CHERRY PUDDING

Light, airy pudding is steamed in individual custard cups

2 eggs
1 c. milk
⅓ c. melted butter or
   regular margarine
2 c. sifted flour
¼ c. sugar
2 tsp. baking powder
1 tsp. salt
2 tsp. vanilla

2 (1 lb.) cans pitted red
   sour cherries
½ c. sugar
2 tblsp. cornstarch
¾ c. water
1 tblsp. butter or regular
   margarine
10 drops red food color

Beat eggs until frothy with rotary beater. Beat in milk and ⅓ c. melted butter; blend well.

Sift together flour, ¼ c. sugar, baking powder and salt. Stir dry ingredients into milk mixture; mixing well. Add vanilla.

Drain cherries, reserving ¾ c. juice. Set aside.

Spoon batter into 8 greased 5-oz. custard cups, filling one-third full. Place 4 to 5 cherries in each cup. Top with remaining batter.

Place cooling rack or trivet in kettle or electric skillet. Add 2" boiling water. Place custard cups on rack. Cover and steam 30 minutes or until puddings test done. Add more boiling water if necessary.

Meanwhile, prepare Cherry Sauce. Combine ½ c. sugar and cornstarch in 2-qt. saucepan. Gradually stir in reserved ¾ c. cherry juice, ¾ c. water, 1 tblsp. butter and red food color. Cook over medium heat, stirring constantly, until mixture comes to a boil. Stir in remaining cherries. Remove from heat.

Remove individual puddings from custard cups and place on serving dishes. Spoon over Cherry Sauce. Makes 8 servings.

Chapter 2

THE HERITAGE OF GERMAN COOKING

German cooking has great variety and scope. It is more compatible with American tastes than some European cooking. The Germans are meat and potato fanciers as we are. They like thick, robust soups made from potatoes and dried peas and beans, and they also prefer creamed soups to clear.

Meat is the mainstay of German cooking; they prepare their meats in much the same manner as we, except that their famed sauerkraut goes with every meat served in some regions of Germany. Our American roasts and pot roasts are similar to theirs. They have cooked stews for centuries and are famous for one-pot meals where meat and vegetables are browned in fat, lightly seasoned with herbs and spices and then simmered in broth until tender. They are fond of dried fruits and began adding them to their meats years ago to provide a welcome break from the winter cabbages and turnips.

Sauerkraut is a star in German cuisine. Our pioneers brought the method of preserving cabbage by pickling from the old country, and in many yards there would be a barrel or two of sauerkraut.

Dumplings play an important role in German cooking, too.

They float in soups and stews and are served as a side dish to accompany meat. They vary in size, shape and texture. Some are even poached in a fruit sauce and served for dessert. Some cooks like to add a pinch of baking powder for lightness. There is a knack to making dumplings, German cooks explain. It takes an experienced hand to turn out perfect dumplings for the humidity in the air affects the amount of flour to be used.

Braised meats are favorites with German cooks. With the less tender, inexpensive cuts of meat, they make wonderful thick gravy that complements their famous dumplings.

Pot roast recipes vary with every region. In the Rhineland white raisins are stirred into a light brown cream gravy, while in other sections the tangy sweet-sour is prevalent and sometimes crusts of rye bread or crumbled gingersnaps are used as thickening.

In fact all German cuisine varies with the location, picking up the flavors of the bordering countries. Food in East Germany favors their Polish and Czech neighbors; there they use caraway seeds, paprika and sour cream often in the preparation of foods. There, too, you will find huge snowy dumplings, sauerkraut and pork. The Rhineland picks up the delicacy of French cooking, fewer sweets-and-sours, but generous amounts of butter, cream and eggs are incorporated into their cooking.

Cabbage, beets and potatoes appear often, especially in the winter months. Noodles are an important part of their diet. Often they are served plain with butter or dressed up with sautéed onions, crumbled bacon or buttered bread crumbs.

Sausages come in all sizes, shapes and degrees of spiciness. There are short stubby knockwurst, bratwurst, liverwurst and summer sausage that keeps for months if hung in a cool spot.

Some of the best bakers in the world are German cooks. Their desserts are rich and irresistible. Apples, cherries and macaroons are buried in clouds of whipped cream. Currant-studded yeast breads, fat, puffy stollens, tissue-thin strudels, spicy cookies and cakes are just a few of the baked goods that make German cooks famous.

German cooking is honest, down-to-earth and simple. We

present recipes that have been part of the American heritage for years; some have not changed while others have been altered to suit family tastes.

SAUERBRATEN WITH GINGERSNAP GRAVY

Every German kitchen boasts at least one recipe for sauerbraten, one of the most renowned of German beef recipes. And every cook has her special marinade. Some are marinated in wine and no vinegar. And in some sections of northern Germany the pot roast is marinated in buttermilk, imparting a distinctive flavor and very tender juicy meat. And instead of gingersnaps, lebkuchen may be broken into the gravy. Our recipe features a two-day steeping in vinegar and spices. The gravy is smooth, mellow and nippy with gingersnaps.

SAUERBRATEN WITH GINGERSNAP GRAVY

Let roast stand 15 minutes before cutting into thin slices

1 medium onion, sliced	1 c. chopped onion
1 c. cider vinegar	1 c. chopped carrots
2 c. water	½ c. chopped celery
2½ tsp. salt	1 c. water
12 whole peppercorns	1 beef bouillon cube
6 whole cloves	1 c. water
3 bay leaves	¼ c. flour
1 (5 lb.) boneless bottom	½ c. water
round, rolled and tied	½ c. crushed gingersnaps
¼ c. cooking oil	

Combine sliced onion, vinegar, 2 c. water, salt, peppercorns, cloves and bay leaves. Pour over roast in large glass dish, turning roast to coat all sides. Cover and refrigerate 2 days, turning meat twice daily.

Remove meat from marinade; dry with paper towels. Reserve 2 c. marinade. Brown meat on all sides in hot oil in Dutch oven, about 15 minutes. Remove meat. Add 1 c. onion, carrots and celery. Sauté until tender (do not brown).

Return meat to Dutch oven. Add reserved marinade and 1 c. water. Bring mixture to a boil. Reduce heat; cover and simmer 3 hours or until meat is tender.

Remove meat to hot platter. Add bouillon cube and 1 c. water to Dutch oven. Bring mixture to a boil.

Combine flour and ½ c. water; stir to blend. Gradually add to hot liquid, stirring constantly. Stir in gingersnaps. Bring mixture to a boil, stirring constantly. Boil 3 minutes. Serve gravy with sauerbraten. Makes 12 servings.

SOUR BEEF AND POTATO DUMPLINGS

Another version of the famous German sauerbraten; this one served with homemade Potato Dumplings. There's a surprise in the center—buttered, browned bread cubes, plus a thick, rich dark gravy to pour over the dumplings.

SOUR BEEF AND POTATO DUMPLINGS

Spicy gingersnaps thicken the gravy in this tangy main dish

4 lbs. stewing beef, cut in 1″ cubes	¼ c. sugar
1½ c. cider vinegar	¼ c. brown sugar, firmly packed
½ c. water	½ c. crushed gingersnaps
½ c. chopped onion	⅓ c. crushed gingersnaps
½ c. raisins	Potato Dumplings (see
1 tblsp. salt	Index)
1½ tsp. pickling spices	

Combine stewing beef, vinegar, water, onion, raisins and salt in 6-qt. kettle. Bring mixture to a boil.

Tie pickling spices in cheesecloth bag. Add to meat mixture. Cover. Reduce heat and simmer 2 hours.

Add both sugars and ½ c. gingersnaps. Simmer 45 more minutes or until meat is tender.

Stir in ⅓ c. gingersnaps and cook 2 minutes or until mixture thickens slightly. Remove spice bag. Serve with Potato Dumplings. Makes 10 servings.

MEATBALLS IN JACKETS

A rich noodle dough rolled paper-thin, filled with a flavorful ground beef mixture, then sealed tightly and popped into hot oil. The meatballs emerge with a crackling crisp crust. Often stewed Tomato Sauce and Creamy Mushroom Sauce are served to give a choice. We sampled a little of both on a pastry—pleasing combination.

MEATBALLS IN JACKETS

These crunchy, meat-filled squares would make great appetizers

1 lb. ground beef	1 tblsp. shortening
½ c. finely chopped onion	3 eggs, beaten
1 clove garlic, minced	2 tblsp. milk
½ tsp. salt	Cooking oil
⅛ tsp. pepper	Stewed Tomato Sauce
6 tblsp. beef broth	(recipe follows)
2½ c. sifted flour	Creamy Mushroom Sauce
1 tsp. baking powder	(recipe follows)
¾ tsp. salt	

Combine ground beef, onion, garlic, ½ tsp. salt, pepper and beef broth; mix lightly, but well. Set aside.

Sift together flour, baking powder and ¾ tsp. salt into bowl. Cut in shortening. Add eggs and milk; mix until moistened.

Divide dough in half. Roll each half to 13″ square. Trim to 12″ square; cut into 9 (4″) squares; reserve scraps of dough. Place 1 heaping tblsp. meat filling in center of each square. Bring corners of squares to center; pinch edges together. Repeat with remaining dough. Roll out scraps to 9″ square. Trim to 8″ square; cut in 4 (4″) squares.

Fry in deep, hot oil (350°) 2 minutes on each side. Drain on paper towels. Serve hot with either Stewed Tomato Sauce or Creamy Mushroom Sauce. Makes 22.

Stewed Tomato Sauce: Sauté 1 tblsp. minced onion and 1 tblsp. minced celery in 1 tblsp. melted butter or regular margarine until tender (do not brown). Add 1 (1 lb.) can stewed tomatoes and ¼ tsp. thyme leaves; simmer 20 minutes. Combine 1 tsp. cornstarch and 1 tblsp. water; stir into tomato mixture. Bring to a boil. Serve over meat pies. Makes 2 cups.

Creamy Mushroom Sauce: Combine 1 (10¾ oz.) can condensed cream of mushroom soup, 1 (3 oz.) can sliced mushrooms (undrained) and ⅓ c. of milk. Stir until smooth. Heat and serve over meat pies. Makes 1½ cups.

PORK CHOP SKILLET DINNER

The Germans are famous for their hearty and nourishing fare. This rib-sticking, down-to-earth dish is perfect to serve on a frosty winter night. When you serve this third-generation German favorite, the men in your family will say, "Let's have this again!"

PORK CHOP SKILLET DINNER

A complete meal-in-a-dish that is ready in one hour

6 lean pork chops	**6 carrots, cut in 1″ pieces**
½ tsp. salt	**(2 c.)**
¼ tsp. pepper	**1½ c. coarsely chopped**
1 tblsp. cooking oil	**onion**
½ tsp. dried savory leaves	**3 medium potatoes, pared**
½ bay leaf	**and quartered**
2 c. tomato juice	**¼ tsp. salt**
½ c. water	
1 small cabbage, cut in 6	
wedges	

Season pork chops with ½ tsp. salt and pepper. Brown chops in hot oil in a large skillet. Add savory, bay leaf, tomato juice and water. Cover and simmer 30 minutes.

Add cabbage, carrots, onion, potatoes and ¼ tsp. salt. Cover. Cook for 35 minutes or until vegetables are tender. Makes 6 servings.

LIVER DUMPLINGS

These German dumplings can be served either in the broth or removed and served as the main course on a bed of tangy sauerkraut. Dip tablespoon in hot broth before dipping into dumpling batter—batter will slide right off the spoon into the hot soup. Dumplings are done when they bob to the surface. Sprinkle with chopped green parsley.

LIVER DUMPLINGS

Parsley-topped, liver dumpling soup makes a tasty first course

4 strips bacon	1 tsp. salt
1½ lbs. beef liver	¼ tsp. pepper
2 tblsp. dry bread crumbs	1 c. flour
½ c. minced onion	3 qts. beef broth
2 eggs, beaten	Chopped fresh parsley

Fry bacon until brown and crisp. Remove and drain on paper towels. Crumble; set aside.

Put liver through coarse blade of food grinder. Combine ground liver, reserved bacon, bread crumbs, onion, eggs, salt, pepper and flour; mix well.

Bring beef broth to a boil in a large kettle. Dip teaspoon into hot broth and then into dumpling mixture, filling ½ full. Drop half of this mixture into boiling broth. Cook in boiling broth 15 minutes or until dumplings rise to surface. Remove dumplings and keep hot. Repeat with remaining mixture, adding more broth if needed. Serve dumplings with broth as a soup and garnish with parsley. Dumplings can also be drained and served with sauerkraut. Makes 6 to 8 servings.

CHICKEN AND PRUNE FRICASSEE

Germans are partial to dried fruits cooked along with meat or poultry. And they always add a bit of spice—a dash of cinnamon or a touch of clove or ginger.

This heirloom from Germany tastes even better the second day, according to the farm wife who sent us this recipe. It is a "must" at their Thanksgiving and Christmas dinners. The family agrees that no one can make it quite like Mom, even though they follow her recipe.

Sometimes dried apricots are substituted for the prunes and it is served with jumbo dumplings.

CHICKEN AND PRUNE FRICASSEE

Succulent, moist chicken pieces served with a gently spiced sauce

½ c. flour
2 tsp. salt
2 (3 lb.) broiler-fryers,
   cut-up
⅓ c. cooking oil
1½ c. pitted prunes
2 c. chicken broth

2 sticks cinnamon
2 strips fresh ginger root
   (2″ long)
1 tblsp. brown sugar, firmly
   packed
3 tblsp. water

Combine flour and salt. Coat chicken pieces with flour mixture. (Reserve remaining flour mixture to thicken sauce.)

Brown chicken on all sides in hot oil in Dutch oven. Remove chicken as it browns. Put chicken back into Dutch oven. Add prunes, chicken broth, cinnamon, ginger root and brown sugar. Bring to a boil. Reduce heat and cover. Simmer 40 minutes or until chicken is tender.

Combine reserved flour mixture with water. Remove chicken and prunes to serving platter and keep warm. Bring sauce to a boil. Slowly stir in flour and water mixture. Boil 2 minutes, stirring constantly. Spoon some of the sauce over the chicken. Pour remaining sauce into serving bowl. Delicious served with rice. Makes 8 servings.

GERMAN BREAD DRESSING

A great-great-grandmother brought this recipe from Germany, but each generation changed it a trifle. The latest revision was the addition of toasted, slivered almonds for crunch and flavor in this marvelous, moist dressing that complements roast goose, duck or turkey. On a cold winter day this Illinois homemaker often makes a pan of the stuffing and browns some sausages for a hearty supper. Fresh, buttered spinach and applesauce complete the meal.

GERMAN BREAD DRESSING

Do try stuffing your next turkey with this popular bread dressing

1 c. chopped celery and celery leaves	3 c. diced unpared apples
½ c. chopped onion	1 c. raisins
1 c. butter or regular margarine	1 c. toasted, slivered almonds
1 (10¾ oz.) can condensed chicken broth	3 eggs, beaten
4 qts. soft bread cubes (½″)	½ tsp. salt
	⅛ tsp. ground cinnamon
	⅛ tsp. pepper

Sauté celery and onion in melted butter in skillet until tender (do not brown).

Add enough water to chicken broth to make 2½ cups.

Combine sautéed vegetables, bread cubes, apples, raisins, almonds, eggs, salt, cinnamon, pepper and chicken broth mixture. Toss gently to mix. Place dressing in greased 13×9×2″ baking dish. Cover with aluminum foil.

Bake in 325° oven 1 hour 15 minutes. Uncover and bake 15 more minutes or until top is golden brown. Makes 8 servings.

EMILIE'S ONION/SAGE DRESSING

A three-generation heirloom, this dressing has been part of a family's holiday meal since the early 1800s. A big pan of dressing is baked the day before the holiday; the flavor improves when it's reheated. But this is also a year-round dressing in this Iowa farm home. It's perfect with pork chops, baked chicken, and the crew especially likes it layered with hamburger and baked—a hearty substantial after a long day in the fields.

EMILIE'S ONION/SAGE DRESSING

To reheat, place in a skillet with a little water and cover

1½ lb. loaf day-old, whole wheat bread, broken in pieces	2 c. chopped celery and celery leaves
1 qt. milk	2 eggs, beaten
1 lb. bulk pork sausage	2 tblsp. rubbed sage
4 c. chopped onion	1 tsp. salt
	⅛ tsp. pepper

Soak bread in milk.

Sauté sausage in 10″ skillet. When meat begins to turn color, add onion and celery. Cook until mixture is well browned.

Add sausage mixture, eggs, sage, salt and pepper to bread mixture; mix lightly. Place dressing in greased 13×9×2″ baking dish.

Bake in 350° oven 45 minutes or until dressing is golden brown. Makes 8 servings.

HOMEMADE GERMAN NOODLES

Homemade noodles often replace potatoes as a meat accompaniment in a German meal. Usually they are boiled, drained and tossed with melted butter. The seasoning depends upon the family's taste. Some like just salt and pepper, while others like crumbled bacon or toasted bread crumbs mingled through the noodles. Thin noodles are preferred for soups, while wider ribbons are popular in hearty stews.

HOMEMADE GERMAN NOODLES

Tender egg-rich noodles are perfect with pot roast and brown gravy

2 c. sifted flour	**3 egg yolks, beaten**
½ tsp. salt	**½ c. lukewarm water**

Combine flour and salt. Stir in egg yolks and water; mix well. Knead on floured surface until smooth and elastic, about 5 minutes. Let dough rest 30 minutes.

Roll out to 18″ square. Let dry 1 hour.

Roll up loosely like jelly roll. Cut dough into ¼″ strips. Unroll strips. Cut in 4″ lengths. Lay out to dry again 1 hour.

Cook in 3 qts. boiling, salted water 18 minutes or until noodles are tender.

Drain in colander. Rinse with hot water. Drain well. Noodles can be served buttered with crumbs or as you would serve packaged noodles. Makes 6 servings.

GERMAN MILK SOUP

There is a quart of milk in this soup, which gives this dish its name. An American farm woman's ancestors brought this soup from Germany in 1810. Several generations ago it was no doubt the mainstay of their diet, as dried beef and vegetables were plentiful. This generation consumes generous portions after a day of skiing and it's a success on their camping trips, too. All the sons have taken the recipe to college and fixed it for their roommates —it makes a big hit every time.

GERMAN MILK SOUP

Serve soup piping hot with lots of homemade biscuits

2 c. chopped onion	**3 c. diced carrots (¼″ cubes)**
1 c. sliced celery	**2 tsp. salt**
¼ c. butter or regular margarine	**⅛ tsp. pepper**
	3 c. water
4½ c. diced pared potatoes (¼″ cubes)	**4 oz. dried beef, cut up**
	1 qt. milk
4 c. coarsely chopped cabbage	**1 c. light cream**

Sauté onion and celery in melted butter in 6-qt. kettle until tender (do not brown).

Add potatoes, cabbage, carrots, salt, pepper and water. Cover. Bring to a boil; reduce heat and simmer until vegetables are tender, about 30 minutes.

Add dried beef, milk and cream. Heat well over low heat (do not boil). Makes about 3 quarts or 9 servings.

CREAM OF TOMATO SOUP

Grated potato makes this a delightfully different tomato soup. Delicately flavored with savory, this soup can be made with fresh tomatoes as well as canned. According to a Michigan farm woman, this zesty soup has been in her family since 1815 when her ancestors came to Michigan from the Old Country. Though she has made the recipe with fresh tomatoes from the garden, her family prefers it when she makes a big batch with her home-canned tomatoes. Everyone has two big helpings of soup and several homemade baking powder biscuits—and creamy rice pudding for dessert. This is a family-request supper at least three times a month in cold weather. If there is any left over, the children take a Thermos of Mom's soup in their lunch box.

CREAM OF TOMATO SOUP

Tomatoes and potatoes are simmered to perfection in this soup

1 (1 lb.) can stewed
tomatoes
2⅓ c. grated pared potatoes
1½ c. chopped onion
2 tblsp. butter or regular
margarine
2 c. water

1 tsp. sugar
1 tsp. salt
½ tsp. summer savory leaves
¼ tsp. pepper
¼ tsp. baking soda
4 c. milk

Combine tomatoes, potatoes, onion, butter and water in Dutch oven. Cover. Bring to a boil; reduce heat and simmer 50 minutes or until potatoes are tender.

Add sugar, salt, savory, pepper and baking soda; mix well. Gradually stir in milk. Heat over low heat. (Do not boil.) Makes about 1½ quarts or 5 servings.

GREEN BEAN AND PORK SOUP

A young German bride brought this recipe to this country in 1865. It was one of the treasures that she brought with her from the homeland and has survived 3 generations. Today her great-granddaughter serves this hearty soup. And it is so nourishing, with a double boost of protein in pork and navy beans. Making this soup is a family tradition when the first beans have been picked from the garden. Each serving is topped with bread cubes that have been sautéed in butter until they are crunchy and golden brown.

GREEN BEAN AND PORK SOUP

Traditionally prunes are substituted for green beans in winter

1 lb. dried navy beans
2 lb. boneless pork shoulder
roast
2 c. chopped onion
2 bay leaves
1½ tsp. salt

2 qts. water
4 c. diced pared potatoes
4 c. cut-up green beans
(1½″ pieces)
2 c. chopped carrots

Wash beans. Cover with water; let stand overnight.

Pour off soaking water; rinse and drain well.

Combine beans, pork, onion, bay leaves, salt and water in 6-qt. kettle. Cover. Bring to a boil; reduce heat and simmer 3 hours or until meat and beans are tender.

Add potatoes, green beans and carrots. Cook, covered, 40 more minutes or until vegetables are tender. Remove pork and cut into chunks. Add pork back to soup mixture. Makes about 3 quarts or 9 servings.

HEARTY SPLIT PEA SOUP

German cooks are artists when it comes to making soup. In Germany there is a soup for every occasion. For a first course, perhaps a clear broth that has been simmered to just the right strength and flavor or a rich, cream soup—green asparagus is a top favorite in the spring. These thrifty cooks have a knack of turning an assortment of leftovers into a rich, nourishing meal.

One of the most popular soups is the Hearty Split Pea Soup, popular with German descendants in the United States. In fact, every family has its special way of preparing this protein-rich soup. For some it must be thick with potatoes and carrots; for others it must have besides the ham some thick slices of bratwurst. Members of each family think their soup is the very best!

HEARTY SPLIT PEA SOUP

Pass lots of crisp saltines with this rib-sticking, homemade soup

3 ham hocks (1½ lbs.)	**8 c. water**
1 lb. dried split peas	**1 tsp. salt**
1¼ c. chopped carrots	**4 whole peppercorns**
(¼″ cubes)	**4 whole allspice**
½ c. sliced onion	**1 bay leaf**

Combine ham hocks, peas, carrots, onion, water and salt in Dutch oven. Cover. Bring to a boil.

Meanwhile, tie peppercorns, allspice and bay leaf in a small piece of cheesecloth. Add to pea mixture. Reduce heat and simmer 45 minutes or until peas are tender. Discard spice bag.

Remove ham hocks from soup mixture. Remove meat from bones. Discard bones. Cut ham up into chunks and add back to soup mixture. Makes 2 quarts or 6 servings.

CREAM OF POTATO SOUP

This hearty, rib-sticking soup has been served in a Wisconsin family for 3 generations. It has been the favorite cold weather supper dish since great-grandmother arrived from Germany. Potatoes, milk and cream were plentiful and it was an economical way to feed a large family. Bowls were filled to brimming and a platter of grilled cheese sandwiches rounded out the meal. Sometimes thin slices of sausage were added as garnish.

CREAM OF POTATO SOUP

Your family will welcome this soup for lunch on a cold day

3 lbs. potatoes, pared and cut up (9 medium)	2½ c. milk
	1 c. light cream
4 whole carrots, pared	⅛ tsp. pepper
1 c. chopped onion	1 tblsp. minced fresh parsley
1½ tsp. salt	

Place potatoes, carrots, onion and salt in Dutch oven. Add water to cover vegetables. Cover. Bring to a boil; reduce heat and simmer 20 minutes or until vegetables are tender.

Drain well. Remove carrots; set aside.

Mash potatoes well with potato masher. Gradually add milk and light cream, mixing well after each addition. Add pepper and parsley. Coarsely chop carrots and add to soup. Heat soup to serve (do not boil). Makes 2 quarts or 6 servings.

RED CABBAGE WITH APPLES

While the pot roast is cooking in a German household or in an American household of German descent—the red cabbage and apples are simmering to tangy goodness. These two foods taste wonderful together. All that is missing is a big bowl of fluffy mashed potatoes or giant dumplings—and deep-brown, rich gravy to ladle over meat and potatoes.

RED CABBAGE WITH APPLES

A tasty vegetable combination that accents both meat and poultry

1 medium head red cabbage, cut in ⅛" strips (about 2 lbs.)	2 tblsp. butter or regular margarine
2 medium apples, pared, cored and cut in ⅛" slices	½ c. red wine vinegar 1 bay leaf
½ c. chopped onion	2 tblsp. sugar ½ tsp. salt

Cook cabbage, apples and onion in melted butter in large skillet or Dutch oven 5 minutes, stirring often.

Add vinegar, bay leaf, sugar and salt. Cover. Bring mixture to a boil; reduce heat and simmer 35 minutes or until cabbage is tender. Remove bay leaf. Makes 12 servings.

HOMEMADE SAUERKRAUT

There are hundreds of methods for preparing sauerkraut that are regional as well as personal. Some cooks like to simmer the kraut until it's very soft and limp. Others like a bit of crunch and reduce the cooking period. The liquids that sauerkraut is simmered in are numerous. Plain water, apple juice and beef bouillon are a few favorites. Caraway seeds are a popular addition. Some cooks always grate a little raw potato into the simmering kraut while flour is often added as a thickener. Then there's the theory that kraut should *never* be thickened.

HOMEMADE SAUERKRAUT

Always rinse sauerkraut with warm water before you use it

You will need roughly 5 lbs. cabbage for every gal. of your crock. For instance, a 10-gal. crock would need about 50 lbs. of cabbage.

Quarter cabbage and shred finely. Place 5 lbs. shredded cabbage and 3½ tblsp. pickling salt in large pan. Mix well with hands. Pack gently in large crock, using a potato masher to press it down. Repeat above procedure until crock is filled to within 5" from the top.

Press cabbage down firmly with potato masher to extract enough juice to cover. Cover with clean cloth. Place a plate on top and weight it down with a jar filled with water.

Keep crock at 65° to ferment. Check kraut daily. Remove scum as it forms. Wash and scald cloth often to keep it free from scum and mold. Fermentation will be complete in 10 to 12 days. (If no bubbles rise, fermentation has ended.)

Pack in hot, sterilized jars to within 1" from top. Add enough juice to cover. If you need more juice, make a weak brine by combining 2 tblsp. salt and 1 qt. water. Cover; screw band tight. Process in boiling water bath 15 minutes. Fifty pounds of sauerkraut makes about 15 quarts.

SPRING LETTUCE SALAD

After a long winter of eating root vegetables, Germans welcomed the first tender leaves of spring lettuce. And the first batch was washed, crisped and coated with a tasty dressing made with light cream, vinegar and sugar. Then the final touch was added —a garnish of chopped eggs and crisp bits of bacon.

"The recipe has been in our family for years, can't imagine any German surviving without it," the Ohio contributor wrote us.

SPRING LETTUCE SALAD

Fresh spinach can be substituted for all or part of the lettuce

4 strips bacon	1 c. light cream
1 tblsp. flour	3 qts. bite-size pieces
1 tblsp. sugar	romaine or leaf lettuce
1 tsp. salt	3 hard-cooked eggs,
2 tblsp. vinegar	chopped

Fry bacon in skillet until crisp. Remove and drain on paper towels. Crumble; set aside.

Pour off bacon drippings, reserving 3 tblsp. Stir in flour, sugar, salt, vinegar and cream. Cook over low heat, stirring constantly, until mixture thickens slightly.

Pour hot mixture over lettuce, eggs and reserved bacon. Toss gently to mix. Serve immediately. Makes 10 servings.

PEARS AND POTATOES

An Oklahoma woman studied violin at the Royal Conservatory in Germany when she was a young girl. One of the dishes she enjoyed was Pears and Potatoes and she carefully copied the recipe.

We found this to be a very different dish and the combination of the fruit and vegetable was subtle and delicious. It's a wonderful accompaniment to a pork roast.

PEARS AND POTATOES

This unusual dish is even better when prepared ahead and reheated

4 strips bacon, diced	3½ c. thickly sliced pared
3½ c. thickly sliced pared	pears (about 4 medium)
potatoes (about 1¼ lbs.)	¼ c. vinegar
1 tsp. salt	1 bay leaf
1 c. hot water	¼ tsp. ground allspice

Fry bacon in Dutch oven until crisp. Remove and drain on paper towels. Crumble and set aside.

Add potatoes, salt and water to bacon drippings. Cover. Bring to a boil; reduce heat and simmer 25 minutes or until potatoes are tender.

Add pears, vinegar, bay leaf, allspice and reserved bacon. Cover and simmer 15 more minutes or until pears are tender. Makes 6 servings.

GERMAN HOT POTATO SALAD

This recipe for tangy potato salad has been in an Illinois family recipe file for 43 years. Every year they have met for a family reunion in August and there's always plenty of this salad on hand to eat with the grilled frankfurters.

The touch of rosemary adds an interesting flavor. There is plenty of dressing and it's perfect—not too sweet and not too tangy.

GERMAN HOT POTATO SALAD

Leftover salad is best if warmed slightly before serving

8 slices bacon, diced	**⅔ c. cider vinegar**
3 tblsp. flour	**⅔ c. water**
⅓ c. sugar	**8 c. diced, cooked potatoes**
3 tsp. salt	**(about 4 lbs.)**
1 tsp. dry mustard	**½ c. chopped onion**
¼ tsp. rosemary leaves	**⅓ c. chopped fresh parsley**
⅛ tsp. pepper	

Fry bacon in 10" skillet until crisp. Stir in flour, sugar, salt, mustard, rosemary, pepper, vinegar and water. Cook over medium heat, stirring constantly, until mixture thickens.

Pour hot sauce over potatoes, onion and parsley. Toss gently to mix. Serve warm. Makes 10 servings.

GERMAN-STYLE POTATO SALAD

Another potato salad that has been around for 75 years—every German family has a pet recipe for this zippy hot salad. And everyone has very definite ideas about ingredients and the balance of sugar and vinegar. This family's recipe calls for sliced potatoes and chopped celery for a little crunch. The thickening is cornstarch rather than flour—some cooks feel it produces a more translucent sauce.

GERMAN-STYLE POTATO SALAD

Everyone will ask for seconds when you serve this tangy salad

5 lbs. new potatoes	**1 tblsp. salt**
1 tblsp. salt	**¼ tsp. pepper**
½ lb. bacon	**2 c. water**
2 tblsp. cornstarch	**1 c. chopped onion**
½ c. vinegar	**½ c. chopped celery**
¼ c. sugar	

Cook potatoes with jackets and 1 tblsp. salt in boiling water until tender, about 30 minutes. Drain. Cool.

Remove peels. Cut potatoes into thin slices.

Fry bacon in skillet until crisp. Remove and drain on paper towels. Crumble bacon; set aside.

Pour off all but ½ c. bacon drippings. Combine cornstarch and vinegar; stir well. Add cornstarch mixture, sugar, 1 tblsp. salt, pepper and water to bacon drippings. Cook over medium heat, stirring constantly, until mixture thickens.

Pour hot sauce over combined potatoes, onion, celery and reserved bacon. Toss gently to mix. Makes 12 servings.

GERMAN POTATO PANCAKES

Crisp and crunchy around the edges, these potato pancakes are great to serve for luncheon or supper. Be sure and have a big bowl of homemade applesauce to eat along with them. Many German families make a complete meal of pancakes and applesauce. A different way to serve potatoes with thin slices of leftover pot roast.

GERMAN POTATO PANCAKES

Also good served with browned pork sausages and apple rings

2 lbs. potatoes, pared and grated (5 c.)	1 tsp. salt
	⅔ c. cooking oil
6 tblsp. flour	Applesauce
¼ c. minced onion	Pancake syrup
2 eggs, beaten	

Combine potatoes, flour, onion, eggs and salt; mix well.

Bake pancakes in hot oil in 10″ skillet, using ¼ c. mixture for each. Cook over medium heat, 4 minutes on each side, or until golden brown and potatoes are tender. Serve with applesauce or pancake syrup. Makes 14 (3½″) pancakes.

POPPY SEED ROLL

This most favorite recipe has been treasured through several generations in a Montana home. It's a great specialty of this German community and a "must" at all family reunions. Poppy seed filling is what makes this so good. The poppy seeds are ground in a coffee grinder or electric blender and mixed with sugar, corn syrup, eggs and cream or evaporated milk—the secret is to spread it thickly, at least ½″ thick on the dough before it's rolled tightly and baked. A 94-year-old German lady from Montana was thrilled when she sampled one of these Poppy Seed Rolls. Her eyes lighted up as she said, "Ah, Moon Kuchen—that's what we call it in the Old Country."

POPPY SEED ROLL

A German coffee bread that's rolled up like a jelly roll

½ c. butter or regular margarine	7 c. sifted flour
⅔ c. sugar	2 c. poppy seeds
1 tblsp. salt	1 c. sugar
2 eggs, beaten	½ c. light corn syrup
2 pkgs. active dry yeast	1 egg, beaten
1 c. lukewarm water	3 tblsp. evaporated milk
1 c. milk, scalded and cooled	

Cream together butter and ⅔ c. sugar until light and fluffy. Add salt and 2 eggs, beating well.

Sprinkle yeast on lukewarm water; stir to dissolve. Add yeast and milk to butter mixture; mix well.

Gradually add enough flour to make a very soft dough. (Dough is sticky.) Place in lightly greased bowl; turn dough over to grease top. Cover and let rise in warm place until doubled, about 1½ hours.

Meanwhile, prepare poppy seed filling. Grind poppy seeds in blender, ½ c. at a time, until smooth. Combine ground poppy seeds, 1 c. sugar, corn syrup, 1 egg and evaporated milk; mix well.

Divide dough in fourths. Roll on floured surface to 15×12" rectangle. Spread with ½ c. of poppy seed mixture. Roll up like jelly roll and pinch seam together. Place on greased baking sheet, seam side down. Repeat with remaining dough.

Bake in 350° oven 20 to 25 minutes or until golden brown. Makes 4 rolls.

STREUSEL KUCHEN

"Just the mention of this Streusel Kuchen has been known to cause pangs of homesickness," a 90-year-old German woman from California says. She received the recipe years ago from a

German immigrant who every Thursday morning would make 3 batches of this luscious crumbed cake. Then there was plenty for anyone who dropped in for coffee or a chat for the tripled recipe made an even dozen. We baked 2 batches, one with the Streusel Topping and the other with a thick coating of brown sugar. They freeze beautifully—good to have on hand for any generation.

STREUSEL KUCHEN

Serve these crumb-topped wedges with plenty of soft, creamy butter

½ c. butter or regular margarine	2 c. milk, scalded and cooled
1 c. sugar	7 c. sifted flour
1 tsp. salt	¼ c. melted butter or regular margarine
1 egg, separated	Streusel Topping (recipe follows)
1 pkg. active dry yeast	
⅓ c. lukewarm water	

Cream together ½ c. butter and sugar until light and fluffy. Add salt and egg yolk, beating well.

Sprinkle yeast on lukewarm water; stir to dissolve. Combine yeast and milk. Add to creamed mixture alternately with flour, mixing well after each addition.

Beat egg white until stiff peaks form. Fold into mixture. Cover bowl with plastic wrap. Refrigerate 8 hours or overnight.

Divide dough in fourths. Pat dough in 4 greased 9″ pie plates. Cover and let rise in a warm place until light, about 1 hour 30 minutes.

Brush kuchens with ¼ c. melted butter. Sprinkle with Streusel Topping.

Bake in 400° oven 20 minutes or until golden. Makes 4 kuchens.

Streusel Topping: Combine ¼ c. flour, ½ c. sugar and 1 tsp. ground cinnamon. Cut in 3 tblsp. butter or regular margarine until mixture is crumbly. Add 1 tsp. vanilla and ¼ c. finely chopped walnuts; mix well.

GERMAN CHRISTMAS BREAD

While many recipes that were brought to this country from Europe remained intact through the years, some were revised and adjusted to suit the family's taste. This German Christmas Bread is an example. The recipe always had citron and white raisins as ingredients but a daughter chose to put 1 tablespoon of citron instead of ½ cup and often omitted it completely. Her family loved raisins so a cup of dark raisins was added, along with a little grated lemon rind. This Nebraska farm woman always makes several batches of fruit-studded bread during the Christmas holidays just as her mother did for years of family celebrations.

GERMAN CHRISTMAS BREAD

Decorate with bits of candied fruits for a more festive look

1½ c. milk, scalded
¼ c. sugar
1 tblsp. salt
2 pkgs. active dry yeast
½ c. lukewarm water
3 eggs
6½ c. sifted flour

1 tsp. grated lemon peel
¼ c. melted butter or
   regular margarine
1 c. golden raisins
1 c. dark raisins
Thin Glaze (recipe follows)

Combine milk, sugar and salt; cool to lukewarm.

Sprinkle yeast over lukewarm water; stir to dissolve. Add yeast, eggs and 2 c. flour to milk mixture. Beat with electric mixer at medium speed until smooth, about 2 minutes, scraping bowl occasionally. Or beat with spoon until smooth.

Add lemon peel, butter and enough remaining flour to make a soft dough that leaves the sides of the bowl.

Turn dough onto lightly floured surface. Knead in raisins. Continue kneading until smooth and satiny, about 10 minutes.

Place dough in greased bowl; turn over to grease top. Cover and let rise in warm place until doubled, about 1 hour 30 minutes.

Divide dough in thirds. Shape each into 8″ round loaf. Place on greased baking sheets. Let rise until doubled, about 1 hour 30 minutes.

Bake in 350° oven 30 to 35 minutes or until golden brown. Cool 10 minutes on racks. Frost with Thin Glaze. Makes 3 coffee cakes.

Thin Glaze: Combine 1 c. sifted confectioners sugar, 2 tsp. soft butter or regular margarine, 2 tblsp. milk and 1 tsp. vanilla; beat until smooth.

OLD-FASHIONED GERMAN KUCHEN

If you visited all the different German communities that dot the Midwest and collected kuchen recipes, you would no doubt have enough to turn out a cookbook on kuchen alone. Every one varies from the other in richness, toppings, shapes and sizes. But they are all buttery and crunchy with nuts and sugar—some of the best sweet doughs in the land. This old-fashioned kuchen is a fine-textured dough, lavish with butter and filled generously with nuts, sugar and cinnamon. Good recipe for the holiday as one batch makes 4 beautiful tea rings. For a bright holiday appearance, substitute chopped maraschino cherries for half the walnuts and decorate the glazed top with bright green citron.

OLD-FASHIONED GERMAN KUCHEN

Freeze these buttery coffee cakes for the Christmas holidays

4 c. sifted flour	½ c. melted butter or
3 tblsp. sugar	regular margarine
½ tsp. salt	1 c. sugar
1 c. shortening	1½ c. finely chopped
1 pkg. active dry yeast	walnuts
¼ c. lukewarm water	1½ tsp. ground cinnamon
1 c. cold milk	Thin Vanilla Icing (recipe
3 egg yolks, beaten	follows)

Combine flour, 3 tblsp. sugar and salt. Cut in shortening with pastry blender or two knives until mixture is crumbly.

Sprinkle yeast over lukewarm water; stir to dissolve. Add yeast, milk and egg yolks to crumb mixture; stir until blended. Cover with aluminum foil or plastic wrap. Refrigerate 12 hours or overnight.

Divide dough into fourths. Roll each on floured surface to 14×11″ rectangle. Brush with melted butter. Sprinkle with combined 1 c. sugar, walnuts and cinnamon. Roll up like jelly roll from narrow side. Pinch seam together. Place on greased baking sheets. Form into a circle; pinch ends together. With floured scissors, make cuts ⅔ of the way through ring at 1″ intervals. Turn each cut section on its side. Let rise until doubled, about 2 hours.

Bake in 350° oven 20 to 25 minutes or until golden brown. Cool on racks. Frost with Thin Vanilla Icing. Makes 4 coffee rings.

Thin Vanilla Icing: Combine 1½ c. sifted confectioners sugar, 1 tblsp. soft butter or regular margarine, 2 tblsp. hot water and 1 tsp. vanilla; beat until smooth.

GERMAN PANCAKES

A New England farm woman grew up with these pancakes. She remembers how she loved to spread the golden pancake with butter, cinnamon and sugar, then roll it up and eat it out of hand. This versatile pancake can serve as dessert or as the main course. Her children love them for every meal: In the morning filled with sausage, at lunch sprinkled with grated cheese and for dessert spread thickly with homemade strawberry jam.

GERMAN PANCAKES

Protein-rich pancakes that are so versatile . . . serve them often

1½ c. sifted flour	2 c. milk
⅔ c. sugar	Red raspberry jelly
1 tsp. salt	Confectioners sugar
4 eggs, beaten	

Sift together flour, sugar and salt.

Combine eggs and milk. Add to flour mixture. Beat with rotary beater until smooth.

Pour ½ c. batter into lightly greased 10″ skillet, tilting skillet back and forth until it coats the bottom evenly. When lightly browned, loosen edges with metal spatula and turn over. Spread pancakes with raspberry jelly and roll up. Dust with confectioners sugar. Makes 6 (10″) pancakes.

BAVARIAN APPLE STRUDEL

Be sure to remove your rings before working with this delicate dough, which you stretch into a tissue-thin sheet. This is one of the most famous German desserts. The finished product with its spiced, apple-raisin filling is handsome when removed from the oven. The dough is golden brown and crisp as a parchment.

BAVARIAN APPLE STRUDEL

This flaky strudel is also delicious made with cherry pie filling

1 tblsp. cooking oil	¼ c. sugar
1 egg, beaten	1 tsp. ground cinnamon
⅓ c. lukewarm water	⅓ c. melted butter or
¼ tsp. salt	regular margarine
1½ c. sifted flour	⅓ c. dry bread crumbs
8 c. sliced pared tart apples	Confectioners sugar
1 c. raisins	

Combine oil, egg, water and salt. Gradually add flour, beating with spoon until a firm dough that pulls away from the sides of the bowl is formed.

Knead dough on floured surface until smooth and elastic, about 5 minutes. Cover and let rest 30 minutes.

Combine apples, raisins, sugar and cinnamon; set aside.

Divide dough in half. Roll each half into 18×12″ rectangle, stretching dough if necessary to make it very thin. Brush with melted butter. Sprinkle dough with half of bread crumbs. Spread half of apple mixture lengthwise in center third of dough. Fold dough over apples on one side and then the other. Brush with melted butter. Place on greased baking sheet. Repeat with remaining dough.

Bake in 400° oven 30 minutes or until golden brown and apples are tender. Serve warm or cold sprinkled with confectioners sugar. Makes 16 servings.

INDIVIDUAL SCHAUM TORTES

This delicate meringue dessert is one of the most elegant and special German desserts . . . pale amber and crunchy on the outside, soft and marshmallowy inside. When strawberries are in season this makes a mouth-watering dessert. Fill the individual meringues with strawberries and frost with a cloud of whipped cream. This tastes equally good with sliced peaches—makes a lovely party dessert to impress your guests.

INDIVIDUAL SCHAUM TORTES

Meringues store well in covered containers for up to two weeks

8 egg whites	2 qts. fresh strawberries,
½ tsp. cream of tartar	sliced and sweetened or
2 c. sugar	3 (10 oz.) pkgs. frozen
1 tsp. vanilla	strawberries, thawed
1 tsp. vinegar	2 c. heavy cream, whipped
	and sweetened

Beat egg whites with electric mixer at high speed until frothy. Add cream of tartar. Beat until egg whites are almost dry.

Slowly add sugar, 2 tblsp. at a time, beating well after each addition. (Total beating time: 20 minutes.) Add vanilla and vinegar, beat 2 minutes. (Mixture should be very stiff and glossy.) Drop mixture by spoonfuls onto greased baking sheets, making 10 tortes.

Bake in 250° oven 1 hour 15 minutes or until pale brown and crusty. Remove from baking sheets; cool on racks.

To serve: Spoon strawberries over each torte and top with whipped cream. Makes 10 servings.

SPICY MOLASSES COOKIES

A young farm girl in Wisconsin baked a batch of her great aunt's German molasses cookies. She offered several along with a glass of lemonade to a neighboring farm boy who was baling hay. After he had demolished 3 cookies and 2 glasses of lemonade he asked her for a date. "Now, I bake them for him and our children every week," she says.

SPICY MOLASSES COOKIES

Crisp and extra spicy cookies that will make a hit every time

1 c. shortening	1 tblsp. ground cinnamon
2 c. sugar	1 tblsp. ground ginger
2 eggs	1 tsp. salt
¾ c. dark molasses	1 tsp. baking powder
1½ tsp. lemon extract	1 tsp. baking soda
5 c. sifted flour	2 tblsp. vinegar

Cream together shortening and sugar until light and fluffy. Add eggs; beat well. Beat in molasses and lemon extract.

Sift together flour, cinnamon, ginger, salt, baking powder and baking soda. Add to creamed mixture with vinegar; mix well.

Roll dough out on floured surface to ⅛" thick. Cut with floured 2" cookie cutter. Place cookies about 1½" apart on greased baking sheets.

Bake in 350° oven 6 to 8 minutes or until brown. Remove from baking sheets; cool on racks. Makes about 15 dozen.

DATE/RAISIN CAKE

According to an Ohio woman's family history her German ancestors settled in Maryland. After fighting in an Ohio regiment

her grandfather moved his family to an Ohio farm and
nine children. This spicy cake was his favorite and he
raised a fuss when it was frosted—a dusting of powdered
was all it needed, he felt.

DATE/RAISIN CAKE

Moist-crumbed raisin cake that is great to eat out of hand

⅔ c. butter or regular margarine	1 tsp. ground allspice
2 c. brown sugar, firmly packed	½ tsp. ground ginger
	½ tsp. salt
2 eggs	1 c. warm coffee
3¼ c. sifted flour	1 c. raisins
2 tsp. baking powder	1 c. cut-up dates
1½ tsp. ground cinnamon	1 c. chopped walnuts
1 tsp. baking soda	1 tblsp. flour
	Confectioners sugar

Cream together butter and brown sugar until light and fluffy.
Add eggs, one at a time, beating well after each addition.

Sift together 3¼ c. flour, baking powder, cinnamon, baking
soda, allspice, ginger and salt. Add dry ingredients to creamed
mixture alternately with coffee, beating well after each addition.

Combine raisins, dates, walnuts and 1 tblsp. flour; mix well.
Stir into batter. Spread batter in greased 13×9×2″ baking pan.

Bake in 350° oven 35 minutes or until cake tests done. Cool.
Sprinkle with confectioners sugar. Cut in 3″ squares. Makes 12
servings.

BLITZ TORTE

A typical German torte, this is a 3-layered beauty. Cake layers
are topped with meringue and baked. Then the layers are filled
with a rich, sour cream mixture and sliced bananas. For those
who worry about calories, substitute a thin layer of whipped
cream and sliced peaches for the sour cream filling. Delicious
both ways!

BLITZ TORTE

A favorite in this Wisconsin family for over four generations

¼ c. butter or regular margarine	¾ c. sugar
	½ c. chopped walnuts
½ c. sugar	5 tblsp. sugar
4 eggs, separated	1 tblsp. cornstarch
1 tsp. vanilla	1 c. dairy sour cream
1 c. sifted flour	1 egg, beaten
1½ tsp. baking powder	1 large banana, sliced
5 tblsp. milk	

Cream together butter and ½ c. sugar until light and fluffy. Add 4 egg yolks and vanilla; beat well.

Sift together flour and baking powder. Add dry ingredients alternately with milk, beating well after each addition. Spread batter in 2 greased and floured 8″ round cake pans.

Beat 4 egg whites until frothy. Gradually add ¾ c. sugar, beating until soft peaks form. Spread meringue carefully over cake batter in both pans. Sprinkle walnuts on top of each.

Bake in 350° oven 30 minutes or until cakes test done. Cool in pans 10 minutes. Remove from pans; cool on racks, meringue side up.

Combine 5 tblsp. sugar and cornstarch in small saucepan. Add sour cream and egg; mix well. Cook over low heat, stirring constantly, until mixture thickens, about 10 minutes.

Place one cake layer, meringue side up, on serving plate. Spread with cream filling. Top with banana slices. Top with other cake layer, meringue side up. Makes 10 servings.

GERMAN REFRIGERATOR COOKIES

Light, golden cookies with crackled tops—a Christmas heirloom always served during the holidays. Cardamom is used in these and many other German cookies and breads during the Christmas season. The crushed ivory-colored cardamom pod adds a special flavor.

GERMAN REFRIGERATOR COOKIES

"I don't remember a Christmas that we didn't have dozens of these"

½ c. butter or regular margarine	1 egg
½ c. lard	2 c. sifted flour
2 c. sugar	1 tsp. baking soda
	½ tsp. ground cardamom

Cream together butter, lard and sugar until light and fluffy. Add egg; beat well.

Sift together flour, baking soda and cardamom. Stir into creamed mixture; mix well. Cover and refrigerate overnight.

Shape dough into 1″ balls. Place about 1½″ apart on greased baking sheets.

Bake in 325° oven 10 minutes or until golden brown. Remove from baking sheets; cool on racks. Makes 5 dozen.

CARAMEL BREAD PUDDING

"My German grandmother always made this simple bread pudding for family and company. The rich caramel sauce made it extra-special," an Indiana farm woman told us. She said it was wholesome, lip-smacking good. We agree. This easy-to-fix dessert simmers for an hour and needs no stirring. Equally good hot or cold.

CARAMEL BREAD PUDDING

A three-layer bread pudding laced with a rich caramel custard

2 tblsp. butter or regular margarine	6 eggs
1 c. light brown sugar, firmly packed	½ c. light brown sugar, firmly packed
6 slices white bread, cut in ½″ cubes	2 c. milk
	⅛ tsp. salt
	1 tsp. vanilla

Generously butter the inside of double boiler top. Place 1 c. brown sugar in bottom and then a layer of bread cubes. (Do not mix.)

Beat eggs well with rotary beater. Gradually beat in ½ c. brown sugar, milk, salt and vanilla. Pour over bread cubes. (Do not stir.) Place over simmering water. Cover and cook 1 hour 30 minutes. Serve hot. Makes 6 to 8 servings.

GERMAN RICE PUDDING

A very creamy pudding in spite of the fact that it contains no eggs. This handed-down recipe originated in Germany and is very popular at church suppers, a Texas farm wife told us. The family prefers it warm with a big dollop of applesauce. For church suppers she makes it early in the morning, then cools it and pours it into a big plastic bowl. Just before she leaves for the supper she dusts the top with a generous layer of cinnamon.

GERMAN RICE PUDDING

Easy-to-fix dessert cooks on top of the range . . . so creamy good

½ c. regular rice	½ tsp. salt
2 c. boiling water	1 tsp. vanilla
3 c. milk	Ground cinnamon
½ c. sugar	

Add rice to boiling water in 2-qt. saucepan. Bring to a boil again; reduce heat and cook, stirring occasionally, until all the water is absorbed.

Stir in milk. Simmer 20 minutes, stirring occasionally. Add sugar and salt; continue cooking 20 more minutes or until mixture is creamy. Stir in vanilla. Serve warm, sprinkled with cinnamon. Makes 6 servings.

Chapter 3

THE HERITAGE
OF DUTCH
COOKING

The Dutch are careful, thrifty and home-loving. Their food is straightforward, simple and hearty. The Dutch have always had a continuous battle with the sea for their land, so dikes predominate the landscape and make possible large areas of rich farmland. Dairying provides creamy milk, butter and cheese, notably the orange-yellow Edam and the pale-yellow Gouda. At one time every farm woman turned out her own cheeses. Dutch country cheese can be bought in three stages; young cheese, which is soft and creamy; old cheese which is heavy, full-bodied in flavor and golden yellow, and aged cheese which is dry and flaky with a piquant flavor.

Because Holland is so rich in coastal areas, much of the Dutch food comes from the ocean. They have been feasting on herring for centuries. In the 15th century, the day before the herring fleet sailed in May was usually a day of celebration.

Like the Germans, they love their soups, usually lusty-full of meat. The national soup in the Netherlands is pea soup. There are as many varieties as there are cooks. Every housewife has her own recipe. According to Dutch legend, any self-respecting Dutch pea soup must be so thick that the spoon will stand up in it.

When a Dutch woman plans her meal she is likely to think first of the vegetables and then the meat. They love vegetables and pride themselves on their preparation of them. Their favorites are carrots, onions, turnips, leeks, spinach, cabbage and beans—they often combine five or six vegetables in one dish. Beans form a large part of their menu and they like them any way they are fixed but especially baked with bacon and molasses. The oldest street in Amsterdam is named for the vegetable growers who lived there in the Middle Ages.

The Dutch taste for almonds, cinnamon, nutmeg and ginger, dates back to the 16th century when the Netherlands gained control of the East Indies.

For breakfast they eat a variety of breads and sliced cheeses and meat. They like pancakes on the large size with sweet or meat fillings. New Year is welcomed in with *oliebollen*. These Dutch doughnuts are a traditional treat on New Year's Eve.

The Dutch get the sharp wind from the North Sea and it builds a hunger for hearty, simple, nourishing fare; they don't go in for elaborate dishes and complicated sauces. The Dutch recipes that found their way to America via immigrants have the same hearty characteristics.

PORK CHOP/SAUERKRAUT CASSEROLE

A third-generation recipe that has been in the family and made every winter since their Dutch ancestors brought it to Ohio. This farm wife varies the meat, using pork chops, sausage or ham layered with apples and sauerkraut. A rich, nourishing meal that everyone enjoys.

PORK CHOP/SAUERKRAUT CASSEROLE

This dish simmers to perfection while you do other chores

2 large tart red apples, pared, cored and cut in ¼″ slices
1 c. chopped onion
1 (1 lb.) can sauerkraut

¼ c. sugar
4 pork chops, ½″ thick
Salt
Pepper

Place apples in bottom of 3-qt. casserole. Top with layer of onion and then sauerkraut. Sprinkle with sugar.

Season pork chops with salt and pepper to taste. Brown well on both sides in skillet, adding cooking oil if necessary. Place browned chops on top of sauerkraut. Cover.

Bake in 350° oven 1 hour 15 minutes. Remove cover. Bake 15 more minutes. Makes 4 servings.

PORK WITH APPLES AND POTATOES

Seventy-two years ago a farmer came to Wisconsin to operate a dairy farm and he remembered eating what he called a Dutch dinner. This robust, economical meal was prepared from all the ingredients that had been grown on their land. Pork, apples and potatoes were cooked together with a spicy bay leaf. Good eating on a cold winter night after chores.

PORK WITH APPLES AND POTATOES

So good with crusty bread to mop up the flavorful juices

1½ lbs. boneless pork shoulder, cut in 1″ cubes	6 medium potatoes, pared and cut in eighths
4 c. water	4 medium, tart red apples, pared, cored and cut in eighths
1 tblsp. salt	
⅛ tsp. pepper	
1 bay leaf	

Place pork cubes, water, salt, pepper and bay leaf in Dutch oven. Cover and bring to a boil. Reduce heat and simmer 1 hour 30 minutes or until meat is tender. Add potatoes; cook 10 minutes. Add apples and cook 20 minutes or until apples are tender. Serve with crusty bread, if you wish. Makes 4 to 6 servings.

DUTCH LETTUCE SALAD

The Dutch combine greens with skill and taste. This tasty salad, an heirloom from Michigan, is popular at family reunions and picnics. Egg and bacon garnish add an attractive note to this tangy salad.

DUTCH LETTUCE SALAD

Wash and crisp the greens ahead . . . toss at the last minute

6 strips bacon
¼ c. cider vinegar
¼ c. water
1 tblsp. sugar
4 hard-cooked eggs, sliced

4 c. bite-size pieces
**   romaine lettuce**
4 c. bite-size pieces fresh
**   spinach**

Fry bacon in small skillet until crisp. Remove and drain on paper towels. Crumble bacon.

Pour off bacon drippings; reserving 2 tblsp. Add vinegar, water and sugar to drippings. Bring to a boil, stirring constantly, cook 1 minute. Pour hot dressing over combined eggs, lettuce, spinach and bacon. Toss gently to mix. Makes 6 to 8 servings.

RAISIN PUDDING CAKE

An old-time recipe from Minnesota that was brought to this country from Holland. There were no measured amounts but through the generations, the recipe was worked up and put on a recipe card to be handed down to the next generation. A homey, old-fashioned cake that goes together quickly and bakes into a sweet pudding with a caramel sauce.

RAISIN PUDDING CAKE

Easy to fix . . . cake bakes on top with a rich sauce underneath

1 c. sifted flour
1 c. sugar
2 tsp. baking powder
¼ tsp. salt
½ c. milk
1 c. raisins

½ c. chopped walnuts
1 c. brown sugar, firmly
**   packed**
1 tsp. butter or regular
**   margarine**
1½ c. boiling water

Sift together flour, sugar, baking powder and salt into bowl. Add milk, raisins and walnuts; mix with spoon until blended. Spread batter in greased 9″ square baking pan.

Combine brown sugar, butter and boiling water; stir well. Pour over batter (do not mix).

Bake in 350° oven 35 minutes or until cake tests done. Serve warm. Makes 6 servings.

GRANDMA'S GLORIFIED GINGERBREAD

This recipe traveled from Holland to Pennsylvania and was passed on through the generations. An Oklahoma farm wife remembers her mother baking it in an old cookstove for the children. It was eaten piping hot with lots of home-churned butter. There was always plenty of sour milk and fresh eggs and when her mother would ask, "Who wants to crack some walnuts for gingerbread?" everyone would volunteer. The recipe is now in the hands of *great*-grandchildren. They use pecans from trees in their back yard.

GRANDMA'S GLORIFIED GINGERBREAD

Mildly spiced gingerbread topped with golden crumbs

2 c. sifted flour	1 tsp. baking soda
1 c. sugar	1 c. sour milk
1 tsp. ground cinnamon	1 egg
1 tsp. ground ginger	¼ c. molasses
¼ tsp. salt	½ c. chopped walnuts
½ c. butter or regular	½ c. raisins
margarine	1 tblsp. flour

Sift together 2 c. flour, sugar, cinnamon, ginger and salt into bowl. Cut in butter with pastry blender or two knives until mixture resembles coarse crumbs. Reserve 1 c. crumbs.

Combine baking soda and sour milk. Add milk mixture, egg and molasses to remaining crumbs, and mix with spoon until well blended. Combine walnuts, raisins and 1 tblsp. flour; stir into batter. Spread batter in greased 9" square baking pan. Top with reserved 1 c. crumbs.

Bake in 350° oven 40 minutes or until cake tests done. Cool in pan on rack. Makes 9 servings.

HOLLAND SPICE COOKIES

Many homemakers in a Dutch community in Wisconsin make this cookie. Each one varies the spices and nuts, and some cover cookies with a light icing, especially during the holidays.

HOLLAND SPICE COOKIES

Ice for the holidays and decorate with bits of candied fruit

1 c. butter or regular margarine	3 tsp. ground cinnamon
1 c. lard	1 tsp. salt
2 c. brown sugar, firmly packed	½ tsp. baking soda
½ c. dairy sour cream	½ tsp. ground nutmeg
4½ c. sifted flour	¼ tsp. ground cloves
	½ c. chopped walnuts

Cream together butter, lard and brown sugar until light and fluffy. Beat in sour cream.

Sift together flour, cinnamon, salt, baking soda, nutmeg and cloves. Gradually add dry ingredients to creamed mixture, mixing well with a spoon. Stir in walnuts. Cover and chill 1 hour in refrigerator.

Shape dough into 4 (6") rolls. Chill in refrigerator overnight.

Cut rolls into ¼" slices. Place 2" apart on greased baking sheets.

Bake in 350° oven 8 to 10 minutes or until golden brown. Remove from baking sheets; cool on racks. Makes 8 dozen.

OLIEBOLLEN

An unusual doughnut filled with apples and raisins, this is served in Holland during the holidays and always on New Year's Day, with big pitchers of milk and freshly brewed coffee. The raisins poke through the dough giving them an unusual shape. A not-too-sweet doughnut that is very moist on the inside and crisp and crusty outside.

OLIEBOLLEN

Serve these doughnuts with hot cider on Christmas Eve

1 pkg. active dry yeast
½ tsp. sugar
¾ c. warm milk
2 c. sifted flour
2 tblsp. sugar
⅛ tsp. salt
2 eggs, beaten

½ c. raisins
½ c. diced pared apple
3 tblsp. chopped, mixed candied fruit
1 tsp. grated lemon peel
Cooking oil
Confectioners sugar

Sprinkle yeast and ½ tsp. sugar on milk; stir to dissolve. Let stand 10 minutes.

Sift together flour, 2 tblsp. sugar and salt into bowl. Make a well in the center. Add yeast and eggs, mix just until blended. Stir in raisins, apple, candied fruit and lemon peel. Cover and let rise in warm place until doubled, about 1 hour.

Drop batter by heaping tablespoonfuls into deep, hot oil (350°), frying until golden brown, about 3 minutes. Drain on paper towels. Dust with confectioners sugar. Makes 15.

Chapter 4

THE HERITAGE
OF SCANDINAVIAN
COOKING

Although Denmark, Norway, Sweden and Finland—usually called Scandinavia—share much in common, each country retains its own stamp of individuality, and this is true also of their cuisines. They are hospitable people and their doors are always open. They use great ingenuity, imagination and skill in preparing and presenting foods. The roots of Scandinavian eating lie with their climate. For centuries these people were forced as a matter of survival to stock supplies ahead to get them through the great blizzards of winter. Nowhere in the world will you find more ways to preserve meat and fish than in Scandinavia.

Denmark is Scandinavia's lush land. The grass is thick and luxuriant, the cows produce the richest milk and the sweetest cream. Their vegetable gardens in the springtime are works of art. Big, well-fed, pink pigs dot the fields each one looking as if it were scrubbed daily. Their foods reflect their land—rich, abundant and colorful. Coffee cakes, rolls and pastries are unequaled —fine, light and crispy and served with strong, perfectly brewed coffee. Open-face sandwiches are as handsome as a painting— breads lavishly spread with butter and heaped with meat or cheese or fish and each one garnished beautifully.

Norway on the other hand, is comprised of breathtakingly beautiful fjords, rocky seashores, huge mountains and acres of thick forests. Country people work hard in Norway; the living is tougher and it's necessary to be sturdy to battle out the long winters in the fjords and mountains.

Norwegian cooking reflects their land; it is simple, sturdy, nourishing and not too rich. They consume much fish and bushels of potatoes. Norwegian housewives make a special dish called *lutfisk* from salted, dry cod. The cod is soaked for several days in water and then put in birchwood ash, which gives it a slightly rubbery consistency. They say you must be Norwegian to like this as it is very bland. But a true Norwegian smothers the lutfisk in plenty of butter and cream and sometimes a touch of mustard and declares it is delicious. This is popular with the older Norwegians in our farm communities today but the young people generally say "no thank you." Norwegian women bake bread and cook with cheeses. Americans of Norwegian descent have adapted Norwegian ideas into American recipes and come up with some interesting dishes.

Sweden is a prosperous country and famous for the *smörgåsbord;* a buffet style of dining originated centuries ago when there were opulent country gatherings. Everyone brought food and it was spread out on a long table for each one to sample a bit of his neighbors' treasures. Smörgåsbord is found in Norway and Denmark but doesn't feature the endless dishes that the Swedish people do.

Smörgåsbord is a deeply rooted Scandinavian tradition. It goes back to the Viking feast days, weddings, christenings and funerals. Distances traveled to get together were long and because they traveled a great many miles, they planned to stay for several weeks. They brought their food with them from all areas. Cheese and greens from the farms, fish from the lake and sea areas, and those from the forest arrived with game. The tables were heavily laden with food and everyone sampled a little of each.

There are similarities in many of the Scandinavian recipes due to the geographical closeness of the countries. Often the recipe of each country has only a slight variation from the other. Recipe terminology and spelling in Scandinavia are highly controversial

—the dialects are different in the provinces and you will find their spellings are old-style, modern or colloquial. A recipe proudly proclaimed the original of one province with its own spelling will show up in other parts of the country with a different name—same ingredients.

Smörgåsbord is popular in our own country, not on as lavish a scale, but the buffet entertaining with a good variety of foods does resemble the Swedish custom. It is enjoyed by all Americans —our numerous potluck suppers so popular in the country are probably a "melting pot" adaptation of the original smörgåsbord.

We offer you a sampling of Scandinavian dishes that have passed down through generations and adaptations in this country.

DANISH PORK ROAST

Danish homemakers are thrifty but cook with imagination and skill. One of the most popular dishes in Denmark handed down through generations is pork, and the Danish cook knows how to prepare it beautifully. One recipe is pork roast stuffed with dried fruits. This recipe has a filling of prunes and a beautiful glaze of currant jelly. This is truly company fare and would be a handsome substitute for the Thanksgiving or Christmas turkey for a change of pace.

DANISH PORK ROAST

Attractive pork roast stuffed with fruits and covered with crumbs

½ tsp. salt
½ tsp. ground cinnamon
½ tsp. ground allspice
½ tsp. pepper
¼ tsp. ground cloves
¼ tsp. ground mace
3 to 3½ lb. boned pork loin
12 pitted prunes
2 medium apples, pared,
   cored and cut into sixths

2 tblsp. raisins
¼ tsp. ground cinnamon
¼ c. brandy or apple juice
1½ tblsp. currant jelly,
   melted
1 c. fresh bread crumbs
¼ c. melted butter or
   regular margarine

Combine salt, ½ tsp. cinnamon, allspice, pepper, cloves and mace. Rub in surface of roast. Cover and refrigerate overnight.

Combine prunes, apples, raisins, ¼ tsp. cinnamon and brandy. Cover and refrigerate overnight.

Cut a long, deep pocket the length of the roast. Stuff with fruit. Sew closed with large needle; tie with kitchen twine. Place roast on rack in roasting pan. Brush roast with liquid left over from fruit.

Roast in 325° oven 1 hour. Remove from oven; brush with jelly. Roll in bread crumbs. Baste with butter; roast 1 hour 30 minutes more or until meat thermometer reads 185°. Let stand 15 minutes before carving. Makes 6 servings.

DANISH CARAMELIZED POTATOES

These shiny, glazed potatoes are served in all Scandinavian countries. Wreathed around a pork roast, they look handsome when brought to the table. They are easy to fix and can be glazed at the last minute.

DANISH CARAMELIZED POTATOES

Tiny potatoes with a delightful, glistening caramel glaze

24 small, new potatoes	**6 tblsp. sugar**
¼ c. butter or regular margarine	**2 tsp. salt**

Cook potatoes in their jackets in boiling water until tender. Drain and peel.

Melt butter in 10″ skillet; stir in sugar, and cook, stirring constantly, until mixture is a light caramel color.

Add potatoes; continue cooking, shaking pan so the potatoes are covered with a thin caramel coating. Sprinkle with salt during cooking. Makes 6 servings.

DANISH DUMPLING AND MEATBALL SOUP

A farm woman from Nebraska wrote us that she married a Dane who begged her to make dumplings like his mother used to make. The bigger and fluffier her dumplings were, the more disappointed her husband became. One Sunday during a visit with a Danish family they were served Danish Dumplings and her husband exclaimed, "These are the dumplings!" She was surprised to learn that the dough was basically a cream puff dough and dropped into a broth or soup along with homemade meatballs.

DANISH DUMPLING AND MEATBALL SOUP

You can also cook the dumplings in chicken broth and serve plain

6 medium potatoes, pared and quartered	1 tsp. parsley flakes
4 medium carrots, pared and cut in 2″ strips	¼ tsp. salt
	1 egg, slightly beaten
2 stalks celery, cut in 1″ diagonal slices	1 tblsp. butter or regular margarine
1 c. chopped onion	1 c. water
6 c. chicken broth	½ c. butter or regular margarine
1 (10 oz.) pkg. frozen peas	1 c. sifted flour
½ lb. ground beef	¼ tsp. salt
¼ lb. ground ham	4 eggs
¼ c. cracker crumbs	

Combine potatoes, carrots, celery, onion and chicken broth in 6-qt. kettle. Cover and bring to a boil. Reduce heat and simmer 30 minutes. Add peas and continue cooking 10 more minutes or until vegetables are tender.

Meanwhile prepare meatballs. Combine ground beef, ham, crumbs, parsley flakes, ¼ tsp. salt and 1 egg; mix lightly but well. Shape into ¾″ balls. Brown on all sides in 1 tblsp. melted butter in 10″ skillet. Cook 10 minutes, turning frequently.

Combine water and ½ c. butter in 2-qt. saucepan; bring to a boil. Stir in flour and ¼ tsp. salt. Continue stirring over medium heat until mixture leaves the sides of the saucepan and forms a ball. Remove from heat. Add 4 eggs, one at a time, beating well with spoon after each addition. Drop by rounded teaspoonfuls into boiling vegetable mixture. Cook 2 minutes or until dumplings rise to top; add meatballs. Serve immediately. Makes 6 to 8 servings.

DANISH CRULLERS

Brought to this country in 1880, these doughnuts have been a big hit in Minnesota ever since. Golden brown and tender and covered with sugar, one batch won't last long even though it makes over 5 dozen.

DANISH CRULLERS

Crisp pastry knots that look so attractive dusted with sugar

2 eggs	1 tsp. salt
½ c. sugar	½ tsp. ground nutmeg
1 c. light cream	Cooking oil
3 c. sifted flour	Confectioners sugar
2 tsp. baking powder	

Beat eggs well. Add sugar and cream, beating well to blend.

Sift together flour, baking powder, salt and nutmeg. Gradually add dry ingredients to egg mixture, stirring just enough to blend. (Do not overmix.) Dough is slightly sticky.

Divide dough in fourths. Roll each on well-floured surface to 12×8" rectangle. Cut into 16 (4×1½") strips. Cut 1" slit lengthwise in center of each strip. Pull one end of strip through slit to form knot.

Fry in deep, hot oil (350°) until golden brown on both sides. Drain on paper towels. Dust with confectioners sugar. Makes 64 crullers.

DANISH CHRISTMAS COOKIES

On Christmas day the Danes feast on goose or pork, salads and chestnuts and then when the main meal is cleared from the table, platters of cookies are brought forth. The recipe for these rich, buttery cookies was brought to this country by a 15-year-old girl years ago. Now an Illinois farm woman, she remembers her grandmother coloring the dough and decorating the cookies. It was difficult to duplicate the cookies, even with the recipe, because Grandmother cooked by "feel," but after much experimentation she believes these cookies taste just like her grandmother's.

DANISH CHRISTMAS COOKIES

Make these buttery cookies a Christmas tradition in your home

1 c. butter or regular margarine	**½ tsp. almond extract**
½ c. sugar	**½ tsp. vanilla**
½ tsp. lemon extract	**2½ c. sifted flour**

Cream together butter and sugar until light and fluffy. Beat in lemon extract, almond extract and vanilla. Gradually stir in flour. Cover with plastic wrap. Chill in refrigerator 30 minutes.

Shape into 13″ roll. Wrap in plastic wrap and refrigerate 8 hours or overnight. (Can be stored 2 days.)

Cut in ¼″ thick slices. Place 2″ apart on greased baking sheets.

Bake in 350° oven 8 minutes or until golden brown. Remove from baking sheets; cool on racks. Decorate with colored sugars or frost with your favorite icing, if you wish. Makes about 4 dozen.

DANISH LAYER CAKE

Desserts rank high in Denmark and they abound in rich butter, eggs and cream. And they look exquisite. This layer cake is an heirloom from Illinois—a high cake filled with pudding and raspberry jam. Surprise the family and make this beauty for a birthday treat or any special occasion. The cake is tender and light as a feather. Cut small pieces as it is rich and caloric.

DANISH LAYER CAKE

This breath-taking cake is six layers high and covered with cream

1½ c. milk	3 tblsp. flour
⅔ c. butter or regular margarine	⅛ tsp. salt
6 eggs	2 c. milk, scalded
3 c. sugar	2 egg yolks, slightly beaten
3 c. sifted cake flour	2 tblsp. butter or regular margarine
3 tsp. baking powder	1 tsp. vanilla
½ tsp. salt	1 c. raspberry jam
2 tsp. vanilla	1½ c. heavy cream, whipped and sweetened
⅓ c. sugar	

Heat 1½ c. milk and ⅔ c. butter to boiling point. Remove from heat.

Beat 6 eggs until thick and lemon-colored, about 5 minutes. Slowly add 3 c. sugar, beating well.

Sift together cake flour, baking powder and ½ tsp. salt. Add dry ingredients to egg mixture, beating at low speed. Continue beating at low speed, gradually adding hot milk mixture and 2 tsp. vanilla. (Batter will be bubbly and quite thin.) Pour into 3 greased and waxed-paper-lined 9" round cake pans.

Bake in 375° oven 25 minutes or until cakes test done. Cool in pans on racks 5 minutes. Remove from pans; cool on racks.

Combine ⅓ c. sugar, flour and ⅛ tsp. salt in medium saucepan. Gradually stir in 2 c. hot milk. Cook over medium heat, stirring constantly, until mixture thickens. Remove from heat. Stir some of the hot mixture into egg yolks, mixing well. Stir back into hot mixture. Cook over low heat 2 more minutes, stirring occasionally. Remove from heat. Add 2 tblsp. butter and 1 tsp. vanilla. Cool completely.

Cut layers in half, making 6 layers. Place one layer on serving plate. Spread with ⅓ of custard filling. Top with cake layer. Spread with ½ of raspberry jam. Repeat layers. Top with cake layer; spread with remaining custard filling. Top with last cake layer. Cover with plastic wrap. Refrigerate until just before serving time.

Spread sweetened whipped cream over surface of cake. Makes 12 servings.

BEEF STEW

In Norwegian, beef stew is called *bankekjøtt* and in Denmark it is named *bankekød*. Both names mean "pounding" or "banging," which is what a Scandinavian cook always does to the cheaper cuts of meat. A typical meal to serve with this spicy stew would be boiled potatoes, pickled beets and lingonberries. Lingonberries are similar to our cranberries and are often served with meats and fish.

BEEF STEW

Basic beef dish with rich, brown gravy . . . good with potatoes

3 lbs. round steak, ½"	**¼ c. cooking oil**
thick	**2 c. hot beef broth**
¼ c. flour	**1 c. chopped onion**
1 tsp. salt	**1 bay leaf**
¼ tsp. pepper	

Pound meat well with meat mallet. Cut in serving-size pieces. Dredge with combined flour, salt and pepper.

Heat oil in Dutch oven. Brown meat on both sides. Add beef broth, onion and bay leaf. Cover and bring to a boil. Reduce heat and simmer 1 hour 15 minutes or until meat is tender. Makes 8 servings.

NORWEGIAN BEEF BIRDS

Both Danes and Norwegians have many recipes for boneless birds as they call them. There are numerous fillings. Some of the most popular variations include mushrooms or chopped anchovies or beef marrow that has been diced and mixed with a little ginger.

NORWEGIAN BEEF BIRDS

Flavorful beef rolls with ground beef and parsley tucked inside

3 lbs. round steak, ½" thick	¼ c. chopped fresh parsley
1 tblsp. salt	¼ c. flour
½ tsp. pepper	3 tblsp. cooking oil
½ tsp. ground ginger	3 c. beef broth
½ tsp. ground cloves	3 tblsp. flour
½ lb. ground beef	⅓ c. water

Pound steak well with meat mallet. Cut in 16 (5×3") pieces.

Season with combined salt, pepper, ginger and cloves. Place 1 tblsp. ground beef in center of each piece. Sprinkle with parsley. Roll up like jelly roll and secure with string. Dredge rolls with ¼ c. flour.

Brown meat rolls on all sides in hot cooking oil in Dutch oven. Return all meat rolls to Dutch oven when all are browned, pour beef broth over all. Cover and bring to a boil. Reduce heat and simmer 1 hour 25 minutes or until meat is tender.

Remove meat rolls from pan; cut string and discard. Keep warm. Skim off excess fat from pan liquid. Combine 3 tblsp. flour and water. Slowly stir into boiling liquid. Boil 1 minute. Serve meat rolls with gravy. Makes 8 servings.

NORWEGIAN-STYLE BROWN HASH

A standard way in which Scandinavian cooks use up leftovers. In some recipes meat and potatoes are browned separately and a pour of cream is added at the very end. In this recipe pork and potatoes are cooked with the onions and tasty beef broth is stirred in and cooked until all moisture is gone and only the flavor is left.

NORWEGIAN-STYLE BROWN HASH

Leftovers taste so good when used to make this great hash

4 c. diced, cooked pork	1½ c. chopped onion
4 c. diced, cooked potatoes	½ tsp. salt
½ c. butter or regular margarine	⅛ tsp. pepper
	1 c. boiling beef broth

Brown pork and potatoes in melted butter in large skillet, stirring occasionally. Add onion, salt and pepper; mix lightly. Stir in beef broth. Cover and bring to a boil. Reduce heat and simmer 45 minutes, stirring occasionally, until all the broth is absorbed. Makes 6 servings.

SAUSAGES AND POTATOES

This down-to-earth main dish is economical and delicious and popular in many Scandinavian homes. The flavor of the sausages trickles through the potatoes giving them a wonderful taste. This is a big favorite with men and field crews. Accompany with cooked carrots for a bright note of color.

SAUSAGES AND POTATOES

Country-style dish that requires little attention while cooking

2 lbs. small, pork sausage links	¼ tsp. pepper
2 c. water	2 lbs. medium potatoes, pared and quartered
2 bay leaves	2 tblsp. chopped fresh parsley
10 whole allspice	
1½ tsp. salt	

Place pork sausages, water, bay leaves, allspice, salt and pepper in Dutch oven. Bring to a boil. Reduce heat and simmer 20 minutes.

Add potatoes. Cover and simmer 20 minutes or until potatoes are tender. Sprinkle with parsley. Makes 6 to 8 servings.

NORWEGIAN CAULIFLOWER SOUP

Norwegians love their soups and manage to make a soup out of every vegetable. This Cauliflower Soup is a family soup often served for supper in this country with assorted cheeses and crackers. In the springtime, fresh peas are added for a colorful note. Just before serving paper-thin radish slices can be stirred into the soup for a bit of crunch.

NORWEGIAN CAULIFLOWER SOUP

An unusual cream soup featuring a favorite wintertime vegetable

2 medium cauliflower	**2 tblsp. flour**
(3¼ lbs.)	**2 egg yolks, slightly**
3 c. water	**beaten**
1 tblsp. salt	**½ c. heavy cream**
2 tblsp. butter or regular	**⅛ tsp. ground nutmeg**
margarine	**3 c. milk**

Trim cauliflower and break into flowerets. Remove stalks and cut into ½" pieces. Place cauliflower, water and salt in Dutch oven. Cover and bring to a boil. Reduce heat and simmer 20 minutes or until tender.

Drain cauliflower, reserving stock. Set aside.

Melt butter in Dutch oven. Add flour. Cook, stirring constantly, 1 minute. Slowly stir in reserved stock. Cover and simmer 10 minutes, stirring occasionally. Remove from heat.

Combine egg yolks, heavy cream and nutmeg. Add 1 c. hot soup to egg mixture; blend well. Add egg mixture back into hot soup, a little at a time, mixing well after each addition. Return to low heat. Add milk and cauliflower and heat well. (Do not boil.) Makes about 2 quarts.

YULE KAGE

Christmas bread that is served in Norway and also in Scandinavian communities in this country. A North Dakota farm woman has been making this for years. She added the glaze for an extra-festive look. Cardamom gives a different flavor which all Norwegians love—it is part of their Christmas taste.

YULE KAGE

Serve lots of soft, creamy butter with this traditional bread

½ c. milk, scalded	1 pkg. active dry yeast
½ c. butter or regular margarine	½ c. lukewarm water
	3¾ c. sifted flour
¼ c. sugar	1 egg
1 tsp. salt	1 c. raisins
¼ tsp. ground cardamom	½ c. mixed candied fruit
1 tblsp. honey	1 egg, slightly beaten

Combine milk, butter, sugar, salt, cardamom and honey. Cool to lukewarm.

Sprinkle yeast over lukewarm water; stir to dissolve.

Add yeast, 1 c. flour and 1 egg to milk mixture. Beat with electric mixer at medium speed until smooth, about 2 minutes, scraping bowl occasionally. Or beat with spoon until batter is smooth.

Stir in raisins and candied fruit. Add enough remaining flour to make a soft dough that leaves the sides of the bowl. Cover and let rise in warm place until doubled, about 1 hour 30 minutes.

Divide dough in half. Shape each into a round loaf and place on greased baking sheet. Cover and let rise 15 minutes.

Snip 1" deep cuts about 1" apart around bottom of loaf with scissors. Press down center of loaf with palm of hand. Brush with 1 beaten egg. Cover and let rise until doubled, about 45 minutes.

Bake in 350° oven 30 minutes or until golden brown. Remove from baking sheet; cool on racks. If you wish, frost with your favorite icing and garnish with bits of candied fruit. Makes 2 coffee cakes.

NORWEGIAN MOLASSES COOKIES

An heirloom recipe from Norway over 100 years old. This North Dakotan's ancestors served this spicy cookie at the Ladies' Aid Meeting. According to her grandmother, in the old days Ladies' Aid meetings started midmorning and lasted all day. Everyone brought a favorite food, big pots of coffee were brewed and the recipes shared.

NORWEGIAN MOLASSES COOKIES

This basic molasses cookie is both crunchy and chewy

1 c. lard	**5 c. sifted flour**
2 c. sugar	**3 tsp. baking soda**
2 eggs	**⅛ tsp. salt**
1 c. molasses	

Cream together lard and sugar until light and fluffy. Add eggs, one at a time, beating well after each addition. Beat in molasses.

Sift together flour, baking soda and salt. Gradually stir into creamed mixture. Cover with plastic wrap. Chill 1 hour in refrigerator.

Shape dough in 1¼" balls. Place 2" apart on greased baking sheets.

Bake in 350° oven 18 minutes or until golden brown. Remove from baking sheets; cool on racks. Makes about 7 dozen.

FATTIGMAN

Christmas is a time of great feasting in Norway. The table is groaning with food. There are always a wide array of cookies and breads. No holiday is complete without a handsome platter piled high with Fattigman. Many farm wives of Norwegian descent make this light-as-air crisp cookie at holidaytime.

FATTIGMAN

These crisp pastry knots are perfect for a coffee break

6 egg yolks	**2¼ c. sifted flour**
½ tsp. salt	**¼ tsp. ground nutmeg**
⅓ c. light cream	**1 tblsp. grated lemon peel**
⅓ c. sugar	**Cooking oil**
1 tblsp. melted butter or	**Confectioners sugar**
regular margarine	

Beat together egg yolks and salt until thick and light. Beat in light cream, sugar and butter.

Sift together flour and nutmeg. Add to egg yolk mixture with lemon peel, mixing well. Chill for 1 hour.

Roll out ¼ of dough at a time, keeping remaining dough chilled. Roll ⅟₁₆″ thick and cut in strips about 1½″ wide with sharp knife. Cut diagonally at 4″ intervals. Make 1″ slits lengthwise in center of each piece. Slip one end through slit.

Fry a few at a time in deep, hot oil at 350° for 1 to 2 minutes or until golden. Remove from oil with slotted spoon. Drain on paper towels and sprinkle with sifted confectioners sugar. Store in an airtight container. Makes 6 dozen.

STUFFED CABBAGE ROLLS

Although this recipe was originally an oriental creation from Turkey, Stuffed Cabbage Rolls have been adopted all over Europe and each country has its own style of preparation depending upon the ingredients available. Scandinavian cooks especially favor the Stuffed Cabbage Rolls using two kinds of meat and adding a little brown sugar for extra flavor and sweetness. Light cream is added to make a rich, flavorful gravy.

STUFFED CABBAGE ROLLS

This hearty supper dish is sure to please your family

1 medium cabbage	2 tblsp. brown sugar, firmly
½ c. regular rice	packed
1 c. water	½ c. beef broth
1 lb. ground beef	2 tblsp. flour
1 egg	¾ c. light cream
1 c. milk	½ tsp. salt
1½ tsp. salt	⅛ tsp. pepper
⅛ tsp. pepper	
2 tblsp. butter or regular	
margarine	

Cut out core of cabbage. Steam cabbage in Dutch oven to soften leaves. Remove leaves gently. Drain on paper towels. Trim center vein from each leaf; set aside.

Cook rice with water in saucepan until water is absorbed. Cool well.

Combine cooked rice, ground beef, egg, milk, 1½ tsp. salt and ⅛ tsp. pepper; mix lightly. Place ¼ c. filling on each cabbage leaf. Roll up and secure with toothpicks or string. (Makes 16 rolls.)

Brown rolls on all sides in melted butter in Dutch oven. Sprinkle with brown sugar. Add beef broth. Cover and bring to a boil. Reduce heat and simmer 45 minutes or until cabbage rolls are tender.

Combine flour and cream. Remove cabbage rolls from Dutch oven and keep warm. Slowly stir cream mixture into pan drippings, stirring constantly. Add ½ tsp. salt and ⅛ tsp. pepper. Cook over low heat until thickened (do not boil). Spoon sauce over cabbage rolls. Makes 6 to 8 servings.

SWEDISH LAMB STEW

Lamb is a particular favorite with Scandinavians and one of their family favorites is lamb stew. The flavor is very delicate and seasoned perfectly. This is a quick and easy main dish to make as the meat is not browned, but simply combined with the vegetables and stock and allowed to simmer to perfection. A shower of chopped parsley added just before serving makes a pretty garnish.

SWEDISH LAMB STEW

Lamb stew tastes especially good on a blustery winter evening

2 lbs. lamb shoulder, cut in 1½" cubes	**½ tsp. marjoram leaves**
	⅛ tsp. pepper
6 medium potatoes, pared and quartered	**1 bay leaf**
	4 c. beef broth or bouillon
6 medium carrots, pared and sliced	**4 tblsp. flour**
	6 tblsp. water
3 medium onions, quartered	**Chopped fresh parsley**

Layer lamb, potatoes, carrots and onions in Dutch oven. Sprinkle with marjoram and pepper. Add bay leaf and beef broth. Cover and bring to a boil. Reduce heat and simmer 1 hour 30 minutes or until meat is tender.

Combine flour and water; mix well. Slowly stir into hot mixture, cook 2 more minutes. Remove bay leaf. Serve sprinkled with fresh parsley. Makes 6 servings.

SWEDISH POT ROAST

Swedish women like to cook with heavy cream, and because of their fondness for fish, they serve pot roast with a hint of anchovies in the rich gravy made with pan drippings and cream. Potatoes that have been browned in butter with a little brown sugar are a popular vegetable to present with this different and delicious pot roast. The gravy never seems to curdle even upon standing. Because of the saltiness of the anchovies, you will need less salt.

SWEDISH POT ROAST

Less expensive roasts are so tender and succulent cooked this way

4 lbs. beef round or rump roast	1½ c. sliced carrots
½ tsp. salt	1 (10½ oz.) can condensed beef broth
¼ tsp. pepper	3 tblsp. flour
2 tblsp. butter or regular margarine	1 c. heavy cream
2 c. chopped onion	1 tsp. anchovy juice

Season beef with salt and pepper. Brown on all sides in melted butter in Dutch oven. Remove from pan. Add onion and carrots; sauté until tender (do not brown).

Place beef back in Dutch oven. Add enough water to beef broth to make 2 c. Add to Dutch oven. Cover and bring to a boil. Reduce heat and simmer 2 hours or until meat is tender.

Remove roast from Dutch oven and keep warm. Pour off pan drippings and reserve 2 c. (Add water if necessary.) Pour back into Dutch oven.

Combine flour, heavy cream and anchovy juice. Slowly add to pan drippings, stirring constantly. Cook over low heat 2 minutes or until mixture thickens slightly. Slice roast and serve with cream gravy. Makes 8 servings.

SCANDINAVIAN HASH

Hash in our country is usually made by combining potatoes, meat and onion and browning until crusty. In Scandinavia, often each ingredient is cooked separately and then combined and seasoned to taste. This hash tastes a bit different and is a delightful way to use that leftover roast. A suggested variation often served in Swedish homes is to pour a cup of cream over the browned hash and reheat thoroughly. It then becomes a creamed hash which is quite unusual.

SCANDINAVIAN HASH

Cream is stirred in at the last minute for extra richness

¾ c. chopped onion	Salt
½ c. butter or regular	Pepper
margarine	1½ c. light cream
3 c. diced, cooked potatoes	3 tblsp. chopped fresh
3 c. ground, cooked beef	parsley

Sauté onion in melted butter in 10″ skillet until tender (do not brown). Add potatoes and beef; sauté until browned. Season with salt and pepper as needed. Pour cream over all and heat well over low heat. Serve sprinkled with parsley. Makes 6 servings.

SWEDISH MEATBALLS WITH SAUCE

If you toured farm homes in Sweden you would likely find a different meatball recipe in every kitchen. These recipes have been handed down through generations and each cook thinks her version is the very finest. They all have a hint of spice however. This version, brought to America, uses unseasoned mashed potatoes to produce a light, tender meatball. The gravy is golden brown and heavy in cream. Wonderful to serve to guests. Just pop these meatballs in a chafing dish and let guests serve themselves.

SWEDISH MEATBALLS WITH SAUCE

Makes a lovely, hot appetizer for the Christmas holiday season

⅓ c. minced onion
2 tblsp. butter or regular
    margarine
1 lb. ground beef
1 c. unseasoned mashed
    potatoes
⅓ c. dry bread crumbs
1 tblsp. minced fresh
    parsley
1 tsp. salt
1 egg

¼ c. heavy cream
2 tblsp. butter or regular
    margarine
2 tblsp. cooking oil
2 tblsp. flour
¼ tsp. ground allspice
½ tsp. bottled browning
    sauce for gravy
1½ c. heavy cream
Chopped fresh parsley

Sauté onion in 2 tblsp. melted butter in small skillet until tender (do not brown). Set aside.

Combine ground beef, potatoes, bread crumbs, 1 tblsp. parsley, salt, egg, ¼ c. heavy cream and sautéed onion. Mix until ingredients are well blended. Shape mixture into ¾″ meatballs. Arrange on tray. Cover. Chill at least 1 hour.

Brown 10 meatballs at a time in 2 tblsp. melted butter and oil in heavy 10″ skillet. Shake pan back and forth frequently to keep meatballs round. Add more oil if needed. Remove meatballs as they brown and place in 2-qt. casserole. Keep hot in 200° oven.

Pour off all but 2 tblsp. pan drippings. Stir in flour, allspice and bottled sauce for gravy. Cook 1 minute, stirring constantly. Remove from heat. Slowly stir in heavy cream. Cook over low heat until slightly thickened. Pour over meatballs. Garnish with chopped parsley. Makes 12 servings.

PICKLED CUCUMBERS WITH DILL

Dill is almost a staple in Swedish cooking. It lends an exquisite distinctive flavor to many foods. In the USA our most common use of dill is in making dill pickles. In Sweden the pretty green sprigs are used as a garnish and ingredient. Here dill teams with cucumbers and vinegar for a delightful sweet-sour salad that has become popular in many American homes.

PICKLED CUCUMBERS WITH DILL

Dill is a favorite herb in Sweden . . . so good with cucumbers

½ c. vinegar
¼ c. sugar
2 tblsp. water
½ tsp. salt

⅛ tsp. pepper
2 medium cucumbers
2 tblsp. chopped fresh dill

Combine vinegar, sugar, water, salt and pepper in saucepan. Bring to a boil. Remove from heat. Cool.

Remove strips of peel lengthwise from cucumbers with vegetable peeler, leaving alternate strips of peel intact. Cut cucumbers in thin slices and place in bowl. Add vinegar mixture. Sprinkle with dill. Toss gently. Cover. Chill 2 to 3 hours. Makes 12 servings.

FISH SALAD WITH PEAS

A handsome dish to add to a buffet dinner; if you happen to have a platter shaped like a fish, this would be a conversation piece. Again the Swedish talent with fish comes through. Even those who are not too fond of fish will take seconds of this delicious dish.

FISH SALAD WITH PEAS

To make dish even more attractive, garnish with bits of pimiento

2 lbs. haddock fillets, cooked, drained and flaked	1½ tsp. prepared yellow mustard
2 tblsp. lemon juice	¾ tsp. salt
2 tblsp. salad oil	¼ tsp. pepper
2 c. cooked peas	1 tblsp. vinegar
2 tsp. lemon juice	¼ c. salad oil
2 tsp. salad oil	⅓ c. melted butter or regular margarine
2 egg yolks, slightly beaten	

Combine haddock, 2 tblsp. lemon juice and 2 tblsp. oil in bowl. Toss gently to mix. Cover with plastic wrap. Chill in refrigerator.

Combine peas, 2 tsp. lemon juice and 2 tsp. oil in bowl. Toss gently. Cover with plastic wrap. Chill in refrigerator.

Combine egg yolks, mustard, salt, pepper, vinegar and ¼ c. oil in small saucepan. Stir in butter. Cook over low heat, stirring constantly, until mixture thickens. Cool well.

Pour sauce over fish mixture. Toss gently to mix. Place fish salad in center of serving dish and surround with peas. Makes 12 servings.

HERRING AND BEET SALAD

One dish that will always be found at the traditional smörgåsbord is Herring and Beet Salad. Swedish cooks have a thousand ways to fix herring but one that has become a favorite in this country is the combination of herring and beet salad with the attractive garnish of chopped egg whites and dill. A good recipe to prepare for company as it can be made several days ahead.

HERRING AND BEET SALAD

Variations of this salad are always included in a smörgåsbord

3 c. diced, cooked beets	¼ tsp. salt
1 c. chopped pickled herring	⅛ tsp. pepper
½ c. diced, cooked potatoes	3 hard-cooked eggs
½ c. diced dill pickle	2 tblsp. vinegar
½ c. chopped pared apples	1 tblsp. prepared yellow mustard
⅓ c. finely chopped onion	¼ c. salad oil
3 tblsp. chopped fresh dill	3 tblsp. heavy cream
2 tblsp. vinegar	1 tblsp. chopped fresh dill

Combine beets, herring, potatoes, pickle, apples, onion, 3 tblsp. dill, 2 tblsp. vinegar, salt and pepper in bowl. Toss gently to mix.

Remove yolks from eggs. Chop egg whites and reserve. Mash yolks with fork in bowl to a smooth paste. Add 2 tblsp. vinegar, mustard and oil; stir well. Stir in heavy cream; blend well. Pour over beet mixture. Toss gently. Cover. Chill at least 2 hours.

Garnish salad with chopped egg whites and 1 tblsp. dill before serving. Makes 8 to 12 servings.

SWEDISH COFFEE CRESCENT

A Michigan farm woman sent this heirloom recipe and told us she makes this often for Christmas bazaars. She has read many Swedish cookbooks and has never found a sweet bread quite like this pretty swirled crescent. The dough is Swedish and the filling with its crushed, vanilla-wafer base is an American adaptation. One recipe makes four crescents and they freeze well. Make several batches for the holidays to give as gifts and serve to friends.

DANISH DESCENDANTS TEAM PORK AND PRUNES. This *Danish Pork Roast* (page 228) is a favorite company dish which a California farm woman always serves on holidays with braised red cabbage, also Danish.

PAELLA, FAMOUS RICE-BASED DISH OF SPANISH ORIGIN. In Valencia, Spanish cooks add sliced pimiento, olives for piquancy. Our adaptation, *Paella Valenciana* (page 133), is a great company dish . . . serve with a salad.

MIDEASTERN KABOBS . . . SKEWERED MEAT. We substitute beef cubes for lamb in *Midwestern Kabobs from the Middle East* (page 259). They are popular cooked outdoors over a grill in the summertime months.

ITALIAN PASTA IS A MAIN DISH AND A SOUP. Our recipes for *Timballo with Cheese Sauce* (page 292) and *Pasta and Bean Soup* (page 296) are favorite adaptations of recipes brought to America by Italian immigrants.

SWEDISH COFFEE CRESCENT

A buttery-rich coffee cake with an unusual vanilla-wafer filling

4 c. sifted flour	5½ c. crushed vanilla
¼ c. sugar	wafers
½ tsp. salt	½ c. melted butter or
1 c. butter or regular	regular margarine
margarine	1 tsp. almond extract
1 pkg. active dry yeast	2 tblsp. water
1 c. milk, scalded and	Vanilla Icing (recipe
cooled	follows)
2 eggs, beaten	

Sift together flour, sugar and salt into bowl. Cut in 1 c. butter with pastry blender or two knives until mixture is crumbly.

Sprinkle yeast over milk; stir to dissolve. Add yeast and eggs to crumb mixture; stirring to mix. Cover with plastic wrap. Refrigerate overnight. (Can be stored 2 days.)

Combine vanilla wafers, ½ c. butter, almond extract and water; set aside.

Divide dough in fourths. Roll each into 15×11" rectangle on floured surface. Sprinkle with 1½ c. of wafer mixture. Roll up like jelly roll from narrow side. Place on greased baking sheet. Shape into a crescent. Snip 1½" cuts 1" apart with scissors around outside edge of crescent. Cover and let rise in warm place until doubled, about 3 hours.

Bake in 375° oven 20 minutes or until golden brown. Remove from baking sheets; cool on racks. Drizzle with Vanilla Icing while still warm. Makes 4 coffee cakes.

Vanilla Icing: Combine 4 c. sifted confectioners sugar, 2 tblsp. soft butter or regular margarine, ½ tsp. vanilla and 4 tblsp. milk; mix until smooth.

ST. LUCIA'S BUNS

In a Swedish household, on December 13 about 5 o'clock in the morning, Santa Lucia, the Queen of Light, enters each bedroom wearing a white robe and lighted crown on her head. Singing the Lucia song, she offers each family member a Lucia Bun and coffee. Traditionally Santa Lucia is one of the young daughters or a relative or friend of the family.

ST. LUCIA'S BUNS

These traditional buns are lovely with their shiny glaze

¾ c. milk, scalded	1 egg
⅓ c. sugar	3½ c. sifted flour
1 tsp. salt	¼ c. golden raisins
¼ c. butter or regular margarine	1 egg white, slightly beaten
$\frac{1}{16}$ tsp. powdered saffron	¼ c. finely chopped blanched almonds
2 pkgs. active dry yeast	2 tblsp. sugar
½ c. lukewarm water	

Combine milk, ⅓ c. sugar, salt, butter and saffron. Cool to lukewarm.

Sprinkle yeast on lukewarm water; stir to dissolve.

Add yeast, egg and 2 c. flour to milk mixture. Beat with electric mixer at medium speed until smooth, about 2 minutes, scraping bowl occasionally. Or beat with spoon until batter is smooth.

Stir in enough remaining flour to make a soft dough that leaves the sides of the bowl. Turn onto lightly floured surface and knead until smooth and satiny, about 8 to 10 minutes.

Place in lightly greased bowl; turn dough over to grease top. Cover and let rise in warm place until doubled, about 1 hour 30 minutes.

Turn dough out on floured surface; let rest 10 minutes.

Cut dough into 18 pieces. Roll each into a 12" long strip; cut in half. Coil both ends of each strip into center of the strip. Place

2 coiled strips back to back to make 1 bun. Place on greased baking sheets. Cover and let rise until doubled, about 30 minutes. Press a raisin in center of each coil. Brush buns with egg white. Then sprinkle with combined almonds and 2 tblsp. sugar.

Bake in 375° oven 15 minutes or until golden brown. Remove from baking sheets; cool on racks. Makes 18 buns.

SAFFRON BRAID

A variation of the Lucia Buns served throughout Sweden during the Christmas holidays. Many cooks make a double or triple batch of dough, shape their Lucia Buns for Santa Lucia Day and make several braids to have on hand when friends and relatives drop in to visit.

SAFFRON BRAID

This lovely golden bread is a must during the Christmas season

1 c. milk, scalded	¼ c. lukewarm water
½ c. sugar	1 egg
2 tblsp. butter or regular margarine	½ tsp. ground cardamom
	4¼ c. sifted flour
½ tsp. salt	1 egg, beaten
Pinch of powdered saffron	Sugar
1 pkg. active dry yeast	

Combine milk, ½ c. sugar, butter, salt and saffron in bowl. Cool to lukewarm.

Sprinkle yeast on lukewarm water; stir to dissolve. Add yeast, 1 egg, cardamom and 1 c. flour to milk mixture. Beat with electric mixer at medium speed until smooth, about 2 minutes, scraping bowl occasionally. Or beat with spoon until batter is smooth.

Gradually add enough flour to make a soft dough that leaves the sides of the bowl. Turn out on floured surface to knead until smooth and satiny, about 10 minutes.

Place dough in lightly greased bowl; turn over to grease top.

Cover and let rise in warm place until doubled, about 1 hour 30 minutes.

Divide dough in half. Divide each half into thirds. Roll each third into a 10″ strip. Braid three strips together. Pinch ends to seal. Place on greased baking sheet. Let rise until doubled, about 1 hour.

Brush braids with beaten egg. Sprinkle with sugar.

Bake in 375° oven 20 to 25 minutes or until loaves sound hollow when tapped. Remove from baking sheets; cool on racks. Makes 2 loaves.

SWEDISH PANCAKES

In every Swedish home you will find a special frying pan used only for making the thin pancakes that measure about 3 inches across. They are served with sugar and jam and are a favorite treat for both youngsters and adults. These thin cakes are always the standard dessert on Thursday, as that is the day many a Swedish homemaker ladles homemade pea soup into bowls for the evening meal. This custom is still followed in some Swedish-American homes.

SWEDISH PANCAKES

Traditionally served with whipped cream and plums

3 eggs	1 tsp. vanilla
1¼ c. milk	Melted butter or regular
¾ c. sifted flour	margarine
1 tblsp. sugar	Sugar
½ tsp. salt	

Blend together eggs and milk with rotary beater. Add flour, 1 tblsp. sugar and salt; blend well. Add vanilla.

Bake in lightly greased 8″ skillet, using ¼ c. batter for each. (Tilt skillet back and forth quickly when batter is added to make a thin coating.) Bake until top is dry; turn and brown other side.

Spread with melted butter and sprinkle with sugar. Roll up. Makes 8 pancakes.

SWEDISH FRUIT SOUP

The Scandinavians are famous for their fruit soups. In the summertime the cloudberry, which is shaped like the raspberry but is yellow in color, and the arctic raspberry are the fruits used to make this sweet soup thickened slightly with cornstarch. In the fall and wintertime mixed dried fruits are stirred into soups with a cinnamon stick and tart lemon juice. Instead of cookies, Swedish cooks fill a platter with crispy rusks to munch along with the soup.

SWEDISH FRUIT SOUP

A most unusual dessert to serve at your next buffet supper

1 (8 oz.) pkg. mixed dried fruit (1½ c.)	1 c. sugar
	½ c. quick-cooking tapioca
2 qts. water	2 sticks cinnamon
1½ c. diced pared apples	Sweetened whipped cream
½ c. raisins	

Soak dried fruit in water overnight. (Do not drain.)

Pour soaked fruit mixture into Dutch oven. Add apples, raisins, sugar, tapioca and cinnamon. Stir until sugar is dissolved. Bring to a boil, stirring constantly. Reduce heat and simmer 1 hour, stirring frequently, until fruit is tender.

Pour mixture into a large bowl. Cover and chill in refrigerator a few hours before serving. Spoon into dessert dishes and top with sweetened whipped cream. Makes 6 to 8 servings.

ALMOND RICE PUDDING

One Swedish dessert specialty is rice pudding that has been combined with lots of whipped cream, almonds, sherry and vanilla. This is often served as a company dessert with a pour of Raspberry Sauce, found in many Swedish desserts. In olden days the fruits were dried and stored until ready to be made into fruit syrups, jams and jellies. These berries form the base for desserts throughout the whole year. Berries are ladled onto every dessert from pancakes to puddings and are often made into fresh-tasting soups.

ALMOND RICE PUDDING

Most Swedish families have this for dessert on Christmas

1¼ c. regular rice
⅔ c. sugar
1 tsp. salt
6 c. milk
⅓ c. cream sherry
3 tsp. vanilla

1⅓ toasted, slivered almonds
2 c. heavy cream
Raspberry Sauce (recipe follows)

Combine rice, sugar, salt and milk in 3-qt. saucepan. Bring mixture to a boil. Reduce heat; simmer uncovered 25 minutes, stirring frequently. Remove from heat.

Pour rice mixture into 13×9×2″ baking dish. Cool slightly. Stir in sherry, vanilla and almonds.

Whip cream until soft peaks form. Fold into rice mixture. Cover. Chill several hours. Serve with Raspberry Sauce. Makes 12 servings.

Raspberry Sauce: Combine 2 (10 oz.) pkgs. frozen raspberries, thawed, 2 tblsp. cornstarch and 2 tsp. lemon juice in a saucepan. Bring to a boil, stirring constantly. Boil 1 minute. Remove from heat. Strain. Cool.

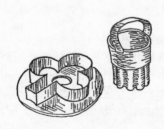

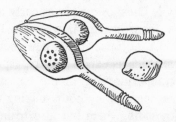

Chapter 5

THE HERITAGE OF
EASTERN EUROPEAN
COOKING

At your next coffee party pass a tray of Czechoslovakian round buns with open pockets displaying luscious fruit fillings. Set a platter of chicken, rosy with paprika and rich with sour cream, on the company dinner table. Carry a baking dish of piping hot pork and sauerkraut, flavored with sour cream, to the buffet. Or please your friends and family by presenting stroganoff for supper.

You will receive compliments on these wonderful foods, which are just a few of the superior contributions people from Eastern Europe made to American cooking. If you are in a town or city where there are bakeries, meat shops and grocery stores operated by descendants of East European immigrants, try some of the foods offered for sale. Their beautiful yeast breads, including a variety of rye loaves with caraway seeds, coffee cakes and sausages of many sizes, shapes and flavors are fascinating.

These European-Americans also continue to make in their own kitchens many of their traditional dishes for special occasions and sometimes for every-day meals. Their neighbors enjoy them so much that they also prepare some of them. The recipes in this chapter are some of the East European specialties made today in American home kitchens.

The first immigrants from Eastern Europe came from what now is Czechoslovakia as early as 1850. They settled mainly on farm lands in the Midwest—in Iowa and Nebraska particularly. Almost at once their new neighbors recognized the Czech-Americans as expert bakers, especially of yeast breads. The immigrants, glorying in the amazingly plentiful supply of wheat flour, spent many hours baking their prized breads, not only to enjoy eating them but also to help overcome homesickness and loneliness.

The big immigration from Eastern Europe started in the 1880s. Many of the families, speaking their native languages until they learned English, settled in industrial areas in closely knit ethnic groups. They had something of their own, even though they were in a new country, to tie them to their former homes and relatives and friends left behind. This was their own style of cooking. Such emotional reliance on foods was not new to them. Many of the nations from which they came had been conquered and ruled by outsiders off and on throughout their history. They had learned that their cooking was one custom they could keep. Treasuring traditions in foods was a way of life and they passed on many of those traditions from one generation to another. They continued to do this in their new American homeland.

While at first they lived in ethnic groups, they gradually entered the American mainstream and enhanced it. They welcomed the bountiful foods in their new country, which they were able to buy with money they earned. They were able to include more meat in their meals. What had been holiday food to them appeared throughout the year.

Hungarian cooking had spread to neighboring European countries in a natural exchange of food ideas and recipes before Hungarian immigrants arrived in America. Many of these dishes were so delicious that they continued to travel to one home from another on this side of the Atlantic. Among the Hungarian-

oriented dishes of the new settlers were noodle specials, goulashes or stews, especially those using paprika and sour cream.
Many Americans consider paprika a bright coloring to sprinkle
on food, but those of Eastern European descent use it for seasoning, not as a garnish. Chicken Paprika (see Index) is one of the
most widely praised specialties inspired by Hungarian-Amer-
icans.

Goulashes have enthusiastic supporters and none deserves
more praise than hearty Pork Goulash (see Index) in which
pork, sour cream and sauerkraut blend. Hungarian Beef Goulash
(see Index) is another favorite of Americans.

While the elegant stroganoff of Old Russia comes to American
dinner tables on special occasions, more frequently ready-to-use
ground beef will substitute for the tiny strips of the most tender
and costly beef cuts (see Hamburger Stroganoff). And sometimes in this burger-loving country, the stroganoff appears in
delicious and satisfying sandwiches (see Beef Stroganoff Sandwiches).

Polish-Americans added many tasty touches to American
meals. Polish sausage (kielbasa) is highly prized and exceed-
ingly popular. And Polish-Americans, as well as Americans from
other Eastern European countries, demonstrate that marvelous
dishes can be fashioned with a humble head of cabbage. Cabbage
with Polish Sausage is wonderfully good, as is Polish-American
Stew (see Index) which in addition to cabbage features sausage,
potatoes, sauerkraut and apples. In fact, all Eastern Europeans
excel in creating splendid dishes with vegetables; they showed
Americans how to use their favorites—especially beets—in interesting combinations. Polish Hot Beet Relish (see Index) is a
good example. It is served as a vegetable dish rather than as a
relish.

Some of the inspiration for cooking meat and vegetables on
skewers derives from southeastern Europe, Georgia and Ar-
menia, as well as from Turkey and other countries in the
Mideast. Our recipe for Midwestern Kabobs from the Mideast
(see Index) is an example.

No consideration of Eastern European contributions to the

American cuisine can omit paying tribute to the superlative and sometimes intricate yeast breads. Many of them are holiday traditionals and they bring happiness to many a Christmas and Easter celebration on this side of the Atlantic. One of the most distinctive breads baked in America is kulich, an old Russian Easter special—tall, stately loaves with dome-shaped tops.

Probably no food contribution of the Czechs (also famous for their noodle dishes and dumplings) is superior to kolaches. These yeast-leavened buns are light in texture and hold a variety of fruit fillings dusted with confectioners sugar. One of the fillings Czech-Americans like best consists of ground poppyseeds cooked with milk and honey. Some home kitchens in Nebraska prize and use poppyseed grinders; others depend on old-fashioned coffee grinders to prepare the seeds. Other Americans, as a rule, prefer the fillings made with dried apricots or prunes, or a combination of the two. These buns are perfect companions to coffee.

MIDWESTERN KABOBS FROM THE MIDEAST

Cookout kings across the United States pay tribute to the kabobs of southwestern Russia, Turkey and other nationalities in the Mideast. They have taken the ancient techniques for cooking vegetables and meats on sticks or skewers and adapted them for use in their own back yards. Americans frequently substitute beef for the lamb universally cooked in the Mideast. And some of the American experts grill the cubes of meat and the vegetables on separate skewers because the cooking times differ.

With beef, only the tender cuts, such as sirloin steak, usually are grilled. In our recipe for Midwestern Kabobs, we use round steak cubes. It is tender enough after chilling overnight in a marinade. This also adds pleasing flavor.

Small onions, green pepper and zucchini slices are parboiled before stringing on skewers. Dip cherry tomatoes and mushrooms in boiling water to prevent splitting. Serve the grilled meat and vegetables on rice.

MIDWESTERN KABOBS FROM THE MIDEAST

You can also cook these over the coals in the summer

2½ lbs. round steak, cut
  1" thick
¾ c. cooking oil
⅓ c. soy sauce
2 tblsp. Worcestershire
  sauce
¼ c. minced onion
3 tblsp. minced fresh
  parsley
1 clove garlic, minced

⅓ c. lemon juice
¼ tsp. pepper
1 large green pepper, cut in
  1½" chunks
12 small onions
3 small zucchini squash,
  cut in 1" slices
16 cherry tomatoes
1 (13½ oz.) can pineapple
  chunks, drained

Cut beef in 32 (1") pieces. Combine oil, soy sauce, Worcestershire sauce, onion, parsley, garlic, lemon juice and pepper; mix well. Pour over beef in bowl. Cover and marinate in refrigerator 24 to 48 hours.

Cook green pepper, onions and squash in water until tender crisp. Drain.

Thread 8 (12") skewers with alternate pieces of beef, vegetables and pineapple, using 4 pieces of meat on each. Broil 4 skewers at a time, 3" from the source of heat, 5 minutes. Turn as needed. Baste with marinade frequently. (Meat will be medium done.) Repeat with remaining skewers. Serve with either Bulgur Wheat Pilaf or Rice Pilaf (recipes follow). Makes 6 to 8 servings.

RICE PILAF

Cook rice and onions in butter until golden—enhances flavors

½ c. chopped onion
1 c. uncooked rice
¼ c. butter or regular
  margarine

1 tsp. salt
2 c. chicken broth, or 1
  (13¾ oz.) can chicken
  broth plus ¼ c. water

Cook onion and rice in butter in heavy saucepan until rice is golden. Stir frequently. Add salt and chicken broth. Bring to a boil. Reduce heat; cover and simmer 20 minutes. Makes 6 servings.

BULGUR WHEAT PILAF

Use bulgur or cracked wheat to make this tasty nut-flavored pilaf

2 c. bulgur wheat
¼ c. butter or regular margarine
1 c. chopped onion
1 (8 oz.) can mushroom stems and pieces
2 (13¾ oz.) cans chicken broth, or 3½ c. chicken broth

1 tsp. salt
½ tsp. dried oregano leaves, crushed
⅛ tsp. pepper

Cook wheat in butter in 10″ skillet until slightly toasted. Stir frequently. Add onion, mushrooms, chicken broth, salt, oregano and pepper. Cover and simmer about 20 minutes or until tender. Makes 8 servings.

PORK AND BEAN CASSEROLE

The recipe for Pork and Bean Casserole comes from an Illinois woman who obtained it from her grandmother while visiting her in Yugoslavia. When she returned, she duplicated the dish, which she describes as "solid farm food," and shared it with neighbors.

Chicken broth is the unusual ingredient. If you have a supply in the freezer, this is a splendid use for it, but commercially canned chicken broth or bouillon also fills the bill. It imparts a subtle flavor, which taste testers usually do not identify. But they agree the dish has an exceptional richness. Wonderful recipe for using dry beans.

PORK AND BEAN CASSEROLE

Unusually good, hearty dish made with dry beans and chicken broth

2 c. navy or Great Northern beans	2 c. chicken broth, or 1 (13¾ oz.) can chicken
Water	broth plus ¼ c. water
1 c. chopped onion	2 tsp. paprika
2 cloves garlic, minced	¼ tsp. crushed, dried red
2 lbs. smoked pork shoulder roll, cut in ½" cubes	pepper

Wash beans. Place beans in Dutch oven and cover with cold water. Bring to a boil; boil 2 minutes. Remove from heat; cover and let stand 1 hour. (Or soak beans overnight.)

Drain beans. Combine with onion, garlic, pork, chicken broth, paprika and red pepper. Bring to a boil; reduce heat, cover and simmer 1 hour 15 minutes. Uncover and simmer about 15 minutes or until most of liquid has cooked away. Stir occasionally. Makes 8 servings.

HAMBURGER STROGANOFF

No other dish imported from Russia pleases American tastes more than beef stroganoff. The magnificent classic, when created in Imperial Russia, was named for the famous Stroganoff family. Slender strips of tender beef, often the filet, take the meat role in the dish, which in Russia is served with potatoes cut exceptionally fine and fried very crisp, similar to our shoestring potatoes.

Americans usually serve their versions of stroganoff over rice, noodles or mashed potatoes. The noodles in the simplified Hamburger Stroganoff are folded into the meat and sour cream mixture just before serving.

For special occasions, many people use sirloin steak to make stroganoff, but for frequent, every-day meals you can make the dish quickly, and thriftily and deliciously with ground beef.

HAMBURGER STROGANOFF

Use this recipe to skip the tedious cutting of tiny meat strips

1 lb. ground beef	2 tblsp. ketchup
½ c. chopped onion	2 tsp. Worcestershire sauce
2 tblsp. flour	1 (8 oz.) pkg. noodles
1 tsp. salt	1 c. dairy sour cream
¼ tsp. pepper	2 tblsp. chopped fresh
1 (8 oz.) can mushroom	parsley
stems and pieces, drained	
1 (10¾ oz.) can condensed	
cream of chicken soup	

Cook ground beef and onion in 10″ skillet until beef is browned. Stir in flour, salt, pepper, mushrooms, chicken soup, ketchup and Worcestershire sauce. Cover and simmer 10 minutes, stirring occasionally.

Meanwhile, cook noodles as directed on package; drain. Stir sour cream into meat mixture. Heat thoroughly, but do not boil. Stir in hot noodles. Turn into serving dish. Sprinkle with chopped parsley. Makes 6 servings.

BEEF STROGANOFF SANDWICHES

Americans have adapted Russian stroganoff, sometimes in ways quite far afield from the original dish. A good example is Beef Stroganoff Sandwiches, which have the good taste of beef plus sour cream.

This is an economical sandwich filling. One pound of ground beef, bolstered by cheese, makes 8 servings. If you are in a rut with supper menus, try these hearty and delicious sandwiches for your main dish. You can make them in less than 30 minutes.

BEEF STROGANOFF SANDWICHES

Complete menu with buttered peas, tossed salad and raspberry parfaits

1 loaf French bread	**1 tsp. salt**
1 lb. ground beef	**⅛ tsp. pepper**
¼ c. finely chopped onion	**1 tsp. Worcestershire sauce**
1 c. dairy sour cream	**1½ c. shredded process**
1 tblsp. milk	**American cheese (6 oz.)**
¼ c. chopped fresh parsley	

Cut bread in half lengthwise. Wrap in foil and heat in 375° oven 10 minutes.

Meanwhile, brown beef with onion, drain off excess fat. Stir in sour cream, milk, parsley, salt, pepper and Worcestershire sauce. Heat, but do not let boil.

Spread meat mixture over cut surface of bread. Sprinkle with cheese. Place on baking sheet and return to oven for 5 minutes. Makes 8 servings.

POLISH-AMERICAN STEW

The Poles, like their neighbors in Eastern European countries, make many marvelous dishes with pork. They are famed internationally for their sausages. Polish-American Stew combines the two meats most successfully. Such dishes are gaining favor because some supermarkets now sell the sausage, usually called *kielbasa*. High school and college students in many Midwestern communities are fond of "hot dogs" using Polish sausage instead of the conventional frankfurter. Cut sausage into frankfurter lengths (sometimes kielbasa is made in individual sausages), heat them, top with sauerkraut and serve in long buns.

Polish-American Stew also contains sauerkraut, as do many dishes in Eastern Europe. The Chinese invented the fermented cabbage long ago; it was an important food in the diet of workers who built the Great Wall. The Tartars carried it to Eastern

Europe and sometime later it was introduced by Austrians into what is now Germany.

Polish people cook all stew ingredients together, but in most American kitchens the potatoes, apples, cabbage and sausage are added toward the end of the cooking. This ends up as a cross between a stew and soup. Serve it in bowls with crusty French bread or arrange the bread slices on individual serving plates and ladle stew over them.

POLISH-AMERICAN STEW

This is a one-pot meal. Good served with a fruit salad

2 lbs. pork, cut in 1" cubes	2 tsp. salt
2 tblsp. cooking oil	¼ tsp. pepper
1 c. chopped onion	1 bay leaf
1 clove garlic, minced	4 medium potatoes, pared and quartered
1 (1 lb.) can sauerkraut	3 c. shredded cabbage
1 c. beef broth, or 1 beef bouillon cube dissolved in 1 c. boiling water	2 apples, pared and sliced
	1 lb. Polish sausage, cut in 1" slices
1 (8 oz.) can tomato sauce	French bread slices

Brown pork in oil in Dutch oven. Add onion, garlic, sauerkraut, beef broth, tomato sauce, salt, pepper and bay leaf. Bring to a boil. Reduce heat; cover and simmer 30 minutes.

Add potatoes; continue simmering 30 minutes. Add cabbage, apples and Polish sausage; simmer 20 minutes. Remove bay leaf. Serve in bowls with French bread. Makes 12 servings.

CABBAGE WITH POLISH SAUSAGE

Of all the ways Polish-Americans have contributed to American kitchens with food, those with cabbage and sauerkraut have caught on most extensively on this side of the Atlantic. You scarcely can miss on a dish when either of these forms of cabbage teams with Polish sausage, available in many markets.

Americans usually adapt the recipes from Eastern Europe. Perhaps the most common change is to cook cabbage a shorter time. The original recipe for Cabbage with Polish Sausage was contributed by a homemaker of Polish descent who lives in the Green Bay area of Wisconsin. It calls for cooking the cabbage 1 hour, while our recipe reduces the time to 20 minutes.

The first step in making the thrifty main dish is to cook the onions in butter or margarine until soft and very lightly browned (in Poland lard usually is used for the fat). The sausage seasons the vegetable delightfully. Even people who normally do not like cabbage are enthusiastic about this dish.

CABBAGE WITH POLISH SAUSAGE

Good with baked potatoes, rye bread and apple salad or dessert

1 c. chopped onion	¾ tsp. salt
2 tblsp. butter or regular margarine	½ tsp. sugar
	¼ tsp. pepper
2 tblsp. flour	3 qts. shredded cabbage
1 c. water	6 Polish sausages, cut in
¼ c. white vinegar	1″ slices

Cook onion in butter in Dutch oven until soft and lightly colored. Blend in flour. Add water and vinegar, and cook, stirring constantly, until mixture comes to a boil. Blend in salt, sugar and pepper. Stir in cabbage and sausage. Cover and simmer about 20 minutes or until cabbage is tender. Stir occasionally. Makes 6 servings.

HUNGARIAN BEEF GOULASH

The national dish of Hungary is *gulyás,* a beef stew that in America we call goulash. Of all meat dishes it is the one most borrowed from Hungarian kitchens. An essential ingredient of the stew is paprika. The production of most Hungarian paprika is mechanized, but in the southern part of Hungary you will sometimes see strings of brilliant red peppers hanging from the eaves of farm houses and drying in the sunshine. This sight reminds one of equally bright peppers hanging from adobe houses in New Mexico.

Hungarian paprika is mild in comparison with some of the pepper products made in America—cayenne, for instance. One reason is that Hungarians grind only the pulp of pepper pods while in cayenne the seeds and pithy interior, the hottest part of peppers, are included. In the Americas, some people combine different kinds, mild to fiery, to obtain the exact taste desired.

Americans make some changes in the goulash recipes that Hungarian immigrants brought to their new home. One is that they usually add sour cream, which is not included in the true Hungarian dish made with beef. And they often omit the caraway seeds, so much used and appreciated in Eastern Europe.

HUNGARIAN BEEF GOULASH

Add ½ tsp. caraway seeds with other seasoning, if you like

2 lbs. stewing beef, cut in 1½″ cubes	½ c. water
½ c. flour	1 tblsp. paprika
3 tblsp. cooking oil	2 tsp. salt
2 c. chopped onion	¼ tsp. pepper
2 cloves garlic, minced	¼ tsp. dried thyme leaves
1 (1 lb.) can tomatoes, cut up	1 c. dairy sour cream
	12 oz. noodles, cooked and drained

Shake stew meat in bag containing flour. Brown meat on all sides in hot oil in Dutch oven. Add onion, garlic, tomatoes, water, paprika, salt, pepper and thyme. Cover and simmer 1 hour 30 minutes, stirring occasionally. Then simmer uncovered about 30 minutes or until meat is tender. Stir frequently.

Stir in sour cream. Heat thoroughly, but do not boil. Serve over hot noodles. Makes 6 to 8 servings.

PORK GOULASH

Women in a Wisconsin club, seeking a new approach to the annual supper given for their husbands, agreed to contribute a dish their ancestors brought to America. Among the dishes that captured the spotlight at the "melting-pot potluck" was Pork Goulash of Hungarian descent. "It was a big surprise to me," one of the hostesses said, "that the ordinary pork and sauerkraut stew which my great-grandmother learned to make in Eastern Europe won so many bouquets."

Our modified recipe for Pork Goulash omits the caraway seeds and tomato purée listed in many European recipes, and calls for marjoram and less sour cream. The rule in Hungary is to cook the onions in lard instead of oil; either may be used—whichever is more available. If your family and friends enjoy sauerkraut, Pork Goulash offers you a good way to please them.

PORK GOULASH

Good served with parsley potatoes, beet relish, celery and a baked apple dessert—cobbler, crisp, pie or dumplings

3 lbs. pork shoulder, cut in 1" cubes	½ c. chicken broth, or 1 chicken bouillon cube dissolved in ½ c. boiling water
2 tblsp. cooking oil	
3 large onions, sliced	
2 cloves garlic, minced	2 (1 lb.) cans sauerkraut, drained and rinsed
1 tblsp. paprika	
1 tsp. salt	1 c. dairy sour cream
½ tsp. dried marjoram leaves	

Brown pork cubes in hot oil in Dutch oven. Remove meat from pan. Cook onions in drippings until golden, stirring frequently. Add pork, garlic, paprika, salt, marjoram and chicken broth. Cover and simmer 30 minutes.

Add sauerkraut; continue simmering 30 minutes or until pork is tender. Stir in sour cream. Heat, but do not boil. Makes 8 to 10 servings.

GROUND BEEF/EGGPLANT CASSEROLE

If members of your family are less than enthusiastic about eggplant, chances are good that you can change their minds with Ground Beef/Eggplant Casserole. It is an autumn favorite in many country homes. Slices of the vegetable are browned and layered in a baking dish with tomatoes, onions and ground beef. The flavors blend delightfully during the baking.

This casserole is a distant relative of the famous Greek moussaka for which there are many recipes. The recipe for Ground Beef/Eggplant Casserole came to Michigan from Romania where ground lamb is more commonly used than beef. This is also true in Greece. Either meat may be used, whichever is the more available.

GROUND BEEF/EGGPLANT CASSEROLE

Serve with green beans and Perfection Salad (see Index)

1 large eggplant (1½ lbs.)	⅓ c. uncooked rice
⅓ c. cooking oil	1½ tsp. garlic salt
1 lb. ground beef	1 tsp. salt
2 c. chopped onion	¼ tsp. pepper
1 (1 lb.) can tomatoes, cut up	

Peel eggplant; cut in 1" slices. Lightly brown eggplant slices in hot oil in large skillet. Remove from skillet. Add ground beef and onion to skillet; cook, stirring frequently, until beef is browned. Add tomatoes, rice, garlic salt, salt and pepper; bring to a boil.

Place half of eggplant slices in greased 2½-qt. casserole. Top with half of beef mixture. Repeat layers. Cover and bake in 350° oven 1 hour. Makes 6 servings.

CHICKEN PAPRIKA

Mention Hungarian cooking almost any place in America and you'll bring to mind rich chicken or meat gravy spiced and tinted by paprika and enhanced by sour cream. Chicken Paprika is a highly esteemed Hungarian-American dish. Its marvelous taste contributes to its popularity, but there is another reason for its wide acceptance. Country women are the world's champions when it comes to collecting and trying promising chicken recipes.

Hungary's best grade of paprika is known as "the rose," which you can find in some specialty food stores. Most women make do with the kind they can buy in the supermarkets. They frequently add seasonings of their own to make up for possible lack of flavor. Bacon is the extra ingredient in the recipe that follows. Everyone who tastes the main dish with the American addition likes the faint, smoky flavor it adds.

CHICKEN PAPRIKA

Serve the chicken and luscious gravy over homemade noodles

8 slices bacon, chopped
1 c. chopped onion
1 clove garlic, minced
1 (3 lb.) broiler-fryer,
   cut up
¾ c. flour
1 tblsp. paprika
1 tsp. salt

1 c. chicken broth, or 2
   chicken bouillon cubes
   dissolved in 1 c. boiling
   water
1 c. dairy sour cream
12 oz. noodles, cooked
   and drained

Cook bacon in 12″ skillet until crisp. Remove and drain on paper toweling. Cook onion and garlic in bacon drippings until soft. Remove and reserve.

Shake chicken pieces, a few at a time, in mixture of flour, paprika and salt in plastic bag. Reserve excess flour mixture. Brown chicken on all sides in bacon drippings in skillet. Pour off all drippings.

Add chicken broth and reserved onion and garlic to skillet; cover and simmer 25 to 30 minutes or until chicken is tender. Remove chicken.

Blend together sour cream and reserved flour mixture. Add to skillet. Cook and stir until mixture is thickened and hot. Do not boil. Add chicken pieces and bacon. Spoon sauce over and heat. Serve over hot noodles. Makes 5 servings.

CABBAGE SKILLET

Cabbage dishes appear in Hungarian meals as often as potatoes do in American country dinners and suppers. Among the Eastern European favorites adopted on this side of the Atlantic Ocean with little or no change is pan-fried cabbage, seasoned with onion, bacon drippings, paprika and sour cream.

For an easy, quick and tasty vegetable dish, make Cabbage Skillet. It is especially good with pork, chicken, ham loaf and other meat dishes. Youngsters insist it is best of all served with hamburgers or frankfurters.

CABBAGE SKILLET

You can make this from start to finish in 15 minutes

8 c. shredded cabbage	**1½ tsp. salt**
2 tblsp. chopped onion	**1 tsp. paprika**
2 tblsp. bacon drippings	**½ c. dairy sour cream**

Cook cabbage and onion in bacon drippings in 10″ skillet about 7 minutes or until tender. Stir frequently. Add salt, paprika and sour cream. Heat thoroughly, but do not boil. Makes 6 servings.

GREEN BEANS AND TOMATOES

Practically all nationalities have vegetable twosomes. Favorite American specials are carrots and peas, corn and lima beans, new potatoes and peas. Green beans and tomatoes get together in Polish kitchens to make a dish called *yelni*. Americans welcome the combination as a way to introduce variety in meals.

The green and red vegetables have the flavorful support of a bit of ham and onion. If you do not have fresh tomatoes, use canned, firm, whole tomatoes, drained and cut up.

GREEN BEANS AND TOMATOES

Attractive way to blend the flavors of two common vegetables

1 (1 lb.) can whole green beans	⅓ c. chopped, cooked ham
	⅛ tsp. salt
2 small tomatoes, peeled and cut up	⅛ tsp. pepper
	1 tblsp. butter or regular
⅓ c. chopped onion	margarine

Drain beans, reserving ¼ c. liquid. Combine beans, bean liquid, tomatoes, onion, ham, salt and pepper in saucepan. Bring to a boil. Reduce heat; cover and simmer about 20 minutes or until flavors are blended. Stir in butter. Makes 5 servings.

CAULIFLOWER POLONAISE

The Polish way of elevating buttered cauliflower above the commonplace has become popular on this side of the Atlantic. The trick is to brown butter lightly, add bread crumbs, chopped hard-cooked egg and seasonings, and spoon the mixture over hot, cooked cauliflower in the serving dish. The vegetable is attractive and the topping enhances its taste and appearance.

CAULIFLOWER POLONAISE

This same topping is also good on cooked green beans

1 medium head cauliflower	1 tblsp. chopped fresh
⅓ c. butter or regular margarine	parsley
	½ tsp. salt
½ c. fine, dry bread crumbs	⅛ tsp. pepper
chopped	⅛ tsp. paprika
1 hard-cooked egg, finely	

Trim base from cauliflower and remove leaves. Break into flowerets. Cook in boiling, salted water 10 to 15 minutes or until tender. (Or cook whole for 15 to 20 minutes.) Drain thoroughly and place in serving dish.

Lightly brown butter. Stir in bread crumbs, egg, parsley, salt, pepper and paprika. Spoon over cauliflower. Makes 6 servings.

POLISH HOT BEET RELISH

Although this well-seasoned, hot beet dish is called a relish by Polish-Americans, many meal planners consider it the second vegetable in the dinner menu. It enjoys special popularity during the hunting season in autumn. The sweet-sour taste complements game, but the beets are equally good in meals when chicken or pork is on the platter.

POLISH HOT BEET RELISH

Serve beets this new way for a delicious change of pace

4 c. shredded, cooked beets	**1 tblsp. sugar**
(8 medium)	**¾ tsp. salt**
2 tblsp. melted butter or	**½ c. dairy sour cream**
regular margarine	**1 tblsp. vinegar**
1 tblsp. flour	

Heat beets in melted butter in saucepan. Stir in flour, sugar and salt. Add sour cream and vinegar. Heat thoroughly, stirring frequently, but do not boil. Makes 6 to 8 servings.

CUCUMBERS IN SOUR CREAM

People of many countries enjoy thinly sliced cucumbers, seasoned and dressed with sour cream. The Poles are no exception, but they prepare the cucumbers somewhat differently. American women who are exposed to the Polish method almost always adopt it in their kitchens. Boiling water is poured over the cucumbers to cover and allowed to stand for 20 minutes. Drain, plunge in cold water for a minute or two, drain again and refrigerate for 30 minutes before combining the slices with the sour cream dressing.

CUCUMBERS IN SOUR CREAM

You can substitute lemon juice for vinegar, chives for dill

2 large cucumbers, peeled and thinly sliced	1 tsp. salt
½ c. dairy sour cream	½ tsp. dried dill weed
2 tsp. sugar	⅛ tsp. pepper
	2 tsp. vinegar

Cover cucumbers with boiling water; let stand 20 minutes. Drain. Cover with cold water; let stand 1 minute. Drain again. Refrigerate 30 minutes.

Stir in sour cream, sugar, salt, dill weed, pepper and vinegar. Refrigerate at least 1 hour to blend flavors. Makes 6 servings.

KULICH

Perhaps the Russian food specialty that most fascinates American women who like to bake bread is kulich, a traditional Russian Easter bread. One Midwestern hostess of Russian ancestry teams the bread with hot tea, which she serves in tall glasses as her grandmother did. It is a good idea to slice one loaf and stand the other in the background to dramatize the tall and stately bread. Place it on a tray and, if served during the Easter season, arrange Easter eggs of bright colors around its base.

One Russian way, and a good one, to cut the loaf is to slice off the puffed-up, rounded top that resembles the dome of a Russian Orthodox church. Cut the loaf, minus its top, in lengthwise halves. Slice each half in pieces about 1½″ thick. Center the top on the serving plate or tray and lay the slices around it.

Our recipe for kulich is for a sweet yeast dough baked in two one-pound coffee cans instead of the Russian pans, shaped like a 12″ piece of stove pipe, which is not generally available. Spread the confectioners sugar frosting over the top and let it dribble down the sides of the loaf; or frost both the top and sides. Sprinkle on tiny, multicolored candies for a final touch.

KULICH

Keep one loaf and give the other for a lovely Easter gift

4½ to 5 c. sifted flour
2 pkgs. active dry yeast
1 c. milk
½ c. sugar
1 tsp. salt
½ c. shortening
2 eggs
½ tsp. vanilla

½ c. raisins
¼ c. chopped, blanched
   almonds
Snowy Frosting (recipe
   follows)
Tiny, multicolored
   decorating candies

Combine 2½ c. flour and yeast in large mixer bowl.

Heat milk, sugar, salt and shortening in saucepan just until warm, stirring to melt shortening. Add to flour-yeast mixture along with eggs and vanilla. Beat at low speed 30 seconds, scraping sides of bowl constantly. Beat at high speed 3 minutes.

Stir in raisins and almonds by hand. Stir in enough remaining flour to make a soft dough. Turn out on lightly floured surface and knead until smooth and elastic, about 5 minutes. Place in greased bowl; turn dough over to grease top. Cover and let rise in warm place until double, 1 to 1 hour 30 minutes. Punch down dough. Let rise again 30 to 40 minutes or until almost double.

Divide dough in half. Form each half into a ball, sealing edges at bottom with fingers. Gently press each ball into well-greased 1-lb. coffee can. Cover and let rise until dough starts to puff over can top.

Bake in 375° oven 40 to 45 minutes. Remove from cans at once; cool on rack. Spread tops with Snowy Frosting, letting it drizzle down sides. Sprinkle with tiny, multicolored decorating candies (or with 2 tblsp. slivered almonds and 2 candied cherries, sliced). Makes 2 loaves.

Snowy Frosting: Mix ½ c. sifted confectioners sugar with 2 to 2½ tsp. milk or light cream, or enough to make frosting of spreading consistency.

KOLACHES

Americans who know kolaches are grateful to the Czechoslovakian-Americans for this taste gift. You sometimes encounter the fruit-topped, yeast-leavened buns in bake shops where many of these people live, such as in Nebraska, Iowa, Minnesota and Wisconsin. You are likely to have them served to you with coffee in the homes in these ethnic neighborhoods. Since American women have a knack for obtaining recipes for a food new to them that tastes exceptionally good, these Bohemian buns are baked by many American women not of Czech descent.

It may not be too easy to achieve perfection in the shape of kolaches baked the first time, but if you follow this recipe faithfully, you should have good results. To make the work easier on baking day, make the filling (or fillings if you want to use more than one) a day ahead, cover and refrigerate. Or you can bake the filled kolaches several days ahead and freeze. (If you do, omit brushing tops of buns with melted butter and sprinkling on confectioners sugar until after you have warmed them just before serving. This last-minute treatment gives them a freshly baked taste.)

KOLACHES

Tempting coffee go-withs—always the talk of the party

½ c. milk	1 tsp. salt
2 pkgs. active dry yeast	4 egg yolks
½ c. warm water (110 to 115°)	4½ c. sifted flour
¾ c. butter or regular margarine	Fillings (recipes follow)
	2 tblsp. melted butter
½ c. sugar	2 tblsp. sifted confectioners sugar

Scald milk; cool to lukewarm.

Sprinkle yeast on warm water; stir to dissolve.

Cream together butter, sugar, salt and egg yolks until light and fluffy. Add yeast, milk and 1½ c. flour. Beat at medium speed 5 minutes, scraping bowl occasionally. Batter should be smooth.

Stir in enough remaining flour, a little at a time, to make a soft dough that leaves the sides of bowl. Place in lightly greased bowl; turn dough over to grease top. Cover and let rise in warm place until doubled, 1 to 1 hour 30 minutes.

Stir down; turn onto lightly floured board and divide into 24 equal pieces. Shape each piece into a ball. Cover and let rest 10 to 15 minutes.

Place dough balls 2″ apart on greased baking sheets; press each ball of dough from center outward with fingers of both hands to make a hollow in center with a ½″ rim around edge. Fill each hollow with 1 level tblsp. filling. Cover and let rise in warm place until doubled, 30 to 40 minutes.

Bake in 350° oven 15 to 18 minutes or until browned. Brush tops of rolls lightly with melted butter and sprinkle lightly with confectioners sugar. Remove from baking sheets and place on racks. Makes 2 dozen.

FILLINGS FOR KOLACHES

Prune: Cook 30 prunes in water to cover until tender; drain. Mash with fork; stir in ¼ c. sugar and ¼ tsp. ground allspice. Filling should be thick. Makes enough for 14 kolaches.

Thick Apricot: Cook 25 dried apricot halves in water to cover until tender; drain. Press apricots through strainer or food mill (or blend in blender). Stir in ¼ c. sugar. Filling should be thick. Makes enough filling for 10 kolaches.

Prune/Apricot: Simmer 1 c. prunes and ¾ c. dried apricot halves in water to cover until tender; drain. Chop and mash with fork. Stir in ½ c. sugar, 1 tblsp. orange juice and 1 tblsp. grated orange peel. Filling should be thick. Makes enough filling for 24 kolaches.

RUSSIAN-AMERICAN CHARLOTTE RUSSE

Collecting recipes for glamorous desserts once popular but largely forgotten is a hobby with some women who like to entertain. Charlotte Russe, the rave of the Gay Nineties, is a good candidate. The beginning of the dessert is obscure, but Americans—especially the Southerners—served it elegantly, garnished with puffs of whipped cream, on antique silver trays or footed, glass cake stands. That was when the South's major industry was agriculture and farm produce plentiful and cheap so that cream and eggs were used lavishly in cooking.

One legend states that a French chef working in Russia created the dessert for a special occasion. Another story is that a French chef invented it for a Russian Czar who was in France on a visit. It was, at any rate, quite the vogue in aristocratic society in the old Imperial Empire.

Our recipe for Russian-American Charlotte Russe, decorated with Ruby Raspberry Sauce, is an adaptation of the old-time dessert. Here's the recipe from an old Maryland cookbook:

MRS. GRAY'S CHARLOTTE RUSSE

Dissolve gelatin in ½ c. water. When dissolved, beat up yolks of 6 eggs and a good-sized cup of sugar. Put in double saucepan with gelatin, and cook until eggs are cooked. Pour into a large bowl to cool. While it cools, beat up 1 quart cream and add to egg yolks and keep stirring until cold enough to mold. Flavor with vanilla. Set ladyfingers in tin or china mold, then pour in the mixture and set away in a cold place.

Now, contrast Mrs. Gray's recipe with our Russian-American Charlotte Russe. Tested recipes of today are easier to use, give better results and avoid waste because guessing has been eliminated.

RUSSIAN-AMERICAN CHARLOTTE RUSSE

Sour cream and raspberry sauce enhance this elegant dessert

2 envelopes unflavored gelatin	1 c. dairy sour cream
¾ c. sugar	2 tsp. vanilla
¼ tsp. salt	12 ladyfingers, split
4 eggs, separated	1 c. heavy cream, whipped
2 c. milk	Raspberry Sauce (see Index)

Stir together gelatin, sugar and salt in heavy saucepan.

Beat egg yolks slightly; add to gelatin mixture along with milk. Cook over low heat, stirring constantly or until mixture coats a spoon. Remove from heat. Blend in sour cream and vanilla. Chill until mixture mounds slightly.

Arrange ladyfingers, rounded sides out, around edge of 9″ springform pan.

Beat egg whites until stiff; fold into custard mixture. Fold in whipped cream. Spoon into pan. Chill until firm, 6 hours or overnight. To serve, remove sides of pan and drizzle dessert with part of the Raspberry Sauce. Pass remaining sauce. Makes 12 to 16 servings.

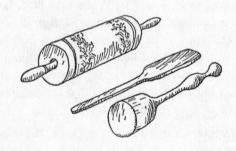

Chapter 6

THE HERITAGE OF ITALIAN AND OTHER MEDITERRANEAN FAVORITES

Hungry Americans love spaghetti in tomato sauce sprinkled with Parmesan cheese. The teen-age crowd gathers at the favorite hangout for hot servings of pizza, dripping melted cheese. No doubt about it, Italian-type foods are a part of the American cuisine.

Since there are many more Italian-Americans than people descended from other nationalities that touch Mediterranean waters, we are including mainly recipes for some of the dishes brought by Italian immigrants to our shores. Most of them, however, have been naturalized in American kitchens. Spain's contributions to our cooking appear in Southwestern Specialties for they came mainly by way of Mexico and South America.

Certain food customs are common to all southern European people, such as the use of olive oil, lemon juice, fresh herbs and local fish. Eggplant dishes are highly regarded (see Index for Eggplant Parmesan).

Many Italian emigrants lived in poverty before they came to America in the early 1900s. Through hard work they were able to buy plentiful foods that previously were luxuries they could not afford. To these Italian-Americans eating was enjoyment.

Italian women in the United States sometimes took paying boarders and served Italian-American dishes that were tasty, substantial and comparatively inexpensive. Reports of these meals circulated and gradually Americans gravitated to them. This was the modest beginning of Italian-American restaurants that today are popular the country over.

The wonderful world of pasta, introduced by Italian-Americans, makes a valuable contribution to meals, particularly when food costs are high. Spaghetti, noodles and macaroni of various shapes and sizes are great "stretchers." Our recipes reflect Italian seasonings and combinations of foods, such as fish and macaroni and cheese in Tuna Bake Italian Style (see Index).

Easy Chicken Tetrazzini, Noodles Parmesan and Two-pan Lasagne are other Italian-American favorites that fit today's lifestyle. Our Pizza Crust is the thin, crisp Neopolitan type and the fillings are exciting and delicious. One is as American as hamburger, another is as Italian as pepperoni, and a third, Texas Pizza, is an example of the "melting pot" influence on food. The pizza is an Italian inspiration and the taco topping of finely shredded lettuce and chopped green onions and tomatoes is a Texas-Mexico addition. Pizzas introduced mozzarella cheese to American kitchens, while pastas established Parmesan as a staple item.

Geography has much to do with what people eat. Mediterranean countries have a climate similar to parts of California. Olives, citrus fruits, figs, grapes and a variety of vegetables, including Italian specials like multiflowered broccoli, artichokes and slim zucchini, grow in both places commercially. Crisp green salads are served with lemon juice or wine vinegar and salad oil dressing. Wine making is a big industry in both Italy and California; raisins are another vineyard product.

Bread loaves frequently are long, slender and crusty; sometimes they are sliced, spread with garlic butter and heated. Italian-type sausages—salami, pepperoni, bologna and others—

are popular in sandwiches and cold plates. Italian-Americans' enthusiasm for good food and the pleasures of cooking have had a great influence in the Golden State particularly.

Italian-American women have the Italian hand in using fresh herbs, such as parsley with flat leaves, sweet basil, oregano, chives, marjoram, tarragon, thyme and bay leaves. They are skilled in using anise-flavored fennel seeds and garlic. These seasonings in Italian-American dishes led to the packaging of mixed Italian spices.

Try the recipes in this sampler of naturalized Mediterranean favorites now enjoyed in homes across the country. America's cuisine is the better for them.

EASY CHICKEN TETRAZZINI

Hostesses have depended on Chicken Tetrazzini to delight their guests since the early 20th century when Luisa Tetrazzini thrilled Americans with her magnificent voice. The dish was created in America for the Italian opera star.

We adapted our version, Easy Chicken Tetrazzini, from the original recipe. Dairy half-and-half substitutes for heavy cream in making the sauce and chicken broth serves as part of the liquid instead of sherry.

EASY CHICKEN TETRAZZINI

We omitted sherry, but you may substitute ⅓ cup for equivalent chicken broth. Leftover turkey also can substitute for chicken

6 tblsp. butter or regular margarine	1 (8 oz.) can mushroom stems and pieces, drained
6 tblsp. flour	
¾ tsp. salt	12 oz. spaghetti, cooked and drained
¼ tsp. pepper	
2 c. dairy half-and-half	½ c. grated Parmesan cheese
1 c. chicken broth	
3 c. cubed, cooked chicken	

Melt butter in 3-qt. saucepan. Blend in flour, salt and pepper. Add half-and-half and chicken broth; cook, stirring constantly, until mixture comes to a boil. Remove from heat.

Stir in chicken and mushrooms. Toss gently with drained spaghetti. Turn into greased 3-qt. casserole. Top with cheese.

Bake in 350° oven 30 minutes. Makes 8 servings.

CHICKEN CACCIATORE

Cacciatore is Italian for a stew in which meat, game, fish or chicken cook in a sauce. The Italian version that Americans like features chicken in a beautifully seasoned tomato sauce. You fry the chicken pieces to a golden brown and then cook it slowly in the sauce.

CHICKEN CACCIATORE

Serve with rice or buttered noodles and broccoli

1 (3 lb.) broiler-fryer, cut up
½ c. flour
½ c. cooking oil
1 medium onion, sliced and separated into rings
½ c. chopped green pepper
2 cloves garlic, minced
1 (1 lb.) can tomatoes, cut up

1 (6 oz.) can tomato paste
1 (4 oz.) can sliced mushrooms, drained
1 tsp. salt
¼ tsp. dried oregano leaves
⅛ tsp. pepper
1 bay leaf

Shake chicken, a few pieces at a time, in bag with flour. Brown chicken on all sides in hot oil in 12" skillet, removing pieces as they brown. Add onion rings, green pepper and garlic to skillet; sauté until tender (do not brown). Drain off excess oil.

Stir in tomatoes, tomato paste, mushrooms, salt, oregano, pepper and bay leaf. Return chicken pieces to skillet, spooning sauce over. Cover tightly and simmer about 30 minutes or until chicken is tender. Remove bay leaf. Makes 4 servings.

TUNA BAKE ITALIAN STYLE

Sicilian fishermen catch almost half the Italian tuna. Many dishes in the island homes are made with the fish. And many of them are seasoned with tomatoes. Dishes made with tuna, fresh or canned in olive oil, are favorites in all parts of Italy.

Tuna Bake Italian Style is exactly what its name implies. It carries some of the same flavors of similar dishes in Italy.

TUNA BAKE ITALIAN STYLE

The tuna-macaroni combination contains tomato sauce and overtones of mixed Italian seasonings and cheese

1 (8 oz.) pkg. macaroni, cooked and drained	1 tsp. instant minced onion
1 (7 oz.) can tuna, drained and flaked	½ tsp. mixed Italian seasoning
1 (15 oz.) can tomato sauce	1 chicken bouillon cube
½ c. grated Parmesan cheese	¼ c. boiling water
1 tblsp. parsley flakes	1 c. shredded mozzarella cheese (4 oz.)

Combine macaroni, tuna, tomato sauce, Parmesan cheese, parsley, onion and Italian seasoning.

Dissolve bouillon cube in boiling water; add to macaroni mixture. Turn into greased 2-qt. casserole.

Bake in 350° oven 30 minutes. Sprinkle with mozzarella cheese. Continue baking 3 to 5 minutes or until cheese is melted. Makes 6 servings.

TUNA/CHEESE CASSEROLE

Inland Americans depend on canned tuna for much of the fish in their meals. They lean heavily on ideas borrowed from Italian kitchens, where tuna was used plentifully. Tuna/Cheese Casserole is a lasagne-type dish in that it contains pasta and three kinds of cheese—but cream, cottage and process American, rather than Italian types. The final touch of genius is sour cream.

TUNA/CHEESE CASSEROLE

This fish special wins praise every time it comes to the table

1 (8 oz.) pkg. cream cheese, softened	1 (7 oz.) can tuna, drained and flaked
½ c. dairy sour cream	2 tomatoes, peeled and sliced
½ c. creamed cottage cheese	¼ tsp. salt
¼ c. sliced green onions and tops	1½ c. shredded sharp process American cheese
¼ tsp. garlic salt	(6 oz.)
1 (8 oz.) pkg. macaroni shells, cooked and drained	

Stir together cream cheese, sour cream, cottage cheese, green onions and garlic salt.

Place half of hot macaroni in bottom of greased 2-qt. casserole. Top with half the cream cheese mixture, all of the tuna, remaining macaroni, then remaining cream cheese mixture. Arrange sliced tomatoes over top; sprinkle with salt.

Bake in 350° oven 30 minutes. Sprinkle cheese over tomatoes. Continue baking 3 to 5 minutes or until cheese is melted. Makes 6 to 8 servings.

TWO-PAN LASAGNE

Americans of all ages often carry a main dish to co-operative meals and lasagne often is the first choice. This recipe for Two-pan Lasagne allows one lasagne to go while the other can stay at home for the family's supper or be frozen for future use.

TWO-PAN LASAGNE

All the ingredients in Two-pan Lasagne are used in Italy, except the cottage cheese, which is a substitute for their fresh ricotta

1½ lbs. ground beef	4 c. creamed cottage cheese
1 c. chopped onion	3 eggs, beaten
1 clove garlic, minced	½ c. grated Parmesan
1 (1 lb. 12 oz.) can	cheese
tomatoes, cut up	2 tblsp. chopped parsley
1 (12 oz.) can tomato	1½ tsp. salt
paste	1 (1 lb.) pkg. lasagne
1½ tsp. salt	noodles, cooked and
1 tsp. dried basil leaves	drained
1 tsp. dried oregano leaves	1 lb. mozzarella cheese,
¼ tsp. pepper	thinly sliced

Cook ground beef, onion and garlic in large skillet until beef is browned. Add tomatoes, tomato paste, 1½ tsp. salt, basil, oregano and pepper. Simmer 30 minutes, stirring occasionally.

Combine cottage cheese, eggs, Parmesan cheese, parsley and 1½ tsp. salt.

Divide ⅓ of lasagne noodles evenly between two greased 9″ square pans. Trim noodles to fit and place trimmings over noodles. Top with ⅓ cottage cheese mixture, ⅓ tomato sauce and ⅓ mozzarella cheese, dividing evenly between the two pans. Repeat layers.

Bake in 375° oven 30 minutes. (If made ahead and refrigerated, bake 45 minutes.) Let stand 10 minutes before cutting in 3″ squares. Each pan makes 9 servings.

LASAGNE FLORENTINE

To Americans, as to the French, Florentine in the name of a dish signifies it contains spinach. Sometimes this designation holds in Italy, but not always. It is as likely to indicate that the dish is prepared the same way as in Florence.

Lasagne Florentine is an Italian-American creation that features a layer of spinach which adds a new flavor note to the baked noodle-cheese dish. This is one easy way to get youngsters to eat spinach.

LASAGNE FLORENTINE

This can be prepared in advance and refrigerated

2 (10 oz.) pkgs. frozen
  chopped spinach, thawed
1 lb. ground beef
1 c. chopped onion
1 (8 oz.) can mushroom
  stems and pieces, drained
1 (15 oz.) can tomato sauce
1 tsp. salt
1 tsp. dried oregano leaves
½ tsp. dried basil leaves
¼ tsp. pepper
1 egg, beaten

½ tsp. salt
1½ c. creamed cottage
  cheese (12 oz.)
1 egg, beaten
1 (8 oz.) pkg. lasagne
  noodles, cooked and
  drained
1 (6 oz.) pkg. sliced
  mozzarella cheese
2 tblsp. grated Parmesan
  cheese

Drain uncooked spinach on paper towels.

Meanwhile, cook ground beef and onion in skillet until beef is browned. Add mushrooms, tomato sauce, 1 tsp. salt, oregano, basil and pepper. Cover and simmer 15 minutes.

Mix together spinach, 1 egg and ½ tsp. salt; set aside.

Combine cottage cheese and 1 egg; mix well. Set aside.

Place ½ of noodles in bottom of greased 13×9×2″ baking dish. Cover with ½ of the cottage cheese mixture, mozzarella cheese slices and meat sauce. Spread all of spinach mixture over sauce. Repeat layers. Sprinkle with Parmesan cheese.

Bake in 375° oven 30 minutes. (If prepared in advance and refrigerated, bake 45 minutes.) Let stand 10 minutes before serving. Makes 8 to 10 servings.

BAKED POLENTA

Early English settlers in New England learned from the Indians that when making cornmeal mush the kernels crushed easier if first heated. Many new Americans ate mush twice a day as the Indians had for many centuries. The colonists named their new food hasty pudding because it reminded them of a grain porridge by that name eaten in their former homeland. Years later, during the Revolutionary War, people were singing:

> Fath'r and I went down to camp
> Along with Captain Goodwin,
> And there we saw the men and boys
> As thick as hasty puddin'.

Colonial women invented dishes made with cornmeal, such as fried mush and Indian pudding. The latter was not named for the Indians but to distinguish their Indian corn from the wheat called corn in England.

Corn reached Italy from the Americas, and the Italians started to make polenta (their name for mush) with it. People in Italy had used mush since ancient days—first made with water and millet, primitive wheat or the flour from chick-peas. Polenta was the field ration of the Roman legions who conquered the ancient world. They heated grain on stones in campfires, crushed it and put it in their haversacks. They added water to it and cooked the mush wherever they might bivouac.

Baked Polenta is an adaptation of a dish introduced in this country by Italian-Americans. The polenta with cheese added is baked and served with a tasty meat-tomato sauce. This main dish is gaining prestige because it is substantial and tasty, also thrifty and nutritious.

BAKED POLENTA

Cook cornmeal in chicken broth to impart a fine flavor to polenta

½ lb. ground beef
1½ c. sliced fresh
    mushrooms (optional)
½ c. chopped onion
1 clove garlic, minced
1 (15 oz.) can tomato
    sauce
½ tsp. salt
1 small bay leaf
¼ tsp. mixed Italian
    seasoning

1 (13¾ oz.) can chicken
    broth
1 c. yellow cornmeal
1 c. water
½ tsp. salt
½ c. grated Parmesan
    cheese
Grated Parmesan cheese

Cook ground beef, mushrooms, onion and garlic in skillet until meat is browned. Add tomato sauce, ½ tsp. salt, bay leaf and Italian seasoning. Cover and simmer 20 minutes. Remove bay leaf. Set aside.

Meanwhile, bring chicken broth to a boil in large saucepan.

Stir together cornmeal, water and ½ tsp. salt. Gradually stir into chicken broth. Cook until thick, stirring frequently. Cover and simmer over low heat 10 minutes. Remove from heat and add ½ c. Parmesan cheese. Turn into greased 11×7×1½" baking dish.

Bake in 350° oven 15 minutes. To serve, cut in squares. Spoon hot meat sauce over top. Sprinkle with additional Parmesan cheese. Makes 6 servings.

PIZZA-STYLE STEAK

When is steak a pizza? Never, of course, but Pizza-style Steak capitalizes on the appeal both the Italian favorite and beef have for Americans. A well-seasoned tomato sauce tenderizes chuck steak, browned first on both sides, then gently simmered in it.

Little pot-watching is required. The topping of cheese, added as the final touch, gives the dish a wonderful taste medley.

PIZZA-STYLE STEAK

The best flavors of pizza and steak are blended to perfection

2 lbs. chuck steak, cut 1" thick	1 tsp. parsley flakes
	1 clove garlic, minced
1½ tblsp. flour	1 tsp. salt
2 tblsp. cooking oil	½ tsp. dried oregano leaves
1 (1 lb.) can tomatoes, cut up	⅛ tsp. pepper
	4 slices mozzarella cheese
¼ c. chopped onion	(3 oz.)

Coat steak with flour. Brown on both sides in hot oil in 10" skillet.

Combine tomatoes, onion, parsley, garlic, salt, oregano and pepper. Pour over steak. Bring to a boil. Place in 11×7×1½" baking dish.

Cover with foil and bake in 350° oven 1 hour 30 minutes to 2 hours or until tender. Top with cheese. Continue baking 2 to 3 minutes or until cheese melts. Makes 6 servings.

SPAGHETTI WITH MEAT SAUCE

One characteristic of the pasta in Southern Italy is the variety of superior sauces served with it. (Naples is called the spaghetti city.) Many of the best ones contain tomatoes. Tomatoes grown in the southern areas are smaller in size than American varieties, and are sweet and flavorful. You sometimes see them hanging in the sunshine on Italian houses. This supply keeps the sauces simmering until the new crop is ready.

Among the tomato sauces that especially appeal to Americans are those that contain beef. Meat sauce on hot, freshly cooked spaghetti was the first Italian ethnic dish Americans adopted widely. American pasta comes largely from Durum wheat, high in protein, grown in North Dakota.

Almost all American kitchens favor a special recipe for the meat sauce, but our recipe definitely is one of the best. Quick-to-use mixed Italian seasonings give our sauce fine flavor.

SPAGHETTI WITH MEAT SAUCE

Double the recipe and freeze half of sauce, ready to use later

1 lb. ground beef	¼ c. chopped fresh parsley
1 c. chopped onion	1½ tsp. mixed Italian
½ c. chopped green pepper	seasoning
2 cloves garlic, minced	1½ tsp. salt
1 (1 lb.) can tomatoes,	1 tsp. sugar
cut up	¼ tsp. pepper
1 (15 oz.) can tomato sauce	Hot, cooked spaghetti
1 (4 oz.) can mushroom	Grated Parmesan cheese
stems and pieces	

Cook ground beef, onion, green pepper and garlic in Dutch oven until meat is browned. Add tomatoes, tomato sauce, undrained mushrooms, parsley, Italian seasoning, salt, sugar and pepper. Cover and simmer 1 hour.

Uncover and continue simmering 20 to 30 minutes or until thick. Stir occasionally.

Spoon meat sauce over hot spaghetti. Pass Parmesan cheese. Makes 6 servings.

AMERICAN SPAGHETTI WITH MEATBALLS

History does not record who first included meatballs in spaghetti sauce. Perhaps it was one of the new Americans who, back home in Italy, sometimes added scraps of meat or fish to the spaghetti sauce. Or it may have been an adaptation of Swedish meatballs to the Italian dish. At any rate, American Spaghetti with Meatballs from FARM JOURNAL COUNTRYSIDE TEST KITCHENS produces a dish that always wins compliments.

AMERICAN SPAGHETTI WITH MEATBALLS

Serve with crusty bread and greens tossed with Italian dressing

1 c. chopped onion	1 lb. ground beef
1 clove garlic, crushed	2 eggs, beaten
2 tblsp. olive or cooking oil	½ c. milk
1 (1 lb. 12 oz.) can tomatoes, cut up	¾ c. dry bread crumbs
1 (12 oz.) can tomato paste	¼ c. grated Parmesan cheese
1½ c. water	1 clove garlic, minced
¼ c. chopped fresh parsley	1 tsp. salt
1 tsp. salt	¼ tsp. dried oregano leaves
1 tsp. dried oregano leaves	⅛ tsp. pepper
½ tsp. dried basil leaves	Hot, cooked spaghetti
¼ tsp. pepper	Grated Parmesan cheese
1 bay leaf	

Sauté onion and 1 clove garlic in hot oil in Dutch oven until soft. Add tomatoes, tomato paste, water, parsley, 1 tsp. salt, 1 tsp. oregano, basil, ¼ tsp. pepper and bay leaf. Cover and simmer 1 hour.

Meanwhile, combine ground beef, eggs, milk, bread crumbs, ¼ c. Parmesan cheese, 1 clove garlic, 1 tsp. salt, ¼ tsp. oregano and ⅛ tsp. pepper. Mix lightly, but well. Shape mixture by rounded tablespoons into balls. Place in 15½ × 10½ × 1" jelly roll pan. Bake in 375° oven 35 minutes.

Add meatballs to sauce; cover and simmer 30 minutes. Remove bay leaf.

Place hot spaghetti on large, deep platter. Top with meatballs and sauce. Pass grated Parmesan cheese. Makes 6 to 8 servings.

MACARONI AND CHEESE WITH BEEF

Among the most tasty macaroni and cheese specials developed in this country are those in which ground beef is an ingredient. Such main dishes are hearty enough to satisfy appetites of hungry men and boys.

Macaroni and Cheese with Beef retains the influences of Italian kitchens since it includes some ingredients frequently used in lasagne—cottage cheese, oregano and tomato sauce. But it is an American dish in its own right, with process American cheese substituting for an Italian type.

MACARONI AND CHEESE WITH BEEF

Great dish to take to church and other co-operative suppers

1½ lbs. ground beef	¼ tsp. pepper
1 c. chopped onion	1 (8 oz.) pkg. macaroni
½ c. chopped green pepper	1 c. creamed cottage cheese
1 (15 oz.) can tomato sauce	1 c. shredded process
1½ tsp. salt	American cheese (4 oz.)
1 tsp. dried oregano leaves	

Cook ground beef with onion and green pepper in skillet until meat is browned. Drain off excess fat. Add tomato sauce, salt, oregano and pepper. Cover and simmer 30 minutes, stirring occasionally. Meanwhile, cook macaroni according to package directions. Drain.

Combine meat mixture with macaroni, cottage cheese and half the American cheese. Turn into greased 2½-qt. casserole.

Bake in 350° oven about 30 minutes or until bubbly. Sprinkle with remaining American cheese. Return to oven about 3 minutes or until cheese melts. Makes 8 servings.

TIMBALLO WITH CHEESE SAUCE

Pasta is the basic food of Southern and Middle Italy. There are endless ways to prepare this favorite, some very plain and others rich and fancy. Our Timballo is a "dressed up" dish that looks and tastes downright elegant.

TIMBALLO WITH CHEESE SAUCE

An unusual pasta main dish in traditional Italian style

1 lb. spaghetti (break strands in half)	2 tblsp. chopped fresh parsley
⅓ c. butter or regular margarine	½ tsp. salt
1 lb. bulk pork sausage	¼ tsp. pepper
1 (4 oz.) can sliced mushrooms, drained	¼ c. dry bread crumbs
3 tblsp. finely chopped onion	2 eggs, well beaten
⅓ c. sliced stuffed olives	¼ lb. mozzarella cheese, shredded
½ c. grated Parmesan cheese	Cheese Sauce (recipe follows)

Cook spaghetti for 10 minutes in boiling salted water. Drain. Toss with butter; coat well.

Sauté sausage in skillet until amost done. Pour off all fat except 2 tblsp. Add mushrooms and onion. Sauté in fat until tender (do not brown).

Toss together spaghetti, sausage mixture, olives, Parmesan cheese, parsley, salt and pepper.

Coat a buttered 9″ springform pan with bread crumbs; reserve some for top. Place half the spaghetti mixture in pan; pour eggs evenly over all. Sprinkle with mozzarella cheese; put remaining mixture on top. Sprinkle with remaining crumbs. Cover with aluminum foil.

Bake in 375° oven 40 minutes. Let stand for 5 minutes. Serve with Cheese Sauce. Makes 6 to 8 servings.

Cheese Sauce: Stir ¼ c. Parmesan cheese and 1 tblsp. chopped fresh parsley into 2 c. of medium white sauce.

McPHERSON COUNTY MACARONI

When soldiers sang of Yankee Doodle and the feather in his cap that he called macaroni, it is doubtful that anyone dreamed that the Italian pasta would be a staple in American homes. This occurred at the end of the 19th century, when cookbooks began including a variety of recipes using pasta. Interestingly enough, this recipe came from a Kansas community ethnically Swedish, further reflecting our melting-pot cuisine.

McPHERSON COUNTY MACARONI

Sour cream gives the casserole a different, distinctive taste

12 oz. macaroni	1 tsp. salt
3 c. shredded process sharp American cheese (12 oz.)	¼ tsp. pepper
	1 tsp. Worcestershire sauce
1½ c. dairy sour cream	½ c. dry bread crumbs
2 tblsp. melted butter or regular margarine	2 tblsp. melted butter or regular margarine
1 tsp. instant minced onion	

Cook macaroni according to package directions; drain.

Stir together cheese, sour cream, 2 tblsp. butter, onion, salt, pepper and Worcestershire sauce. Combine with macaroni. Turn into greased 2-qt. casserole.

Toss bread crumbs with 2 tblsp. butter. Sprinkle on top of casserole.

Bake in 350° oven 30 minutes or until heated through. Makes 6 servings.

NOODLES PARMESAN

In China, noodles—called *mein*—were made and enjoyed for thousands of years before America was discovered. It is believed that Marco Polo on his return home over the Old Silk Route introduced the pasta to Italy. Regardless of how the southern Europeans learned to make noodles, they invented many glorious dishes including them, such as those containing cheese, made in and near the city of Bologna. Noodles Parmesan is one American interpretation of these rich and delicious noodle-cheese combinations which Italian immigrants brought with them to

America. Be sure to serve the noodles promptly after tossing the hot, seasoned pasta with the cheese.

NOODLES PARMESAN

Marvelous with chicken—cheese extends protein content

1 (8 oz.) pkg. thin noodles	1 c. grated Parmesan cheese
6 tblsp. butter	½ c. dairy half-and-half
½ c. dairy half-and-half	

Cook noodles according to package directions; drain.

Melt butter in skillet; cook over low heat until lightly brown. Stir in ½ c. half-and-half; heat until bubbly. Add noodles and toss with two forks. Add cheese and ½ c. half-and-half in three additions, tossing after each. Makes 8 servings.

SKI COUNTRY VEGETABLE SOUP

Wedges of ducks honking overhead signal cold weather on the way and soup-making days at hand. Soups are as varied as the people of the world.

Italian vegetable soups not only vary from region to region but also with the foods on hand at the moment. Ski Country Vegetable Soup contains two varieties of canned beans, a can of condensed onion soup and canned tomato paste. The tomato and the Parmesan cheese tie it to soups of Italy.

SKI COUNTRY VEGETABLE SOUP

This Italian-type soup is filling after a day on the slopes

2 lbs. stewing beef, cut in 1"cubes	¼ tsp. pepper
	2 c. sliced pared carrots
1 (6 oz.) can tomato paste	1 c. sliced celery
1 (10 oz.) can condensed onion soup	1 (1 lb.) can green beans
	1 (15 oz.) can kidney beans
5 c. water	½ c. grated Parmesan cheese
1½ tsp. salt	
1 tsp. dried basil leaves	

Combine meat and tomato paste in Dutch oven. Stir in onion soup, water, salt, basil and pepper. Bring to a boil. Reduce heat; cover and simmer about 1 hour 30 minutes or until meat is tender.

Add carrots, celery, undrained green beans and kidney beans. Continue simmering 30 to 40 minutes or until all vegetables are tender. Stir in Parmesan cheese. Makes 3¾ quarts.

PASTA AND BEAN SOUP

At least once a week in Southern Italy, this hearty, thick soup is served in Italian homes. Some regions feature a thinner soup, using more liquid. Our recipe has been handed down through several generations of good Italian cooks.

PASTA AND BEAN SOUP

Nourishing main dish soup that will please the heartiest appetite

1 lb. dry Great Northern beans	**1 (1 lb.) can stewed tomatoes**
2 qts. water	**½ bay leaf**
2½ tsp. salt	**½ tsp. dried oregano leaves**
1 large, whole carrot	**½ tsp. salt**
6 strips bacon	**¼ tsp. pepper**
½ c. chopped onion	**¼ c. water**
½ c. chopped celery	**1 c. ditalini, or small elbow macaroni**
1 small clove garlic, minced	

Soak beans 8 hours or overnight. Rinse and drain. Combine beans, 2 qts. water, 2½ tsp. salt and carrot; simmer in 6-qt. pot for 2 hours or until beans are tender.

Fry bacon in skillet until crisp. Remove and drain on paper towels. Crumble and set aside.

Reserve ¼ c. bacon drippings. Add onion, celery and garlic. Sauté until tender (do not brown). Stir in tomatoes, bay leaf, oregano, ½ tsp. salt, pepper and ¼ c. water. Bring to a boil; reduce heat. Simmer 30 minutes.

Cook macaroni according to package directions. Drain.

Purée half of the beans. Remove carrot and cube. Combine all ingredients in pot. Heat thoroughly. Makes 3½ quarts.

GREEN BEANS ITALIAN

Italians were quick to accept the New World vegetables, including snap beans. They planted seeds and were gratified to discover that they grew successfully. The art of cooking them developed over many years. Green Beans Italian illustrates what seasonings can do to a commonplace vegetable.

GREEN BEANS ITALIAN

Cheese, lemon juice and garlic bring out the best bean flavor

2 lbs. green beans, cut up,
  or 2 (9 oz.) pkgs. frozen
  cut green beans
½ c. chopped onion
1 clove garlic, minced
3 tblsp. butter or regular
  margarine

3 tblsp. lemon juice
½ c. grated Parmesan
  cheese
¼ tsp. pepper

Cook beans in boiling salted water until tender; drain.

Meanwhile, sauté onion and garlic in butter until tender. Add lemon juice, cheese and pepper. Pour over hot beans. Makes 6 to 8 servings.

EGGPLANT PARMESAN

Supermarket shoppers selecting a shiny, purple eggplant probably are planning to prepare a dish of Mediterranean origin. Eggplant Parmesan is a favorite on the west side of the Atlantic. The recipe for this herb-seasoned casserole underwent almost no change in American kitchens although vegetable oil, due to cost and taste differences, usually replaces olive oil. Americans generally use oils from crops they grow on a large scale, such as soybeans, corn and cotton (seed), while Italians and people of other nationalities in the Mediterranean region use the oil their olive groves provide.

EGGPLANT PARMESAN

The vegetable-cheese casserole is a good main dish for lunch. Serve with fruit salad and hard rolls

1 large eggplant (1½ lbs.)	1 tsp. dried oregano leaves
2 eggs, beaten	1 tsp. dried basil leaves
2 tblsp. water	½ tsp. salt
¾ c. dry bread crumbs	½ lb. mozzarella cheese,
¾ c. cooking oil	sliced
½ c. grated Parmesan cheese	3 (8 oz.) cans tomato sauce

Peel eggplant; cut in ¼" slices. Dip slices in mixture of beaten eggs and water, then in bread crumbs. Brown on both sides in hot oil, removing slices as they brown.

Combine Parmesan cheese, oregano, basil and salt. Place ⅓ of eggplant in greased 2-qt. casserole; sprinkle with ⅓ of Parmesan cheese mixture. Top with ⅓ of mozzarella cheese slices and 1 can tomato sauce. Repeat layers twice.

Bake in 350° oven 30 minutes or until sauce is bubbly. Makes 6 servings.

EASTER EGG BREAD

The fascinating Easter egg breads in Italian bakery windows can be baked at home—as easy to make as to bake sweet rolls. Our Easter Egg Bread consists of the sweet-roll dough baked around individual eggs tinted in bright colors. Italian-American bakers form the dough in fancy shapes, such as lambs, other animals, little men and roses. They then place the colorful eggs in the desired positions and frame them with strips of dough.

Our Easter Egg Bread is easier. You shape the dough in rings around the eggs, which make individual rolls. The only decoration is a sprinkling of tiny, multicolored candies.

EASTER EGG BREAD

Combination main dish for a gala Easter Sunday breakfast

12 eggs	**½ c. shortening**
Easter egg coloring	**Grated peel of 2 lemons**
4½ c. flour	**2 eggs**
2 pkgs. active dry yeast	**1 egg, beaten**
1 c. milk	**Tiny, multicolored**
½ c. sugar	**decorating candies**
1 tsp. salt	

Wash 12 raw eggs. Tint shells with egg coloring; set aside.

Combine 2½ c. flour and yeast in large mixing bowl.

Heat milk, sugar, salt and shortening just until warm, stirring occasionally to melt shortening. Add to flour mixture along with lemon peel and 2 eggs. Beat at low speed 30 seconds, scraping sides of bowl constantly. Beat at high speed 3 minutes, scraping bowl occasionally. By hand stir in enough remaining flour to make a soft dough. Turn out on lightly floured surface, knead until smooth and elastic, about 5 minutes. Place in greased bowl; turn dough over to grease top. Cover and let rise in warm place until double, about 1 hour. Punch down; cover and let rise again until almost double, about 30 minutes.

Divide dough into 12 equal balls. Form each into a ring around a tinted egg. Cover and let rise until double, about 30 minutes.

Brush 1 egg evenly over dough. Sprinkle with decorating candies. Bake in 375° oven about 15 minutes or until lightly brown. Serve warm. Makes 12.

PIZZA CRUST

Pizza and spaghetti are the two Italian food contributions young Americans today most enjoy and many grownups endorse this selection. Pizza, according to food historians, dates back to the Neolithic Age, but it became really popular in Italy when tomatoes were introduced from the New World in the 16th century. Italians improved on the Inca tomato and created the fabulous sauces made in America 200 years later.

Although many American communities have thriving "pizza parlors," the "made-from-scratch" version is favored in many households. After numerous tests in FARM JOURNAL KITCHENS, the final choice of taste panels was for the Pizza Crust recipe that follows.

The dough is partially baked 6 to 8 minutes and cooled. The crust is later filled and baked. Or the crusts can be frozen for later use. The pizza can also be prepared and frozen before final baking for meals or snacks.

PIZZA CRUST

A baking sheet is a handy, giant spatula to lift pizza from oven

2 pkgs. active dry yeast	**1 tsp. salt**
7 c. sifted flour	**2½ c. warm water (110 to 115°)**

Combine yeast, 2½ c. flour, salt and warm water in large bowl. Beat at low speed 30 seconds, scraping sides of bowl constantly. Beat at high speed 3 minutes. Stir in enough remaining flour to make a very stiff dough. (As dough becomes stiff, flour can be kneaded in.)

Knead on lightly floured surface until smooth and elastic, 8 to 10 minutes. Shape into a ball; place in greased bowl and turn dough over to grease top. Cover and let rise in warm place until doubled, about 45 minutes.

Punch down dough; divide in fourths. Roll each part to make an 11" circle. Stretch each circle to fit a greased 12" pizza pan or place on greased baking sheet and make ½" rim around edges.

Bake in 500° oven 6 to 8 minutes or until crust starts to brown. (Crust will be somewhat uneven due to baked-in air bubbles, but they will not affect finished pizza.) Remove from pans; cool on racks. You can leave partially baked crusts at room temperature 24 hours before making pizza. Makes 4 pizza crusts.

To freeze Pizza Crusts: Freeze Pizza Crusts in pans or on baking sheets. When frozen, remove from pans or sheets. Wrap each crust separately in foil or freezer paper and freeze. Thaw before using in one of the following recipes.

To freeze prepared pizzas: Top Pizza Crusts with fillings using the following recipes. Freeze in pans or on baking sheets. When frozen, remove from pans or sheets. Wrap each pizza separately in foil or freezer paper and freeze.

To heat: Place frozen pizza on baking sheet. Place on oven rack at lowest position. Bake in 500° oven 10 minutes or until bottom of pizza is golden brown.

CHEESE/MUSHROOM PIZZA

In every crowd there are mushroom fans who prefer this one

1 Pizza Crust	1 (4 oz.) can mushroom
1 (8 oz.) can pizza sauce	stems and pieces, drained
¼ c. grated Parmesan	1½ c. shredded mozzarella
cheese	cheese (6 oz.)

Place Pizza Crust on baking sheet. Spread with pizza sauce. Sprinkle with Parmesan cheese and mushrooms. Top with mozzarella cheese. Place on lowest rack in oven.

Bake in 500° oven 7 to 8 minutes or until bottom of pizza is golden brown. Makes 1 (12″) pizza.

HAMBURGER PIZZA

Excellent way to extend ground beef—a change from burgers

1 Pizza Crust	½ c. chopped green pepper
1 (8 oz.) can pizza sauce	½ c. chopped onion
¼ c. grated Parmesan	½ tsp. salt
cheese	1½ c. shredded mozzarella
½ lb. ground beef, cooked	cheese (6 oz.)
and drained	

Place Pizza Crust on baking sheet. Spread with pizza sauce. Sprinkle evenly with Parmesan cheese, ground beef, green pepper, onion, salt and mozzarella cheese. Place on lowest rack in oven.

Bake in 500° oven 7 to 8 minutes or until bottom of pizza is golden brown. Makes 1 (12") pizza.

SAUSAGE/CHEESE PIZZA

Tastes good—like pizzas baked in the best Italian restaurants

1 Pizza Crust	½ lb. bulk pork sausage,
1 (8 oz.) can pizza sauce	cooked and drained
¼ c. grated Parmesan	1½ c. shredded mozzarella
cheese	cheese (6 oz.)

Place Pizza Crust on baking sheet. Spread with pizza sauce. Sprinkle with Parmesan cheese, sausage and mozzarella cheese. Place on lowest rack in oven.

Bake in 500° oven 7 to 8 minutes or until bottom of pizza is golden brown. Makes 1 (12") pizza.

PEPPERONI PIZZA

Sliced, "hot" Italian sausage makes this a sure winner

1 Pizza Crust	1 small green pepper, cut in
1 (8 oz.) can pizza sauce	strips
½ c. grated Parmesan	1½ c. shredded mozzarella
cheese	cheese (6 oz.)
2 oz. thinly sliced pepperoni	

Place Pizza Crust on baking sheet. Spread with pizza sauce. Sprinkle with Parmesan cheese. Arrange pepperoni and green pepper over top. Sprinkle with mozzarella cheese. Place on lowest rack in oven.

Bake in 500° oven 7 to 8 minutes or until bottom of pizza is golden brown. Makes 1 (12") pizza.

INDEX

312INDEX

Tennessee Turkey Hash, 26
Tetrazzini, Easy Chicken, 281
Texas Beans and Hominy, 136
Thousand Island Dressing, Easy, 40
Timballo with Cheese Sauce, 293
Toad-in-the-Hole, 171
Tomato(es)
  Aspic with Vegetables, 62
  Baked, California, 141
  /Corn Soup, 144
  Green Beans and, 271
  Sauce, Stewed, 191
  Scalloped, 56
  Soup, Cream of, 198
Topping, Streusel, 208
Torte, Blitz, 216
Tostadas, Chicken, 132
Trifle, English, 177
Tuna
  Bake Italian Style, 283
  /Cheese Casserole, 284
  Club Sandwiches, 38
Turkey
  /Cheese Sandwiches, Midwestern,
    39
  Hash, Tennessee, 26
  Roast, Perfect, 21
    Guide for, 21
  Stuffing Casserole, 25

Uncle Jim's Oatmeal Cookies, 173
Upside-down Apple Pie, 80

Vanilla
  Icing, 249
    Thin, 211
  Pie, Amish, 87
  Sauce, 181
  Wafer Crumb Crust, 89
Vegetable(s), *see also* names of
    vegetables
  /Beef Stew San Juan, 143
  Relish, Zuni, 142
  Scallop, Indian, 140
  Soup, Ski Country, 295
  Tomato Aspic with, 62
Virginia Peanut Brittle, 113

Waldorf Salad, Party, 63
Welsh Rarebit, 168
White
  Christmas Cookies, 106
  Mountain Frosting, 105
Wilted Spinach Salad, 66
Winter
  Corn
    Chowder, 32
    Pudding, 45
  Squash Bake, 51

Yankee Pot Roast, 8
Yorkshire Pudding, 170
Yule Kage, 238

Zuni Vegetable Relish, 142